MARKETING PROFESSIONAL SERVICES

PHILIP KOTLER
Northwestern University

PAUL N. BLOOM
University of Maryland

PRENTICE-HALL, INC., *Englewood Cliffs, NJ*   07632

Library of Congress Cataloging in Publication Data

KOTLER, PHILIP.
  Marketing professional services.

  Bibliography: p.
  Includes index.
  1. Professions—Marketing. I. Bloom, Paul N.
  II. Title.
  HD8038.A1K67 1984   658.8   84-4816
  ISBN 0-13-557620-2

Editorial/production supervision and interior design: Maureen Wilson
Cover design: Lundgren Graphics, Ltd.
Manufacturing buyer: Ed O'Dougherty

Printed in the United States of America
10 9 8 7 6 5 4 3 2 1

ISBN 0-13-557620-2   01

PRENTICE-HALL INTERNATIONAL, INC., *London*
PRENTICE-HALL OF AUSTRALIA PTY. LIMITED, *Sydney*
EDITORA PRENTICE-HALL DO BRASIL, LTDA., *Rio de Janeiro*
PRENTICE-HALL CANADA INC., *Toronto*
PRENTICE-HALL OF INDIA PRIVATE LIMITED, *New Delhi*
PRENTICE-HALL OF JAPAN, INC., *Tokyo*
PRENTICE-HALL OF SOUTHEAST ASIA PTE. LTD., *Singapore*
WHITEHALL BOOKS LIMITED, *Wellington, New Zealand*

This book is dedicated to those
professionals who strive for excellence
in solving their clients' problems

Contents

PART 3

**MANAGING

THE MARKETING PROGRAM**

PREFACE

We have spent nearly our entire professional careers—a combined total of more than forty years—teaching, writing, and consulting in the field of marketing. As close observers of developments in this field, we have witnessed an enormous surge of interest in marketing over the last decade from sectors of our society which formerly ignored or disdained marketing, such as hospitals, educational institutions, and government agencies. But nowhere in our experience have we seen the acceptance and adoption of marketing occur as rapidly and as massively as it has occurred recently in the professions. Accountants, lawyers, management consultants, architects, interior designers, engineers, dentists, doctors, and other professionals are turning to marketing with great enthusiasm and commitment. And marketing, in turn, is creating fundamental and lasting changes in their professions.

In spite of the great enthusiasm and commitment that professionals have shown toward marketing, there have been only very limited amounts of resource materials made available to guide the adoption and implementation of professional service marketing programs. We have been constantly told by professionals that a need exists for written materials that recognize the distinctive problems of marketing professional services (versus more conventional goods and services) and provide sound, in-depth advice on how to deal with those problems. This book represents an attempt to fill such a need.

We have written a book that carefully explains how marketing concepts can be applied to the problems commonly faced by professional service organizations when they seek to improve their practice development programs. The book provides guidance on how to think *strategically* and *analytically* about marketing in professional service settings. We have gone beyond the offering of a collection of marketing tips and ideas and sought to integrate the thinking of numerous individuals into a book that teaches both the "how" and the "why" of various professional service marketing approaches. In other words, this is not just a "how-to" book, but neither is it a book that overemphasizes the theoretical and impractical. We attempt to give the professional a solid grounding in *usable* marketing principles and theories which can be readily applied with profitable results. As Clive Porter, an active marketing consultant to professionals, has stated to us: "Professionals must have the right marketing *premises* before they can start applying their own logic."

One other feature of this book is its use of examples from a wide variety of professions. Although we recognize that each profession faces certain unique circumstances, we do not treat the marketing problems of each profession separately. We believe that the various professions have a considerable amount in common when it comes to marketing problems. Practitioners in one profession can gain helpful insights into their own problems by reading and learning about the problems of practitioners in other professions. Although for convenience we use the term "clients" throughout the book to refer to the organizations and individuals served by professionals, the book is intended to have value for all types of professionals and practices, including those whose clients are typically called "patients."

A book like this can only be written with the help and guidance of numerous people. We would first like to thank the many practicing professionals who have freely discussed their marketing problems and programs with us over the last few years. We especially appreciate the ideas offered by Gary Fossett (MIICORP), David Hirzel (Sasaki Associates), William Novelli (Porter, Novelli and Associates), and Karl Hellman (formerly with the Management Analysis Center).

In addition, we appreciate the careful reviews of earlier drafts of this book provided by Clive Porter (Marketing Science International), Richard Connor (Synergy Corp.), Valarie Zeithaml (Texas A&M University), Terry Shimp (University of South Carolina), and Darlene Smith (University of Maryland). The encouragment and support of our past Prentice-Hall editor, John Connolly, and our present editor, Elizabeth Classon, are also deeply appreciated. Finally, our families (Nancy, Amy, Melissa, and Jessica Kotler, and Diane and Jonathan Bloom) deserve considerable thanks for allowing us the time to pursue this endeavor.

1

PROFESSIONAL MARKETING FOR PROFESSIONALS

Jack Newman has seen the CPA firm he founded following World War II grow from a solo practice to a 53-person firm with offices in two major East Coast cities. Jack's firm has prospered by providing specialized auditing, tax planning, write-up, and management advisory services to construction firms, local governments, and small businesses. At the age of 64, Jack is thinking seriously about retirement, and in the last few years he has gradually relinquished many of his managerial responsibilities to his partners. But Jack is deeply troubled by several recent developments affecting his firm, and he fears serious financial difficulties for his partners if he does not stay on to help steer them through a turbulent period.

The firm recently lost a long-standing audit engagement with a local municipality when one of the "Big Eight" national firms "low-balled" in a competitive bidding situation, offering to do the job for a much lower fee than Jack's firm could afford to do it. In addition, many of the firm's current audit clients have been targeted directly by competing CPA firms, influencing many of these clients to request "rebids" for audit and management services work for the first time. Advertising has begun to be used regularly by a few competing firms, and this has been backed up by fancy brochures, newsletters, and proposals. Jack even heard about one competing firm that sent all of its partners to the Dale Carnegie School to teach them how to "sell" more effectively.

Jack feels it is time his firm got involved with actively marketing its services. For this reason, he had a local marketing consultant give the firm's staff a half-day seminar on marketing accounting services. Jack reacted enthusiastically to the seminar and came away with several concrete actions he thought the firm should take to commence a serious and productive marketing program. Now all Jack has to do is convince his skeptical, conservative

1

partners to go along with his ideas about marketing. Then maybe he can retire with a clear conscience.

Marketing has become a pervasive and influential force throughout the professions. In a few short years, marketing has shed its old image of being something unethical and unnecessary and has, instead, become viewed as an essential ingredient in building and maintaining a rewarding and profitable professional practice. The 1980s have become "The Era of Marketing" in most of the professions, as new ways of designing, pricing, distributing, and promoting professional services are appearing constantly. Consider the following developments:

Legal and dental clinics have become commonplace. Multioffice clinics offering routine services at low fees now exist in all major metropolitan areas. These clinics have located themselves in highly visible and accessible offices in shopping areas and have made extensive use of advertising and other promotional techniques. Many have achieved considerable success.

Large retailers such as Sears and Dart Drug have decided to apply some of their marketing know-how to the provision of professional services. They have become heavily involved with marketing tax advisory, legal, and optometric services, offering a serious competitive challenge to more conventional professionals competing in these fields.

Prepaid legal and health-care services are now available in many localities. Clients of organizations offering these services merely pay a fixed fee per time period to receive all the services they might need. They are not required to pay on a fee-for-service basis.

The boundaries between various traditional services such as banking, insurance, real estate, and stock brokerage are blurring as giant U.S. firms—Sears, American Express, Citibank, and Merrill Lynch—enter and interface these businesses. For example, Merrill Lynch offers a relocation management service to corporations whose executives are moving to new locations. Merrill Lynch will help executives find new homes, buy them through their real estate brokers, arrange finance through affiliated banks, and insure the mortgage through their insurance subsidiary.

Design-build firms are acquiring an increasing share of the business historically obtained by architects, engineers, and construction firms. The design-build firms offer clients the opportunity to obtain *all* the services they may need to build a building from a single supplier.

Marketing research studies involving surveys of clients are being done with increasing frequency. Several "Big Eight" accounting firms, for instance, regularly interview chief financial officers of large corporations to learn more about what influences the selection of auditors and consultants. The results of these studies are being used to formulate improved, sophisticated business development strategies.

Consultants specializing in marketing professional services have been receiving considerable attention and usage. Seminars offered by these experts have had large enrollments and their consulting services have been sought frequently. For instance, one consulting firm that specializes in this area experienced a 400% growth in billings during 1981.

Thus traditional professions find themselves in a whole new competitive environment. There are new types of firms offering new types of services in new types of locations. Fees and prices are being billed in new ways and selling and advertising are being done using new, overt (rather than covert) techniques. Clearly, firms like Jack Newman's—as well as much smaller and much larger firms in all of the professions—are rapidly recognizing a pressing need to become more sophisticated about marketing.

But what exactly is this thing called marketing that is turning the professions upside down? And why have so many professionals who formerly disdained marketing become so attracted to its potential? What demand situations can marketing help a firm confront? And what are the distinctive problems associated with marketing a professional service that can prevent marketing from achieving what its newly won adherents expect from it? Finally, what type of organizational orientation gives a professional service firm the best chance of achieving success with marketing? These are the major questions we will address in this chapter. In answering them, we will introduce several basic concepts and topics that will receive repeated discussion throughout the book.

WHAT IS MARKETING?

Marketing has been maligned and misunderstood for most of its existence. Some people see marketing as manipulative, wasteful, intrusive, and unprofessional. Or they equate marketing primarily with advertising or selling. These beliefs have made it difficult for marketing to gain acceptance outside of the conventional business world.

But the image of marketing is changing rapidly. Marketing has recently gained widespread acceptance as an essential part of the management practice of numerous hospitals, educational institutions, government agencies, and other nonprofit organizations.[1] And professionals from fields such as law, accounting, architecture, engineering, dentistry, and optometry are taking an increasing interest in marketing. People are coming to recognize that there are different *styles* of marketing that an organization can adopt. Some firms choose a marketing style characterized by hard sell and intrusiveness. Others choose a marketing style that adheres to traditional professional standards and avoids advertising and hard selling techniques. In fact, it is possible for a sound marketing program to make only minimal use of advertising and selling, relying instead on careful design of services, creative pricing, and effective distribution to achieve profitable results. As well-known management theorist Peter Drucker noted: "The aim of marketing is to make selling superfluous."[2]

Marketing is something that can be done with as much professionalism as the work of a lawyer, CPA, or doctor. The *professional marketer* is someone who is skilled at *understanding, planning, and managing exchanges.* This professional knows how to conduct research to obtain an understanding of the needs of those with whom he seeks to establish exchange relationships; how to design a valued offering to meet these needs; how to communicate the offer effectively; and how to present it at the right time and place.

To be more precise, we offer the following definition of marketing:

> **Marketing** is the analysis, planning, implementation, and control of carefully formulated programs designed to bring about voluntary exchanges of values with target markets for the purpose of achieving organizational objectives. It relies heavily on designing the organization's offering in terms of the target markets' needs and desires, and on using effective pricing, communication, and distribution to inform, motivate, and service the markets.

Several things should be noted about this definition of marketing.

First, marketing is defined as a managerial process that manifests itself in carefully formulated programs—and not just haphazard actions—designed to achieve desired responses. If the managing partner of a law firm simply urges all partners to spend more time seeking out new clients, this is *not* a program, and it is bound to produce disappointing results. The partners are not given direction as to whom to call on, what to say about the firm, and how to arrange follow-up discussions. They are being asked to do *selling* without the benefit of having a *marketing* program to support them. Marketing takes place *before* any selling takes place and involves the development of carefully formulated plans and programs.

Second, marketing seeks to bring about *voluntary* exchanges of values. Marketers seek a response from another party, but it is not a response to be obtained by any means or at any price. For example, coercive actions, such as a threat to file a lawsuit against a client if a competing professional is retained, have no place in a marketing program. Marketing is the philosophical alternative to coercion. The marketer seeks to formulate a bundle of benefits for the target market of sufficient attractiveness to produce a voluntary exchange.

Third, marketing means the selection of target markets rather than a quixotic attempt to serve all markets and all needs. Marketers routinely distinguish among possible market segments and decide which ones to serve, on the basis of market size, profit potential, firm mission, or some other basis. An engineering firm with special competence in civil engineering will not bid for any type of engineering work. Rather, it will go after opportunities in civil engineering with clients possessing narrowly defined geographic, size, or other characteristics.

Fourth, the purpose of marketing is to help organizations insure survival and continued health through serving their markets more effectively. Whether the organization's objective is profit maximization or the achievement of some social benefit, marketing can be useful. However, effective marketing planning requires that an organization be very specific about its objectives.

Fifth, marketing relies on designing the organization's offering in terms of the target market's needs and desires rather than in terms of the seller's personal tastes. Marketing is a democratic rather than an elitist technology. It holds that efforts are likely to fail that try to impose on a market an offering that is not matched to the market's needs and wants. Thus, a management consulting firm that recommends a similar organizational structure for all its clients, and fails to account for the unique needs of each client, is likely to have few clients. Effective marketing is user oriented, not seller oriented.

Sixth, marketing utilizes and blends a set of tools called the *marketing mix*—the design of offerings, pricing, communication, and distribution. Too often the public equates marketing with only one of its tools such as advertising. But marketing is oriented toward producing results, and this requires a broad conception of all the factors influencing the buying behavior of clients. The success of an architectural firm, for example, may be attributable to more than its ability to promote itself through winning design awards or getting press coverage about its work. The firm's practice of constantly communicating with clients about even the smallest details, as well as its record of finishing jobs on time and within budget, may have much more to do with its prosperity.

WHY ARE PROFESSIONALS TURNING TO MARKETING?

Jack Newman, whose plight was described in the opening of this chapter, has become attracted to marketing in a manner similar to many other professionals. Jack has turned to marketing to help him cope with a rapidly changing and difficult-to-understand environment. He sees a strong commitment to marketing as something that can help his firm strengthen its relationships with existing clients, attract additional clients, and improve the efficiency of its business development efforts.

Major transformations in the environments of all the professions are leading many professional service organizations down the same path that Jack's firm has been following. Marketing has become extremely attractive to professionals who have been confronted with changes such as:

1. A Revised Legal and Ethical Climate

Restrictions against the use of advertising, solicitation, competitive bids, and certain promotional tools have essentially been eliminated in all of the professions. A series of highly publicized 1970s court cases—brought by consumer groups, federal agencies, and members of the professions themselves—spurred the elimination of those restrictions from both professional codes of ethics and selected state statutes.[3] And recent attempts by the American Medical Association and others to lobby Congress to obtain an exemption for the professions from being under the control of the Federal Trade Commission—thereby allowing the reinstatement of certain restrictions—have not proven successful.[4] While some restrictions remain, professionals are essentially free today to promote their services however and wherever they want, as long as they do not make any deceptive or misleading claims. This new-found freedom has sparked a wave of intensifying promotional and competitive activity in most of the professions. Many professional service organizations are finding that their survival hinges on being able to compete in this new climate.

2. An Oversupply of Professionals

One of the reasons more intense competition can be expected in many professions is that there will be more professionals. The legal, architectural,[5] and dental professions are already facing oversupply conditions, and similar conditions hae been predicted for the medical professions.[6]

> For example, the number of lawyers in the United States rose from 131,000 in 1968 to 500,000 in 1979. This is a much faster growth rate than that of the population as a whole. In the State of California, there is one lawyer for every 365 persons.
>
> The number of dentists has climbed from 112,000 in 1975 to 136,000 in 1978. The average number of patients per week declined from about 62 in 1978 to 60 in 1982.

Moreover, the oversupply of certain professional services will intensify as more paraprofessionals (e.g., paralegals, midwives) provide services previously offered by only licensed professionals. Economic theory tells us that when supply exceeds demand, more vigorous competition for customers occurs. Insufficient demand for their services is leading many professionals to intensify their efforts to attract clients.

3. Increased Dissatisfaction with Professionals

Members of the learned professions no longer enjoy the high esteem they received in past years. Substantial numbers of people see lawyers as ambulance chasers, accountants as tax loophole finders, architects as avant-garde elitists, and dentists as overpriced mechanics. Influenced by unflattering portrayals of professions in the media and best-selling books, clients have become much more likely to question the judgment of professionals or to offer strong complaints. Consumerism has struck in the professions, taking the form of malpractice suits and other overt challenges to professionals of all types.[7] Clearly, professionals need to take actions to enhance their public image and to improve the satisfaction levels of their clients.

4. Rapidly Changing Technologies

Technological changes in communications, data processing, medical science, and other areas are having a profound influence on the professions. Technological breakthroughs are making some professional services obsolete while at the same time creating profitable opportunities for other services built around the new technologies. For example, marketing research firms are finding that many of their traditional ways of collecting data for clients are becoming obsolete because of the availability of data collection methods involving two-way cable television, computerized supermarket checkouts, and portable microcomputers. Professionals are finding that they must be prepared to react quickly to technological change. They need to be able to introduce a new service or adjust fees on short notice after a technological breakthrough has modified the operations of competitors or clients.

IN WHAT DEMAND SITUATIONS CAN MARKETING BE HELPFUL?

Marketing can help professional service organizations deal with the challenges identified above. Whether environmental forces are pushing the demand for an organization's services up, down, or into some irregular pattern, marketing can be of assistance. Indeed, *marketing manage-*

ment's task is to influence the level, timing, and character of demand in a way that will help the organization achieve its objectives.

Marketing can be used to contend with seven different demand situations:

1. *Negative demand.* A market is said to be in a state of negative demand if a major part of the market dislikes the offering and in fact may even pay a price to avoid it. Many people have a negative demand for wills, estate planning, and computer systems. Still others show a negative demand for vaccinations, dental work, vasectomies, and gall bladder operations. The marketing task is to analyze why the market dislikes the offering, and whether a marketing program can change the market's beliefs and attitudes through redesign of the offering, lower prices, and more positive promotion.

2. *No demand.* Targeted clients may feel uninterested or indifferent toward an offering. Thus someone who has never needed to retain a lawyer may have no demand for a prepaid legal services program. And a college administrator planning a building renovation may feel indifferent about consulting an architect. The marketing task is to find ways to connect the benefits of the product or service with the person's natural needs and interests.

3. *Latent demand.* A substantial number of clients may share a strong desire for something that cannot be satisfied by any existing offering. There is strong latent demand for accurate economic forecasts, painless divorce settlements, and fast and successful treatment for alcoholism. The marketing task is to measure the size of the potential market and develop goods and services that will satisfy the demand.

4. *Falling demand.* Every organization, sooner or later, faces falling demand for one or more of its offerings. Architects have seen the demand for designing school buildings dissipate, and attorneys periodically see declines in demand for real estate work. The marketer must analyze the cause of market decline and determine whether demand can be restimulated through finding new target markets, changing the offering's features, or developing more effective communications. The marketing task is to reverse the declining demand through creative remarketing of the offering.

5. *Irregular demand.* Many organizations face demand which varies on a seasonal, daily, or even hourly basis, causing problems of idle capacity or overworked capacity. Many accounting firms are flooded with work during tax "season" but underutilize their staff during the rest of the year. Pediatricians must see more patients during the winter cold and flu seasons. The marketing task is to find ways to alter the time pattern of demand through flexible pricing, promotion, and other incentives.

6. *Full demand.* Organizations face full demand when they are pleased with the amount of business they have. The marketing task is to maintain demand at its current level in the face of the ever present possibility of changing client preferences and more vigorous competition. The organization must keep up its quality and continually measure client satisfaction to make sure that it is doing a good job.

7. *Overfull demand.* Some organizations face a demand level which is higher than they can, or want to, handle. Having too much work may

prevent certain key individuals of a firm from having the kind of involvement with each case or project that they find satisfying and rewarding. Or too much demand may lead to a deterioration in the quality of the work performed. The marketing task, called *demarketing*, requires finding ways to reduce the demand temporarily or permanently. General demarketing seeks to discourage overall demand and consists of such steps as raising prices and reducing promotion and service. Selective demarketing consists of trying to reduce the demand coming from those parts of the market which are less profitable or less in need of the service. Demarketing does not aim to destroy demand but only to reduce its level.

Professional service marketers may face several of these demand situations as they work with a given organization.

TEN DISTINCTIVE PROBLEMS IN
MARKETING PROFESSIONAL
SERVICES

In confronting any of the demand situations described in the previous section, professional service marketers cannot assume that the marketing approaches and techniques that have worked in other industries will automatically work for them. The marketing of professional services *is* different, and what has worked to sell detergent, steel, or even banking services may not be transferable to the situations found in many professions. We have identified ten distinctive problems that make the marketing of professional services different, and often more difficult, than the marketing of other goods and services. We introduce these problems here, and will refer to them throughout the entire book.

Problem 1: Third-Party Accountability

Sound marketing involves making a strong commitment to serving the needs and desires of target markets. Marketers of commercial products like automobiles or breakfast cereals therefore generally give primary consideration to how to fully satisfy their consumers. Some consideration is given to how government regulatory agencies, stockholders, and employees react to their activities, but this is given only secondary consideration. On the other hand, marketers of professional services must give substantial consideration to how third parties other than their clients will react to their marketing programs.

Professionals typically cannot go to quite as great lengths to produce satisfied "customers" as conventional commercial marketers can. A CPA cannot offer to overlook a client's financial irregularities; a doctor cannot continuously prescribe addictive narcotics to a patient; and an engineer cannot accede to cost-cutting pressures of clients and use unsafe building materials. Professionals should always recognize that in serving one type of client they are also serving other third-party "clients" such as investors, insurance companies, government agencies, and the members of their own profession. To go overboard in serving one type of client could lead to a loss of trust with important third parties—and a loss of the legal certification or licensing that allows one to be a professional in the first place.

Problem 2: Client Uncertainty

People face uncertainty in all types of buying situations, and uncertainty is particularly high for buyers of professional services.[8] Not only do buyers of professional services face the common problem of having difficulty evaluating the performance characteristics of an offering prior to purchase and use, but they also frequently face the problem of not being able to evaluate performance characteristics *after* purchase and use. A patient may not be convinced that he should have had surgery for a certain ailment; and a plaintiff may not be convinced that his lawyer should have settled out of court. There is a mystery and complexity associated with many professional services that clients often do not comprehend.

High levels of client uncertainty create unique challenges for professional service marketers. Client *education* must play a much bigger role in the marketing of professional services than in the marketing of other offerings. Clients must be educated about what criteria to use in evaluating professionals and about how to employ professionals productively. Furthermore, in some cases people must even be educated about when they really need to seek out the services of a professional.

Problem 3: Experience Is Essential

Although buyers of professional services are frequently uncertain about the criteria to use in selecting a professional, one criterion is almost always prominently considered: *prior experience with similar situations.* People prefer to use accountants and management consultants who have worked in their industry before, lawyers who have litigated cases just like theirs, architects who have built buildings like the one they want to build, and surgeons who have successfully performed the needed surgical procedure hundreds of times.

The need to have this kind of experience to obtain clients produces problems for many professional service organizations. Firms with expertise in limited areas often find it difficult to diversify into new lines of work. And inexperienced professionals often find it difficult to find any work at all. "Newness" cannot be readily promoted as a favorable attribute in most professions, as might be done with a new soft drink or banking service. This situation makes it especially important for professionals to do extensive marketing planning to help them determine the future market potential associated with the different specialized services they are considering providing.

Problem 4: Limited Differentiability

Marketers typically attempt to differentiate their offerings from those of their competitors. They desire to have target markets perceive their offerings as having certain unique and superior characteristics. Differentiation is carried out by actually producing an offering with unique characteristics and/or by persuading buyers through advertising and selling that the offering possesses unique characteristics.

The differentiation of offerings is difficult for most marketers to achieve, but it is an especially difficult task for marketers of professional services. The innate differentiability of many professional services is quite limited. It is hard to differentiate an accounting audit, a title search, and an eye examination. Unlike the case of a consumer product like breakfast cereal, one cannot accomplish differentiation through simply sprinkling on a new coating or stamping out a new shape. The amount of variation in the way a professional service can be provided may be quite limited, particularly if certain professional standards restrict methods of provision. Additionally, even if a service is provided that really is different than competing services, it may be difficult to get clients, who may be experiencing great uncertainty, to perceive and recognize the real differences.

Problem 5: Maintaining Quality Control

Keeping high-quality control levels is a challenging task for service marketers in general,[9] and for professional service marketers in particular. Services do not come off production lines where statistical sampling can be done to check on levels of quality. Instead of fine-tuning a machine to maintain quality, people-intensive service organizations must emphasize finding good people and exhorting them to work conscientiously.

Many professional service organizations have to contend with the additional problem that the quality of their service often depends on the behavior of their clients. A consultant's or doctor's services will usually be more helpful to those persons who follow the professional advice they have received. Uncooperative clients can, unfortunately, produce poor results and a poor track record for a professional to try to build upon.

Problem 6: Making Doers into Sellers

Before "buying" professional services, people like to meet and become acquainted with the professionals who will be serving them. It is a way for them to reduce their uncertainty. The use of only salespersons or full-time presenters to sell the services of unseen professionals is therefore ill advised. The professionals who will be the "doers" of certain kinds of work need to become involved with the selling of that work. But convincing many professionals that they should become actively involved with selling their own services can be exceedingly difficult. And teaching these people improved selling skills can be even more difficult. Many lawyers, accountants, architects, doctors, and other professionals simply do not want to have anything to do with selling, and many others do not have personal characteristics that would make them good at selling.

Problem 7: Allocating Professionals' Time to Marketing

Since professionals can bill clients for time they spend providing professional services, but cannot bill anyone for time they spend marketing their services, many firms are reluctant to allocate very much of professionals' time to marketing. Moreover, even if professionals devote substantial time to marketing, decisions must still be made about how much of this time to devote to existing clients, new prospects, and more general public relations work. And in some firms a problem can arise when certain key people spend much too much time with marketing— accepting every speaking invitation and proposal-writing opportunity— and not enough time being a doer and helping to maintain the firm's quality control. Clearly, the need for professionals to be both doers and marketers creates many time management problems.

Problem 8: Pressure to React Rather than Proact

A problem related to the time allocation problem has to do with the constant demands many professionals face to provide services on short notice. Clients tend to want their work done for them "yesterday," and this can frequently cut into time that has been set aside for marketing planning. Being proactive while clients are putting time pressure on you can be quite difficult.

Problem 9: The Effects of Advertising Are Unknown

The use of advertising is still so new in the professions that a sophisticated understanding of its effects has not been obtained. Knowledge about the most effective appeals, media, and spokespersons to use to promote particular professional services has not been accumulated. Also, knowledge about the types of advertising that may "backfire" for professionals has not been developed. Backfiring could occur because many people are not accustomed to seeing professional service advertising. They could interpret some messages as suggesting that an advertiser lacks competence (or else why would advertising be needed to obtain business?) or possesses other negative features. Undoubtedly, more experience and research are needed with professional service advertising before clear guidelines—such as have appeared for advertising other goods and services—will be available.

Problem 10: A Limited Marketing Knowledge Base

In addition to not having much knowledge available to guide them in making advertising decisions—a problem that we feel deserves special notice—professional service marketers do not have much knowledge available to guide them in making *all* marketing decisions. The relative newness of marketing in the professions has not left much time for many books, scholarly articles, or trade journals to appear on the subject.[10] Meetings and conferences focusing on marketing professional services have also been in short supply. Unlike marketers in other industries, marketers of professional services cannot rely on reading materials or discussions with colleagues in similar situations to provide them with much guidance. There is a tendency for those involved with marketing professional services to keep silent about many of their approaches out of fear of losing some type of "competitive edge." In general, marketers of professional services find it necessary to fend for themselves to a greater extent than do other marketers.

These ten problems will face different organizations with varying intensity. Nevertheless, we believe all professional service organizations face these problems to some degree. Much of this book is therefore devoted toward suggesting approaches for dealing with these problems. Some problems, like "third-party accountability" and "client uncertainty," will be addressed throughout the book. Other problems, like "maintaining quality control" and "making doers into sellers," will be treated primarily within appropriate chapters.

WHAT ORIENTATION IS NEEDED FOR A SUCCESSFUL MARKETING PROGRAM?

A final topic we need to address in this opening chapter is the necessity of developing a *marketing orientation.* The development of such an orientation should be the very first mission of a professional service organization seeking to become effective at marketing. This task involves much more than introducing a *marketing function.* The mere appointment of a marketing director or completion of a marketing research study will not, by itself, be enough. What a marketing orientation is can best be described by contrasting it to three other orientations that organizations can have. They are described below.

Production Orientation

Many organizations focus their attention on running a smooth production process, even if human needs must be neglected to meet the requirements of the production process. For example, some doctors' offices are run as though they are processing objects instead of people. Patients come in, wait for long stretches, tell their story to a nurse or assistant, see the doctor for a few seconds, pick up their prescriptions, fill out their insurance forms, pay their bills, and leave. One does not get the impression that the office personnel exist to serve the needs of patients but, rather, that the patients exist to meet the needs of the "system." As another example, consider the tax accountant who completes dozens of returns during the weeks just prior to April 15, focusing on how many he can finish (without asking for extensions) and taking as little time as necessary to discuss them with clients. We define a production orientation as follows:

> A **production orientation** holds that the major task of an organization is to pursue efficiency in production and distribution.

Product Orientation

Many organizations can be found which are in love with what they sell. They believe strongly in its value even if their target markets are having second thoughts. They would strongly resist modifying it even if this would increase its appeal to others. Thus, architects stick with a certain design philosophy even though many potential clients find it distasteful. And investment counselors continue to offer essentially the same investment portfolio to all their clients even though many have commented that it appears too risky. We define a product orientation as follows:

> A **product orientation** holds that the major task of an organization is to put out offerings which it thinks will be good for the public.

Sales Orientation

Some organizations believe they can substantially increase the size of their market by increasing their selling effort. Rather than change their offerings to make them more attractive, these organizations will increase the budget for advertising, personal selling, public relations, and other demand-stimulating activities. Thus, a law firm reacts to a decline in billings by starting an advertising campaign and urging its partners to make more speeches and public appearances. These sales-oriented steps may work to produce more clients in the short run. But their use in no way implies that the firm has moved into a marketing orientation that would generate more clients in the long run. A sales orientation is defined as follows:

> A **sales orientation** holds that the main task of the organization is to stimulate the interest of potential clients in the organization's existing offerings.

Marketing Orientation

We can now clarify the meaning of a marketing orientation against the background of these other orientations. Some organizations have discovered the value of focusing their attention not on production, offerings, or sales, but on meeting the changing needs and wants of their clients. They recognize that production, offerings, and sales are all means of producing satisfaction in target markets. Without satisfied clients, these organizations would soon find themselves "clientless" and tailspin into oblivion.

"Client-centeredness" is attained in an organization through hard work. The organization must systematically study clients' needs, wants, perceptions, preferences, and satisfaction—using surveys, group interviews, and other means. The organization must act on this information to improve its services constantly to meet its clients' needs better. The professional staff must be well selected and trained to feel that they are working for the client (rather than the boss). A client orientation will express itself in the friendliness with which the organization's telephone operators answer the phone and the helpfulness of various staff members in solving client problems. Staff members in a marketing-oriented organization will work *with* clients rather than *on* clients. We define a marketing orientation as follows:

> A **marketing orientation** holds that the main task of the organization is to determine the needs and wants of target markets and to satisfy them through the design, communication, pricing, and delivery of appropriate and competitively viable offerings.

Of course, the previously identified problem of "third-party accountability" will influence the nature of the marketing orientation a professional service firm can adopt. Client-centeredness must be carried out with a strong regard for the interests of relevant third parties. In a sense, the professional service organization must center itself around a broader group of clients than other types of organizations. How to set up an organization to do this is the focus of our next chapter.

SUMMARY

The 1980s have become "The Era of Marketing" in most of the professions. Marketing has helped to bring about a whole new competitive environment for professional service organizations. There are new types of firms offering new types of services in new types of locations. Fees are being billed in new ways and selling and advertising are being implemented using new, overt techniques.

Marketing is not something that is inherently unethical or manipulative. Different styles of marketing exist and marketing can be carried on with as much professionalism as the work of a lawyer, CPA, or doctor. The professional marketer is someone who is skilled at understanding, planning, and managing exchanges. A "marketing mix"—involving the design of offerings, pricing, distribution, and promotion—is developed by the marketer to achieve voluntary exchanges with target markets.

Professionals are turning to marketing to help them cope with increasing competition, greater public dissatisfaction with the professions, and several other changes in their external environments. They are finding marketing helpful in dealing with a variety of demand situations, including negative demand, falling demand, and overfull demand.

Professional service marketers cannot assume that the marketing approaches that have worked in other industries will automatically work for them. The marketing of professional services is different, with several distinctive problems that must be confronted. Professional service organizations must deal with high levels of client uncertainty, limited product differentiability, quality control difficulties, and several other obstacles to mounting a successful marketing effort.

The development of a marketing orientation should be the very first mission of a professional service organization seeking to become proficient at marketing. Such an orientation involves having the entire organization give primary attention to serving the needs and wants of clients and patients.

NOTES

1. See Philip Kotler, *Marketing for Nonprofit Organizations,* 2nd ed. (Englewood Cliffs, N.J.: Prentice-Hall, 1982).

2. Peter F. Drucker, *Management: Tasks, Responsibilities, Practices* (New York: Harper and Row, 1973), pp. 64–65.

3. See Paul N. Bloom, "Advertising in the Professions: The Critical Issues," *Journal of Marketing,* July 1977, pp. 103–10.

4. "FTC Gets Full Budget; Senate Kills AMA Rider," *Advertising Age,* December 27, 1982, p. 2.

5. See Deborah Silver, "Architects Refocus Plans to Build Business," *Crain's Chicago Business,* November 1, 1982, pp. 25–30.

6. See Paul Starr, "Too Many Doctors?", *Washington Post,* March 13, 1977, p. C3; Susan Tompor, "Doctors Turn to Marketing to Get Patients," *Wall Street Journal,* September 1, 1981, p. 1.

7. See "Those #*X/!!! Lawyers," *Time,* April 10, 1978, pp. 56–66; "The Troubled Professions," *Business Week,* August 16, 1976, pp. 126–38; "More Trouble for Doctors and Lawyers," *Business Week,* April 25, 1977, p. 102.

8. See Aubrey Wilson, *The Marketing of Professional Services* (London: McGraw-Hill, 1972); Warren J. Wittreich, "How to Buy/Sell Professional Services," *Harvard Business Review,* March–April 1966, pp. 127–36.

9. See *Marketing Consumer Services: New Insights,* Report No. 77–115 (Cambridge, Mass.: Marketing Science Institute, 1977).

10. See Wilson, *The Marketing of Professional Services;* Weld Coxe, *Marketing Architectural and Engineering Services* (New York: Von Nostrand, 1971); James J. Mahon, *The Marketing of Professional Accounting Services* (New York: Wiley, 1978); Christopher C. Gilson, Linda C. Cawley, and William R. Schmidt, *How to Market Your Law Practice* (Germantown, Md.: Aspen Systems, 1979); Irwin Braun, *Building a Successful*

Professional Practice with Advertising, (New York: AMACOM, 1981); Stan G. Webb, *Marketing and Strategic Planning for Professional Service Firms* (New York: AMACOM, 1982); Larry E. Greiner and Robert D. Metzger, *Consulting to Management* (Englewood Cliffs, N.J.: Prentice-Hall, 1983); Edward W. Wheatley, *Marketing Professional Services* (Englewood Cliffs, N.J.: Prentice-Hall, 1983).

2

ORGANIZING FOR BUSINESS DEVELOPMENT:

Creating a Marketing Organization

It was a public relations nightmare. One of New York City's largest and most reputable law firms, Stroock & Stroock & Lavan, was the first target of a clerical union's organizing drive among New York's big legal factories. Stroock resisted the union and the union responded by filing a complaint with the National Labor Relations Board, alleging unfair labor practices on the part of the law firm. The complaint was not all Stroock faced: it also found itself in the middle of a spate of bad publicity.

Quickly following came an accusation that the 170-lawyer firm had violated Florida bar rules by sending one of its Manhattan partners to represent clients in Stroock's new Miami office, even though the partner wasn't a member of the Florida bar. The law firm's slip was showing, and predictably reporters were once again pouncing on the indiscretion.

For Stroock & Stroock & Lavan, the proper course of action seemed obvious: it hired a public relations company to help it handle press inquiries and present a more favorable image. "We thought we ought to get some professional advice," recalls William Perlmuth, one of the partners who was instrumental in bringing in the outside public relations help. "We always give everyone else advice, so we thought we'd seek some ourselves."

Today, almost two years later, the unpleasantness over Stroock's unlicensed Florida law firm and its alleged union-busting tactics has faded. The firm accepted a general rebuke from the Florida Supreme Court, and the clerical workers' union withdrew its organizing bid (and its NLRB complaint) after failing to gain much support from those it would have represented. But Stroock's need for public relations has only intensified in the meantime. Stroock is now using its public relations company, Harshe-Rotman & Druck, to set up speaking engagements and interviews for Stroock's partners, suggest subjects for articles, and counsel the law firm in its relations with the media. According to public relations firms that work with lawyers, standard fees for such work could easily cost $25,000 to $100,000 a year.

Among law firms, Stroock isn't alone in its use of a public relations firm. And that, in turn, says something about the rapidly changing legal business. In an age of intense competition for new clients, many law firms have recently begun turning to skilled professionals in advertising, public relations, and marketing to help them gain an advantage in the scramble—however seemly—for business.

Source: Excerpted from John A. Jenkins, "Selling the Law," *TWA Ambassador,* August 1981, p. 52, with the permission of author and publisher. Copyright © 1981, Trans World Airlines, Inc.

The New York law firm's story illustrates one path that can be followed by a professional service organization in initiating a commitment toward marketing: the hiring of outside marketing and public relations experts to guide the organization. But this is only one approach among many that can be utilized. And for this approach to be most successful the entire staff of the professional service organization must become involved with marketing and not leave most of the marketing to be done by the outside experts. As indicated in the last chapter, it is necessary to make the "doers" of professional services into "sellers" and to create a marketing orientation throughout the organization.

The task of organizing a responsive, marketing-oriented organization is essential. Yet it is in performing this task that many professional service organizations seriously undermine their marketing effort. In fact, Richard Connor, a leading consultant on marketing professional services, has stated that the three most critical mistakes made in marketing professional services are related to how firms organize for marketing. These mistakes are:

1. Defining and limiting marketing to "getting new clients."
2. Misunderstanding or refusing to examine the organizational implications for effective marketing.
3. Neglecting to tie individual marketing effort into the firm's appraisal system.[1]

This chapter addresses how to avoid these mistakes and create an organization that understands, facilitates, and rewards marketing. We cover how to complete this task at the very beginning of the book because of its primary importance in establishing a successful professional service marketing program. The specific questions we will examine are:

1. Does a professional service organization need a formal marketing office in order to be effective in its marketing?

2. If an organization decides to establish a formal marketing office, what should be its level and job description, and where and how should the marketer be recruited?

3. What can this person do to accomplish results quickly?

4. How can the marketing function be elaborated over time?

5. What steps can be taken to make the whole organization more responsive and marketing oriented?

ASSESSING THE NEED FOR MARKETING

The issue of whether a professional service organization should install a formal marketing office is not the issue of whether it should do marketing. All organizations do marketing whether or not they organize it in a formal way or call it marketing, business development, or practice development. Figure 2–1 makes the points that various people in a professional service firm carry out some marketing work, consisting of identifying prospects, converting them into clients, doing market analysis, studying possible locations, and so on. The shaded areas indicate the relative amount of marketing work carried on in each job position. While the marketing office (if it exists) is totally involved in marketing work, the marketing function is larger than the work occurring within the marketing office. That is, a marketing office carries on only a small part of the total marketing work taking place in a professional service firm.

Historically, many professional service organizations have informally designated people as:

- "Finders": those who find business
- "Minders": those who take care of and develop the account
- "Grinders": those who service the account
- "Binders": those who hold the firm together and lead it[2]

The marketing issue confronting many firms is whether the informal use of certain partners and principals as finders should be supplemented by a more formal, extensive, and expensive marketing function. Should people be given marketing titles and assigned various marketing responsibilities?

Source: Modified from E. Gummesson, "Marketing Cost Concept in Service Firms," *Industrial Marketing Management*, Vol. 10 (1981), p. 178. Reprinted by permission of the publisher. Copyright 1981 by Elsevier Science Publishing Co., Inc.

FIGURE 2–1.   The marketing function (shaded area) in a professional service firm

Most professional service organizations would prefer to operate without a formal marketing office. They would like their reputations to draw in all of the clients they could ever want, eliminating the need to spend any time or money on marketing. In this ideal world, virtually 100 percent of all professionals' time would be billable (except for time spent in retraining to improve skills). Moreover, the ideal workload would consist of many highly "leveraged" projects—those with major portions of their billable hours attributed to lower-level or junior professionals who would perform the more routine work (i.e., "grinders"). Such an arrangement would tend to relieve senior people from having to do less stimulating tasks. It would also tend to help profitability, since junior people can often be billed out at greater "multiples" of their hourly cost to the firm than can senior people.[3]

But few professional service organizations find themselves in the ideal world we just described. The real world for most professionals will make it advisable to establish some type of formal marketing function. And the more likely it is that a firm will face (1) target markets in which the firm has no reputation and limited experience, (2) active marketing efforts by competitors, and (3) unpredictable and demanding clients, the more formal and extensive the marketing function will need to be.

Unfortunately, the installation of formal marketing responsibilities will have to either add to a firm's overhead expenses or cut down on the billable hours of its professionals. This, in turn, will tend to make it even more imperative to find highly leveraged projects—to compensate for the overhead and nonbillable hours that will be spent on marketing. However, if too many highly leveraged projects are pursued, service quality levels could suffer, as senior people might become less involved with the work. This could damage a firm's reputation and its ability to attract future clients. Thus, a fear of these possible developments often contributes to resistance to establishing more formal marketing responsibilities.

What we are saying is that for some firms the hiring of marketing personnel or the reassigning of existing personnel to marketing duties is a step that may appear too risky. Take, for example, a small law firm consisting of three partners who all recognize a need to get more involved with marketing. These partners may be reluctant to cut back any of their own billable hours—or, alternatively, to hire someone permanently to perform marketing tasks—because of a concern about having to compensate for this move by obtaining more ongoing matters and by having more of the work for those matters done by the firm's young associates and paralegals. They may fear a decline in quality in the firm's work. Or they may fear that clients will feel mistreated (even if quality is unaffected) by not having as much contact with the partners. (Assume they have ruled out the possibility that they could compensate for the move by raising their hourly fees because they do not believe their clients would accept this.)

Makeshift Marketing Approaches

Firms that reject the installation of a formal marketing office for reasons similar to those we have just described, or for any other reasons, can still take some concrete actions to improve their marketing resources. They can:

1. Send key people to marketing seminars and workshops to learn marketing, hoping they will somehow apply what they learn when they return to their old responsibilities.
2. Invite help from the marketing faculty of a business school, such as using a marketing research class to research a problem facing the organization.
3. Hire a marketing consulting firm, marketing research firm, advertising agency, or public relations firm to do specific projects when needed.
4. Rely on marketing support and assistance provided by a professional association. (See Exhibit 2–1 for an example.)

EXHIBIT 2–1. Example of marketing assistance provided by a professional association

A good example of the burgeoning trend toward health services marketing can be found in Operation Outreach, a three-tiered marketing program orchestrated by the American Dental Association (ADA), Chicago.

The scope of the plan is broad—involving dentists, local societies, and the national organization. More importantly, said Robert Roach, ADA assistant executive director of communications, the program represents a digression from the association's previous marketing efforts which focused on educating and informing consumers on the need for dental care.

In a recent *Journal of the American Dental Association (JADA)* article, Roach said Operation Outreach will expand those efforts into the areas of "motivating and influencing the public to seek dental care," a practice shunned by some but deemed necessary by others in order to combat the "busyness" problem facing dentists today.

Busyness, or the lack of it, in dental offices can be attributed to many factors including a depressed economy, long-term emphasis on preventive care, improvements in dental technology and increasing competition, the *JADA* said.

The new ADA marketing program emerged from an examination of the concerns expressed by member practitioners who were seeking guidance and leadership from their national organization. "Organized dentistry," Roach said, "will display an ancillary role, supporting, assisting, and supplementing the grassroots efforts of practitioners.

"In addition, the association will be responsible for collecting and disseminating proven dental marketing information, serving as a clearinghouse on the most current and successful programs," he said.

"How-to" materials and workshops for practitioners comprise the first tier of the plan, which has been designed to aid individual dentists in improving their skills at building and maintaining traditional dental practices, the *JADA* article said.

Materials available for purchase or rental by dentists include:

- A dental market planner workbook offering a step-by-step approach to developing a tailored, personalized marketing plan.
- Marketing starter kits containing sample recall cards, patient audit forms, staff questionnaires, patient newsletters, practice brochures, etc.
- Target marketing packages including marketing tools and promotional ideas to reach the more than 100 million Americans who do not regularly visit the dentist.
- Marketing idea files, a collection of the latest literature on specific marketing techniques and topics described in the dental market planner.
- Practice-building seminars in selected locations throughout the United States, as well as a national videoteleconference on "Dental Practice Promotion."
- A quarterly marketing newsletter covering developments in dental mar-

keting, resource materials, literature, abstracts, interviews with experts, and information on other health care activities.

"The society materials are designed to help constituent, component, and allied dental organizations implement broad-based community outreach marketing activities," the article said. Dental society materials, which are more generic in nature than those offered to practitioners, include:

- Dental society marketing planner workbook.
- Consulting services offering practical, on-site assistance in strategy development, goal setting, materials assessment, and development of specific marketing program activities.
- Conferences and workshops to review the latest in dental marketing research and programs.

The third tier of the program is represented by the new marketing service department at ADA headquarters, which will supervise the development of all materials and program activities and serve as a central advisory and coordinating agency for all written and audiovisual materials that have potential marketing applications, the article said.

The new department also will seek corporate funding for national educational and marketing activities which are too expensive or inappropriate for implementation at the state or local level.

They are:

1. *The elderly* with their special needs (dentures, for example) and problems (lack of insurance, limited or fixed incomes, reduced mobility).
2. *Working people* who may fail to obtain needed dental care because of job obligations and other variables.
3. *The poor and minority groups* who do not seek dental care for financial and other reasons.
4. *The disabled or handicapped* who may find dental service inaccessible or difficult to secure, based on their particular needs.
5. *Preschool children and their parents* who may be unaware of the importance of dental care for primary teeth.
6. *Unmotivated consumers* who shun dental care out of fear, a low priority on appearance or overall health, or who view dental service as inconvenient or inaccessible.

For each of these primary target groups, specific motivational messages were designed by the ADA to break down perceived barriers and to encourage the use of dental services, the article said.

Several such projects, which have already been launched or are under development, include:

- A pilot project, cosponsored by the ADA and the Colgate-Palmolive Co., designed to upgrade dental health education in inner city schools.

• A promotion, underwritten by Procter & Gamble Co., designed to promote dental office visits through a refund offer on Crest toothpaste which requires proof of a dental office visit.

• A bat boy/bat girl "Funstakes" designed to promote visits to the dentist. Previously operated by the ADA, the sweepstakes offers children a chance to be selected as bat boy or bat girl at the All-Star major league baseball game. Corporate sponsorship is being sought for 1984.

The *JADA* article said several manufacturers will also underwrite the cost of new patient education leaflets such as "How to Become a Wise Dental Consumer," recently revised with funding from Johnson & Johnson.

The initial step in developing the marketing program was extensive marketing research undertaken by the ADA to assess the needs and desires of the profession, determine the present state of dental marketing, etc. The article said it was that early research which helped identify six target markets of individuals who have either underused dental care services or who have been underserviced by the profession.

"Dentists have just begun to realize that dentistry is a business, and few businesses can survive without marketing," said James Pride, founder and codirector of the Pacific Institute, a firm specializing in dental office management.

"For some dentists, marketing will consist of getting a little bit nicer business card and learning to say, 'Good morning,'" he said. "For others, marketing will involve nothing short of TV."

The ADA marketing program can be tailored to the personality of the individual practitioner. Nevertheless, the article said, many dentists are suspicious of marketing and perceive it as unprofessional.

Their resistance stems from a disdain for commercialism and the equating of marketing with selling. Dental service marketing, however, is not a novel concept, the ADA's research disclosed. Both individual dentists and dental societies have used some form of marketing for years, normally under another name, such as "education."

"It should be understood at the outset," Roach said, "that the marketing plan is not to be regarded as a panacea for the busyness problem. Genuine and lasting improvement in dental practice weighs heavily on the efforts of individual practitioners.

"The marketing program will assist dentists and dental societies by pointing the way and providing certain tools. But the actual implementation of the program and its ultimate sucess depend largely on the skill and dedication of dentists themselves."

Source: "Operation Outreach Seeks to Expand Dental Market," *Marketing News,* February 18, 1983, p. 1. Reprinted from *Marketing News,* published by the American Marketing Association.

Although these makeshift ways of acquiring marketing services will not do the full job of creating a marketing-oriented organization, they will often produce good value in the short term and allow a firm to move gradually closer to installation of a formal marketing function. Nevertheless, certain precautions must be exercised. Seminars and workshops should be seen as providing only a very brief introduction to marketing.

They will not turn people into marketing experts overnight. They cannot take the place of years of real-world marketing experience or semesters of coursework in marketing. Similarly, one cannot expect unusually perceptive advice to come from student projects, since students typically have limited amounts of relevant experience upon which to base their recommendations.

On the other hand, the many years of marketing experience that may be obtained by employing outside marketing firms should also be viewed with caution. That experience may have been in industries that bear little resemblance to the relevant profession. Moreover, experienced marketers vary in quality. The good ones will talk about doing research on markets and building strong long-term relationships with clients. The poor ones will recommend quick-hitting advertising or public relations campaigns and growth for growth's sake.

Finally, the option of relying on professional associations seems potentially valuable. But programs like the American Dental Association's (see Exhibit 2–1) are still so new that their value has not been documented.

The Marketing Task Force

Eventually, firms confronted with difficult markets, tough competitive marketing actions, and/or demanding clients will probably perceive the risks associated with establishing a formal marketing function as relatively small. To reach a final decision on this matter, a *marketing task force* should be appointed and charged with three objectives:

1. Identifying marketing problems and opportunities facing the organization.
2. Assessing the felt need of key people throughout the organization for professional marketing assistance.
3. Recommending whether the organization should establish formal marketing positions.

The marketing task force should include representatives from a cross-section of the organization's groups or departments that might have a stake in marketing. Thus, a consulting firm's marketing task force should contain the people in charge of the various forms of consulting that the firm provides, as well as any people involved with proposal writing and public relations. The task force might also include an outside marketing consultant to provide professional guidance. The task force should gather information from various people—clients, referral sources, staff members, experts—as to: how they see the opportunities and threats in the organization's environment; what they see as the organization's strengths and weaknesses; what they view as the actual and desired strategy for the organization; how they perceive the marketing problems facing the organization; and so on. Many surprising, if not shocking, things will be discovered in this process.

The task force should digest the information and prepare a report for the president, managing partner, or principal-in-charge of the organization. The report should first present major findings about marketing problems and needs of the organization. Second, it should present recommendations as to courses of action. The recommendations can be divided into short-term actions (which can be implemented early and normally at low cost) and long-term actions (which take more time to implement and involve a higher cost). Ideas about how to formalize the marketing function should be prominent among the suggested actions.

This report of marketing findings and recommendations is called a *marketing audit* (see Chapter 14, pp. 277-82). Although it is an "inside" audit done primarily by a task force of nonmarketers, it is likely to be highly useful. The organization always has the option of hiring a marketing consultant or consulting firm to do a full-scale marketing audit, which will cost more but be likely to yield even greater value if an independent, objective, and experienced auditor is used.

ESTABLISHING MARKETING

At some point, the professional service organization may wish to establish a formal marketing office. The organization may find the makeshift use of outside marketing resources to be too costly or unreliable, or it may find that its marketing needs are extensive enough to hire a full-time marketing person or at least have someone devote a substantial block of time each week to marketing. The organization should recognize that establishing a marketing office is undertaken at some risk if the rest of the organization is resistant and/or if the new appointee is not given sufficient authority to carry out his or her responsibilities. However, if the organization decides to move forward, it must decide on (1) the level at which to hire or appoint someone, (2) the job description, and (3) the recruiting or selection strategy.

The major issue concerning level is whether to hire or appoint a middle-level or upper-level person to direct and coordinate the organization's marketing effort. Selection of the middle-level option would involve the designation of a marketing director, marketing coordinator, or marketing manager who would not be a partner or principal. This person would basically act as a resource person or internal marketing consultant to various other persons in the organization who need marketing services. This middle-level marketer would help define marketing problems, arrange for marketing research, and hire advertising agency services as needed. A job description for a middle-level "Director of Marketing Services" is provided in Table 2–1.

Alternatively, an organization could hire or appoint an upper-level person to lead the marketing effort. Such a person would be given partner or principal status and hold a position with more scope, authority, and influence. With a title such as "partner in charge of marketing" or "vice president of marketing," this person would not only coordinate

TABLE 2–1
JOB DESCRIPTION FOR A DIRECTOR
OF MARKETING SERVICES

Position Title: Director of Marketing Services

Reports to: Chief Executive Officer of the firm

Scope: Firm-wide

Position Concept: The Director of Marketing Services is responsible for providing marketing guidance and services to the entire firm.

Functions: The Director of Marketing services will:

> 1. contribute a marketing perspective to the deliberations of top management in its planning of the firm's future.
> 2. prepare data that might be needed by firm personnel on a particular market's size, segments, trends, and behavioral dynamics.
> 3. conduct studies of the needs, perceptions, preferences, and satisfactions of particular markets.
> 4. assist in the planning, promotion, and launching of new services and programs.
> 5. assist in the development of communication and promotion campaigns and materials.
> 6. analyze and advise on pricing or fee questions.
> 7. advise on new client development.
> 8. advise on satisfaction levels of current clients.

Responsibilities: The Director of Marketing Services will:

> 1. contact individual officers and small groups in the firm to explain services and solicit problems.
> 2. prioritize the various requests for services according to their long-run impact, cost-saving potential, time requirements, ease of accomplishment, cost, and urgency.
> 3. select projects of high priority and set accomplishment goals for the year.
> 4. prepare a draft of the annual marketing plan, with relevant budget requests, to be reviewed and modified by top management.
> 5. prepare an annual report on the main accomplishments of the office.

---

and supply marketing services for others, but would also participate in the setting of policy and direction for the organization. This person would be responsible for planning and managing relations with all of the organization's clients.

Which position should it be initially? Some organizations prefer to appoint a middle-level person on the idea that the position costs less, its value can be tested, and, if the person proves effective, he or she can be promoted to an upper-level post. Other organizations feel that a middle-level person can only accomplish minor things because he or she would not have the ear of the most influential people and would not participate in the making of important strategic decisions. Our own view is that the upper-level option should be adopted initially, although we acknowledge the difficulty in finding the right person to fill such a position. Among other things, this approach makes it easier to accomplish the necessary task of transforming the thinking of key people into a marketing mode.

Suppose, however, that the organization decides initially to appoint a middle-level director of marketing services to occupy a position like the one described in Table 2–1. Before searching for a qualified person to fill the job, the organization will want to define further the desirable age of the person, years and type of marketing experience, salary range, and planned budget for the job. The organization may decide that it wants a person with substantial marketing training and experience in any industry in preference to a person who has worked in its profession—whether accounting, law, dentistry, or engineering—but who has only weak training in marketing. The organization may feel it is easier to educate a person about the nuances of its profession than to train the person as a marketer. The major drawback to this approach is that a lack of relevant professional credentials (e.g., J.D., CPA, M.D.) may provide an obstacle to the promotion to partner or principal of a middle-level marketer, making that person feel like he or she is in a "dead-end" position. Such a perception can hurt performance and also lead to short job tenures.

Normal recruitment channels should be used to locate promising candidates—job ads in newspapers, professional journals, or the *Marketing News* (published by the American Marketing Association); phone calls to business school professors for leads; use of executive search firms; and so on. This should produce a large number of leads, leaving the organization to prune the list and interview a few of the most promising candidates and make a choice among them.

THE FIRST MARKETING PROJECTS

A newly appointed marketing director, marketing vice president, or other top marketing executive will want to demonstrate quickly that marketing thinking can contribute value to the professional service organization. Many members of the organization will be critical of marketing, arguing that it is inappropriate or a waste of money. Others will be puzzled about what marketing is or does. Only a few will see it as a strong opportunity for the organization.

In the face of this skepticism, the new "director" must carefully choose initial projects which, if successfully executed, demonstrate the value of marketing. The marketing director must, in essence, *market marketing,* and should therefore spend considerable effort determining what the target markets—in this case, the other people in the organization—think and feel about various marketing projects. The director should not assume that he or she knows what others want, but should conduct interviews and group discussions to get opinions and ideas about various projects. Some people may be cool to the idea of conducting a small-scale research project to find out more about the organization's image, while others might suggest a strong desire for a small study of client perceptions of the organization's fees.

Obtaining feedback about possible projects should build goodwill and understanding with various people in the organization and lead to many project ideas, often more than can be handled by a single marketing director operating with a small budget. The director should not promise to do work on any project until he or she reviews the possible projects and chooses the best ones. The best early projects to undertake would have four characteristics:

1. A high impact of making money or saving money for the organization
2. A relatively small cost to carry out
3. A short period of time for completion
4. A high visibility potential if successful

Projects possessing these characteristics will vary by organization and by profession. For some organizations the best initial projects might involve exercises in introspection for top management, where the mission of the organization and the clients it should be targeting are given careful examination. For other organizations the best initial projects will involve small, narrowly targeted promotional efforts, such as the sending of a reprint of a journal article, written by someone in the organization, to prospective clients who are likely to be facing the problems discussed in the article.

MORE ELABORATE MARKETING ORGANIZATIONS

If the "marketing director" (regardless of level) does a good job and this is recognized by others in the organization, then more resources will become available. The director may want to hire one or more assistants to specialize in marketing research, client communications, new services evaluation, and other marketing functions. It pays to hire a full-time expert in any specialized marketing function that the organization needs to cover on a continuous basis. For example, one of the Big Eight CPA firms recently appointed a vice president of marketing who is provided with staffs to support him in three areas: (1) research/information, (2) communications/public relations, and (3) sales support (presentations and sales training).

Although most professional service organizations will never need highly elaborate marketing departments, it is useful to provide a list of the variety of job positions found in full-scale marketing departments in major corporations. A description of these job positions is presented in Table 2–2. They suggest the many functions that must be absorbed by the small marketing groups (or single marketing person) of most professional service firms.

Normally, the first step in expanding a marketing department is to add functional specialists, such as a marketing researcher and/or a communications manager. But at some point the organization will want to give serious consideration to establishing a product/service management system, market management system, or both. A product/service management system would call for appointing a different person to head the marketing effort for each major product/service offered by the organization. For example, Burke Marketing Research—a well-known marketing research firm based in Cincinnati—introduced a service management system a few years ago with the following statement:

> The marketing concept at Burke involves the assignment of responsibility for the planning, research and marketing of new and existing services to those Burke personnel experienced with each specific service. These individuals will have the specific responsibility for evaluating the potential of their particular product/service as well as identifying target clients. Responsibility will also include developing appropriate promotional materials, preparing and making presentations to new and existing clients and counselling the Burke staff in the most effective use of the new product/service.[4]

Burke appointed people to manage the following services that it offers:

1. Focused group discussions
2. Wide Area Telephone Service (WATS) studies
3. Personal and telephone interviews among professionals (i.e., businessmen, doctors, computer operators, etc.)
4. Central location studies
5. Custom market area sampling
6. Cathode ray tube interviewing
7. Day-after recall testing
8. Management development seminars[5]

TABLE 2–2
GENERIC MARKETING POSITIONS

MARKETING MANAGER

1. Other names: vice president of marketing, marketing director, chief marketing officer, marketing administrator.

2. The marketing manager heads the organization's marketing activities. Tasks include providing a marketing point of view to the top administration; helping to formulate marketing plans of the organization; staffing, directing, and coordinating marketing activities; and proposing new products and services to meet emerging market needs.

PRODUCT/SERVICE MANAGER

1. Other names: program manager, brand manager.

2. A product/service manager is responsible for managing a particular product/service, or program of the organization. Tasks include proposing product objectives and goals, creating product strategies and plans, seeing that they are implemented, monitoring the results, and taking corrective actions.

MARKET MANAGER

1. Other names: market segment manager, industry manager.

2. A market manager is responsible for managing the marketing program for a particular market segment. Tasks include proposing market objectives and goals, creating strategies and plans for the market, seeing that they are implemented, monitoring results, and taking corrective actions.

MARKETING RESEARCH MANAGER

1. Other names: marketing research director.

2. The marketing research manager has responsibility for developing and supervising research on the organization's markets and publics, and on the effectiveness of various marketing tools.

COMMUNICATIONS MANAGER

1. Other names: advertising manager, advertising and sales promotion director.

2. The communications manager provides expertise in the area of mass and selective communication and promotion. Person is knowledgeable about the development of messages, media, and publicity.

SALES MANAGER

1. Other names: vice president of sales.

2. The sales manager has responsibility for recruiting, training, assigning, directing, motivating, compensating, and evaluating sales personnel and agents of the organization, and coordinating the work of sales personnel with the other marketing functions.

TABLE 2–2 *(cont.)*

New-products/Services Manager

1. Other names: new-products services director.

2. The new-products/services manager has responsibility for conceiving new products and services; screening and evaluating new product ideas; developing prototypes and testing them; and advising and helping to carry out the innovation's introduction in the marketplace.

Distribution Manager

1. Other names: channel manager, physical distribution manager, logistics manager.

2. The distribution manager has responsibility for planning and managing the distribution systems that make the organization's products and services available and accessible to the potential users.

Pricing Manager

1. Other names: pricing executive.

2. The pricing manager is responsible for advising and/or setting prices on the organization's services and programs.

Customer Relations Manager

1. Other names: customer service manager, account manager.

2. The customer relations manager has responsibility for managing customer services and handling customer complaints.

Government Relations Manager

1. Other names: legislative representative; lobbyist.

2. The government relations manager provides the organization with intelligence on relevant developments in government and manages the organization's program of representation and presentation to government.

Public Relations Manager

1. Other names: public affairs officer.

2. The public relations manager has responsibility for communicating and improving the organization's image with various publics.

Territory Manager

1. Other names: regional manager, district manager, area manager.

2. The territory manager has responsibility for managing the organization's products, services, and programs in a specific territory.

Source: Adapted from Philip Kotler, *Marketing for Nonprofit Organizations,* 2nd ed. (Englewood Cliffs, N.J.: Prentice-Hall, 1982), pp. 140–41.

A market management system, on the other hand, would call for appointing a different person to head the marketing effort for each major market segment served by the organization. For example, a marketing research firm such as Burke could have different market managers for government agency clients, retailer clients, consumer product manufacturer clients, and so on. Similarly, a CPA firm could have different market managers lead the marketing programs developed for the banking industry, the publishing industry, and other major industries served by the firm.

Both systems have many advantages. A product/service management system helps insure that each major product/service provided by the organization is given adequate attention and developed to its fullest potential. Additionally, the competition that can develop internally between product/service managers—if not allowed to become too heated—can also be healthy for an organization, stimulating the use of more creative marketing approaches. Similarly, a market management system helps insure that each major market segment is given adequate attention and that creative competition between market managers occurs. These managers can become experts on the needs and wants of their assigned markets, improving the organization's ability to develop effective promotional appeals and new service ideas.

The advantages associated with both systems often make it attractive to utilize both within a *matrix organization.* But the expenses associated with a matrix approach can often outweigh its benefits. A good way to proceed is to install a few product/service and market managers on a trial basis (using existing personnel) to see what the system produces and costs the organization.

CREATING A RESPONSIVE
ORGANIZATION

Whether a professional service organization pursues marketing by relying on outside marketing consultants or by building an elaborate formal marketing structure, achieving excellence in marketing requires the creation of a responsive organization. We define this type of organization as follows:

> A **responsive organization** is one that makes every effort to sense, serve, and satisfy the needs and wants of its clients within the constraints of (1) the legal and ethical standards of its profession and (2) its financial resources.

The responsive organization receives rave reviews from the vast majority of its clients. These people become the best advertisements for the organization. Their goodwill and favorable word-of-mouth make it easier for the organization to attract and serve more people.

Being responsive means answering telephone calls courteously and returning telephone calls promptly. It means politely putting people on hold for a few seconds at the outset of a phone conversation in order to locate their file and quickly become familiar with the matter that prompted their call. It means taking the time to talk with clients about their problems and about services the organization offers that might help alleviate their problems. And it means constantly seeking information from both current and previous clients about their satisfaction with the organization's services and their thoughts about where services can be improved.

Some professional service organizations may already be reasonably responsive and may require only the addition of a more formalized marketing function to achieve marketing excellence. But for those professional service organizations which have been deficient in their "client" orientation, the process of becoming a responsive, marketing-oriented organization can take a long time. Convincing experienced professionals that they must make fundamental changes in the way they deal with clients—and teaching them how to do so—is not something that can be accomplished overnight. Older partners or principals may be set in their ways because they feel their ways have worked in the past or they have "paid their dues" and should not have to make an investment in new learning. Moreover, convincing new, less experienced profession-als to contribute to a marketing effort can be just as difficult. Many young professionals do not have strong, long-term commitments to their organi-zations. They prefer to focus their energies on developing their technical professional skills rather than on developing marketing or selling skills.

In the face of these obstacles, attempts to reorient an organization require a plan. The plan must be based on sound principles for producing organizational change. Achieving a marketing orientation calls for sever-al measures, the sum of which will hopefully produce a responsive organization within a few years. These measures are described below.

Top Management Support

A professional service organization is not likely to develop a strong marketing orientation until its chief executive officer (CEO)—the found-ing partner, chairman, managing partner, president, or other organiza-tional leader—believes in it, understands it, wants it, and wins the support of other high-level people for building this function. The CEO is the organization's highest "marketing executive," and has to create the climate for marketing by talking about it and agitating for it. By setting the tone that the organization must be service-minded and responsive, the CEO prepares the groundwork for introducing further changes later.

Effective Organization Design

The CEO cannot do the whole marketing job. Eventually, a marketing office must be introduced into the organization in one of the forms discussed earlier in this chapter. Marketing involves hard work, and this work cannot be done effectively by people who are doing marketing on only an occasional basis. A managing partner who is highly respected and well versed in marketing should ideally head the function. Working for him should be a full-time marketing director who has no chargeable hours to achieve personally.

In-House Marketing Training

An early task of the person taking charge of the marketing effort is to develop a series of workshops to introduce marketing to various groups in the organization. These groups are likely to have incorrect ideas about marketing and little understanding of its potential benefits.

The first workshop should be presented to top management. Their understanding and support are absolutely essential if marketing is to work in the organization. The workshop may take place at the organization's headquarters or at a retreat; it may consist of a highly professional presentation of concepts, cases, and marketing planning exercises. From there, further presentations can be made to lower-level people to enlist their understanding. These presentations should cover such topics as market opportunity identification, market segmentation, market targeting and positioning, marketing planning and control, fee setting, selling, and marketing communication. Updated information on how marketing concepts are being implemented by the firm can be provided through the use of internal marketing newsletters, something used by numerous CPA and consulting firms.

Improved Hiring Practices

Training can only go so far in inculcating the right attitudes in staff members. For example, a group of engineers who have spent most of their careers working on highly technical matters and talking mostly to one another may never be able to develop marketing and selling skills. An organization must therefore think about trying to rectify such a situation gradually by hiring more client-centered, marketing-oriented people. Some individuals are more naturally service-minded and friendly than others, and this can be a criterion for hiring.

New staff members should go through a training program that emphasizes the importance of creating satisfied clients. They can be taught how to handle complaining and even abusive people without getting riled up. Skills in listening and client problem solving would be part of the training.

Facilitating and Rewarding Marketing-Oriented Actions

One way for top management to convince everyone in the organization of the importance of marketing-oriented attitudes is to facilitate and reward marketing-oriented behavior. The following example illustrates how this might be done:

> A large public accounting firm made the decision recently that practitioners should spend approximately one-fourth of their time in practice development. Management, however, realized that this would be a pious utterance unless backed by incentive and budget. Practitioners could not be expected to work a longer day. Nor could they be expected to cut down their current "billable" time. The only solution was to create a budget account for business development which could support the practitioners' club memberships, luncheons, and charges to billable time.
>
> Furthermore, the desired behavior still wouldn't come about unless practitioners found that their effectiveness at business development was included as a factor in determining their annual bonuses. In addition, the firm created a new position that, among other things, organized seminars to help practitioners improve their planning and sales skills. The office designed planning forms that are filled out by the practitioners each year describing their intentions in the areas of cross-selling, prospecting, referral source work, favorable awareness activities, etc. These plans are reviewed quarterly for accomplishment and for redesign where necessary.[6]

We will provide further details about how to insure that staff members will perform their marketing duties when we cover the subject of controlling the marketing program (Chapter 14). We will also address the question of how much time each professional should allocate to marketing (is the one-fourth figure cited above an appropriate one?) when we cover the subject of selling (Chapter 10). The important thing to note here is that marketing should not be seen by staff members as a costly activity for them to pursue. Marketing should be made easy, exciting, and financially rewarding for professionals to become involved with.

SUMMARY

All professional service organizations carry on marketing whether or not they acknowledge this. The issue is whether they should utilize marketing more formally. Organizations can draw on marketing resources in a number of ways, such as inviting help from marketing professors, hiring marketing firms (advertising agencies and marketing research firms), and sending their staff to marketing seminars. When the organization feels ready to establish a formal marketing function, it can hire a middle-level marketing services director, whose job is to supply marketing assistance and services to others in the organization. Or it could hire an upper-level vice president of marketing whose job is to participate with top management in strategy and policy formulation. A careful search should be made for the right person, who understands both marketing and the relevant profession. This person should choose initial marketing projects that promise to have a high impact on the organization for a relatively small cost in a reasonably short period of time. If marketing's contribution is strong, its size will expand over time to cover different marketing functions, services, markets, and territories. The presence of a marketing department, however, does not mean that the organization as a whole is marketing oriented, since this department may have limited influence. To create a truly marketing-oriented organization requires several things: top management support, effective organization design, in-house marketing training, improved hiring practices, and the facilitation and reward of marketing-oriented behavior.

NOTES

1. Richard A. Connor Jr., "Marketing Professional Services—Insights and Action Steps," paper presented at the Special Conference on Services Marketing of the American Marketing Association, Orlando, Fla. Februrary 8–11, 1981.

2. See David H. Maister, "Balancing the Professional Service Firm," *Sloan Management Review*, Fall 1982, pp. 15–29.

3. Ibid.

4. Burke Marketing Research, Inc., "Burke Implements Marketing Concept," *The Burke Investigator*, December 1976, p. 1. Reprinted with permission.

5. Ibid.

6. Philip Kotler and Richard A. Connor, Jr., "Marketing Professional Services," *Journal of Marketing*, January 1977, p. 75.

3
STRATEGIC PLANNING FOR MARKETING

Bill Novelli watched the returns from the 1980 presidential election with great interest. He realized that if Ronald Reagan won the election a whole new strategic direction would be required for Porter, Novelli and Associates, the seven-year-old consulting firm which Bill headed with his colleague, Jack Porter. The 40-person, Washington, D.C.–based firm had enjoyed steady growth throughout its existence, establishing a reputation as the top "social" marketing consulting firm in the country. By specializing in providing marketing advice to government agencies and nonprofit organizations involved with promoting socially beneficial causes, Bill's firm had helped programs involved with "selling" high blood pressure control, physical fitness, smoking cessation, and other offerings. But a Reagan victory would most likely bring substantial budget cuts to most federal health and welfare agencies, limiting their ability to use the services of firms like Porter, Novelli.

As the television networks came through with their predictions of a Reagan landslide, Bill turned to his wife, Fran, who worked with him at Porter, Novelli, and lamented: "We're never going to be able to get as much work from the feds as we have in the past. Unless we find a new target market, we'll have to let some people go. Maybe we should focus on the states— although the conservative swing in this election tells me that they'll be hit by budget crunches too. And I'm not sure how charities and nonprofits will be affected by any tax changes Reagan pushes through. I don't know, maybe we'll have to rethink our whole mission and modify our positioning as a 'social marketing' firm. It looks like we're going to have to figure out some type of strategy to get work from big corporations, trade associations, and others who might have money to spend on consultants."

Bill had to laugh as he thought of the irony of where events were taking him. He had started his marketing career as a product manager with Lever

Brothers and then spent some time in account management with a major New York advertising agency. He left the commercial world in the early 1970s to become advertising director for the Peace Corps. He found he liked selling social causes better than selling soap and therefore opened his consulting firm. Now he was coming full circle and having to return to the commercial world. He thought the skills his firm had acquired in selling social causes would be useful to profit-making organizations. But he had to figure out a strategy for presenting and promoting these skills to this new target market. Bill thought about the discussions he had held recently with the management of Needham, Harper, and Steers—a major advertising agency with accounts like Xerox and Honda—about a merger between their firms. Maybe such an action would provide a good way for his firm to reach and obtain commercial clients.

Sophisticated organizations in all industries are increasingly turning to strategic planning as the major systematic theory for adapting to changes like the one that faced Bill Novelli. We define strategic planning as follows:

> **Strategic planning** is the managerial process of developing and maintaining a strategic direction that aligns the organization's goals and resources with its changing marketing opportunities.

Professional service organizations have to pay attention to *market evolution* and *strategic fit.* All markets undergo evolutionary development marked by changing clients, competitors, technologies, and laws. A firm should be looking out of a *strategic window* watching these changes and assessing the requirements for continued success in each market.[1] There is only a limited period when the fit between the requirements of a particular market and the organization's competencies is at an optimum. At these times the strategic window is open, and the organization should be investing in this market. In some subsequent period, the organization will find that the evolutionary path of this market is such that it can no longer be effective and efficient in serving this market. It should then consider disinvesting and shifting its resources to areas of growing opportunity—as Bill Novelli was doing in contemplating a shift from federal agencies to profit-making firms.

The major steps that an organization should take to remain strong in a changing environment are shown in Figure 3–1. First, the organization should carry out a careful analysis of its *environment,* both today's envi-

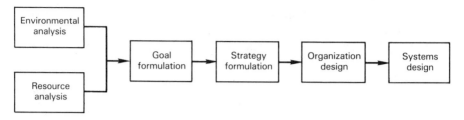

FIGURE 3-1. Strategic planning process

ronment and tomorrow's probable environment, to ascertain its major opportunities and challenges. Then it should review its major *resources* as indicating what it can feasibly hope to do. The environment and resource analysis lead the organization to formulate new and appropriate *goals* to pursue in the coming planning period. Goal formulation is followed by *strategy formulation* in which the management chooses the most cost-effective strategy for reaching its goals. The development of a *marketing strategy* is an important part of this step. Finally, attention is turned to the *organization's structure* and *systems* to see if they permit carrying out the strategy effectively. When all of these components are aligned, they spell performance.

In this chapter, we show how people like Bill Novelli can use the strategic planning process in Figure 3-1 in making decisions about target markets, mergers, and other basic matters. Our coverage essentially provides an introduction to the steps of strategic planning, with more detailed discussions of certain steps coming later in the book. The material here is particularly important for laying the groundwork for learning how to develop a marketing plan—a topic covered in our concluding chapter (Chapter 14).

ENVIRONMENTAL ANALYSIS

The first step in strategic planning is to analyze the environment in which the organization operates, trying to identify the leading trends and their implications for the organization. A high-level person, internal committee, or external consultant should be charged with the task of studying the changing environment, using the organization's marketing information system (see Chapter 7) for guidance.

The major components of a professional service organization's environment are:

1. *Internal environment,* consisting of the internal publics of the organization, specifically, the *board of directors* (if one exists), *partners, principals, officers, associates,* and *staff.*

2. *Market environment,* consisting of the individuals and other organizations that the professional service organization directly works with to accomplish its mission. The main components of the market environment are *clients, collaborating professionals, referral sources,* and *suppliers.*

3. *Public environment,* consisting of other groups and organizations that take an interest in the activities of the organization. The public environment consists of *activist publics, media publics, regulatory agencies, professional societies,* and the *general public.*

4. *Competitive environment,* consisting of individuals and organizations that compete for attention and loyalty from the markets and publics of the organization.

5. *Macroenvironment,* consisting of large-scale fundamental forces that shape opportunities and pose threats to the organization. The main macroenvironmental forces that have to be watched are the *demographic, economic, technological, political,* and *social* forces. These forces largely represent "uncontrollables" in the organization's situation to which it has to adapt.

A firm's strategic planners should research each major environment component following a four-step procedure. The procedure consists of (1) listing the major factors and subfactors making up the environment component, (2) describing the major trends in each factor, (3) describing the implications of these trends for the organization, and (4) converting these implications into specific opportunities and threats.

Threat Analysis

Every professional service organization must attempt to identify the major threats it faces. We define threat as follows:

> An **environmental threat** is a challenge posed by an unfavorable trend or specific disturbance in the environment which would lead, in the absence of purposeful marketing action, to the stagnation, decline, or demise of an organization or one of its services.

Not all threats warrant the same attention or concern. Strategic planners should assess each threat according to two dimensions: (1) its *potential severity* (measured by the amount of money the organization would lose if the threat materialized), and (2) its *probability of occurrence.* Suppose the managing partner of a CPA firm identified the following four threats:

1. The firm might lose four audit clients, worth $150,000 in fees, if proposed mergers are carried out between the clients and larger corporations.
2. The cost of hiring the five new junior accountants the firm attempts to bring in annually might increase 15 percent next year.
3. The firm might lose $40,000 worth of small-business audit work to

competing CPA firms which offer to conduct less expensive "reviews" instead of audits for small clients.

4. The firm might be hit with a multimillion-dollar liability suit from a dissatisfied stockholder of a major client.

A chart such as that shown in Figure 3–2 can be developed as part of the threat analysis. The most serious threats are those shown in the upper left cell (in this example, number 1), and they require the firm to come up with contingency plans. The least serious threats are shown in the lower right cell and they can safely be ignored. The other two cells contain threats of medium seriousness and they should at least be monitored, although contingency plans are not necessary. By identifying and classifying threats, a firm knows which environmental developments to plan for, monitor, or ignore.

Probability of occurrence

	High	Low
Potential severity **High**	1	4
Potential severity **Low**	2	3

FIGURE 3–2.   Threat matrix

Opportunity Analysis

Opportunity analysis is as important as threat analysis, and probably more important. By managing its threats successfully, an organization stays intact but it doesn't grow. But by managing its opportunities successfully, the organization can make great strides forward. Here we are concerned with marketing opportunities. We define marketing opportunity as follows:

> A **marketing opportunity** is an attractive arena of relevant marketing action in which a particular organization is likely to enjoy superior competitive advantages.

Every level of an organization should make an effort to identify several opportunities facing the organization. Suppose the president of a large management consulting firm perceives the following opportunities:

1. The firm could introduce a "marketing audit" service for professional service organizations to capitalize on the great interest in marketing among accountants, lawyers, architects, and so on.

2. The firm could start a "personal computer assistance program" designed to give advice to the growing number of business firms that are considering giving personal computers to their sales forces and other personnel.

3. The firm could open a branch office in a thriving "Sunbelt" city where the existence of many growing businesses might provide numerous consulting opportunities.

4. The firm could offer a series of seminars for managers on "stress management."

Not all opportunities are equally attractive. An opportunity can be assessed in terms of two basic dimensions: (1) its *potential attractiveness* (measured by the amount of revenue or other results that an organization might value), and (2) its *success probability* (measured by the ability of the organization to develop the opportunity). The results of assessing the preceding opportunities is shown in the opportunity matrix of Figure 3–3. Offering marketing audits for professional service organizations seems to be the best opportunity for the firm since it will produce a good revenue stream, provide a way of spreading good word-of-mouth about the firm to the business clients of the audited professionals, and have a high probability of being done competently and effectively by the firm's staff of marketing consultants. Opportunities in the upper left cell deserve specific plans to be designed. On the other hand, the stress seminars fall in the lower right cell, which means they should be rejected since heavy competition in the "help with stress" market will limit revenue possibilities and make success unlikely. Opportunities in the other two cells are worth monitoring, although specific planning is not warranted.

The activity of identifying threats and opportunities can result in four different findings on the organization's situation. The organization might be lucky and find that it faces many strong opportunities and few threats (an ideal situation). It might find that it faces strong opportunities and strong threats (a speculative situation). It might find that it faces only strong threats (a threatening situation). Or it might find that it faces neither significant threats nor opportunities (a mature situation).

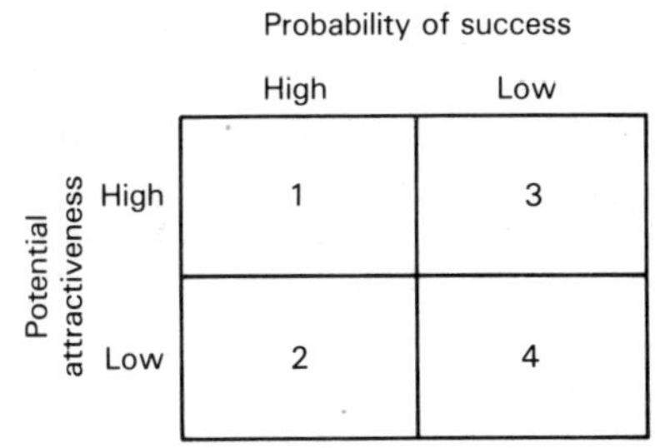

FIGURE 3–3. Opportunity matrix

RESOURCE ANALYSIS

Following the environmental analysis, a firm's strategic planners should undertake an analysis of its resources and capabilities. The purpose is to identify the major resources that the organization has (its *strengths*) and lacks (its *weaknesses*). The premise is that an organization should pursue goals, opportunities, and strategies which are suggested by, or congruent with, its strengths and avoid those where its resources are too weak.

Figure 3–4 shows a form that the organization can use, with appropriate modifications, to develop a *resource audit.* The major resources listed are people, money, facilities, systems, and market assets. Management indicates whether its position with respect to each resource constitutes a strength (high, medium, low), is neutral, or constitutes a weakness (low, medium, high). Suppose the checks reflect a law firm's evaluation of its resources. The firm believes that it has very adequate and skilled professionals who, unfortunately, are not very enthusiastic, loyal, or service-minded. As for money, the firm has several big corporate clients who are very loyal, because of old ties to certain partners, and who provide a base amount of revenues that the firm can rely upon to avoid financial problems—at least for the near future. The firm's physical facilities are somewhat lacking, with no spare office space to allow for firm growth, a poor library, antiquated filing and typing equipment (with only limited word processing capabilities), and an inconvenient location for both staff members and clients. Its management systems for information, planning, and control are quite weak. Finally, the firm is in a relatively strong position with respect to clients, contacts, and general reputation.

In considering opportunities, the organization should generally avoid those for which necessary resources are weak or inadequate. If a law firm is considering making a bigger commitment to tax law, but has few staff members with good accounting backgrounds and/or tax experience, then the idea should be dropped. As we stated in Chapter 1, *experience is essential* in the marketing of professional services. However, in some circumstances an organization may be able to obtain experienced people, or other resources it lacks to carry out a particular venture, by hiring new professionals or entering into mergers or joint ventures.

As a clue to its best opportunities, the organization should pay attention to its distinctive competencies. *Distinctive competencies* are those *resources and abilities that the organization is especially strong in.* If a law firm happens to have two people who are well known and experienced in handling large negligence cases, then it might want to consider expanding its practice in this area. Organizations will find it easiest to work from their strengths rather than trying to build up a more balanced set of strengths.

(H = high; M = medium; L = low; N = neutral)

(Checks ✔ are illustrative)

Resource	Strength			N	Weakness		
	H	M	L	N	L	M	H
People							
1. Adequate?	✔						
2. Skilled?	✔						
3. Enthusiastic?						✔	
4. Loyal?							✔
5. Service-minded?						✔	
Money							
1. Adequate?		✔					
2. Flexible?					✔		
Facilities							
1. Adequate?					✔		
2. Flexible?						✔	
3. Location quality?						✔	
Systems							
1. Information system quality?					✔		
2. Planning system quality?						✔	
3. Control system quality?						✔	
Market assets							
1. Client base?		✔					
2. Contact base?	✔						
3. General reputation?		✔					

FIGURE 3-4. Organization resource analysis

At the same time, a distinctive competence may not be enough if the organization's major competitors possess the same distinctive competence. As we discussed in Chapter 1, an organization should seek to differentiate itself from its competitors, even though this is often hard to do in the professions. Thus, an organization should pay close attention to those strengths in which it possesses a *differential advantage*—that is, it can outperform competitors on that dimension. For example, a law firm may not only have a distinctive competence in antitrust law, but by having a former commissioner of the Federal Trade Commission as a firm partner it may have a differential advantage in pursuing clients who face FTC complaints. The differential advantage permits the firm to achieve a sustainable competitive position in the marketplace.

In evaluating its strengths and weaknesses, the professional service organization should not rely on its own perceptions, but should go out and do an *image study* of how it is perceived by its key publics. For example, an architectural firm may feel it designs beautiful modern office buildings, but an image study may reveal that facilities managers in most local corporations perceive the firm as designing sterile, unimaginative, expensive glass boxes. Image studies frequently yield information about organizational strengths and weaknesses that managers have not considered. We will provide more information about how to do image studies in the next chapter and in Chapter 7.

GOAL FORMULATION

The environmental and resource analyses are designed to provide the necessary background and stimulus to management thinking about its basic goals as an organization. The professional service organization needs to establish goals to enable it to determine what it should be doing, develop effective plans, set objectives for individuals' performances, and evaluate results. Without goals, anything the organization does or achieves can be considered acceptable; there is no standard for planning and control.

The task of establishing organizational goals breaks into two distinct steps, namely, (1) determining what the current goals are, and (2) determining what the goals should be. Even the image of the current goals will differ from person to person and group to group in the organization. For example, one partner in a CPA firm may see the primary goal as increasing the number of clients served by the firm. Another partner may see the primary goal as increasing the amount of services provided to (and revenues received from) existing clients. A third partner may see the primary goal as expansion of the firm's management consulting revenues. To discover the current goals requires interviewing several individuals and groups as to what they think the organization's goals and their own goals are, and trying to make sense out of the resulting data. The data will show that the organization is really a coalition of several groups, each giving and seeking different things from the organization.

Determining what the goals of the organization should be is even a harder task. In principle, the chairman or CEO of a CPA firm can unilaterally set new goals for the firm for the next decade, or even longer. Increasingly, however, top management has found it useful to involve others in the process of goal formulation. Their ideas on proper goals may not only be valuable, but are more likely to be embraced and supported because of their involvement in the goal formulation process.

Goal formulation involves the organization in determining an appropriate mission, objectives, and goals for the current or expected environment. The three terms are distinguished below:

- *Mission:* the basic purpose of an organization, that is, what it is trying to accomplish.
- *Objective:* a major variable which the organization will emphasize, such as reputation or profitability.
- *Goal:* an objective of the organization that is made specific with respect to magnitude, time, and who is responsible.

We shall examine these concepts in the following paragraphs.

MISSION.   An organization's mission is usually clear in the beginning. Over time, however, its mission may become unclear as the organization grows and develops new services and markets. Or the mission may remain clear but some people may have lost their interest in the mission. Or the mission may remain clear but may lose its appropriateness to new conditions in the environment—as was the case for Porter, Novelli in this chapter's opening example.

For these reasons, an organization should reexamine its mission from time to time. It should periodically reconsider what "business" it wants to be in. A consulting firm has to decide whether it wants to be in the *government contracts business,* the *expert testimony business,* the *corporate strategy development business,* or any of numerous other options. Similarly, a law firm has to decide whether it wants to be in "businesses" such as *corporate law, negligence law, personal injury law, marital law,* and so on. Defining its mission is critically important to an organization because it affects everything else it does.

A growing number of organizations have taken to writing formal *mission statements* to gain needed clarity. A well-worked-out mission statement provides everyone in the organization with a shared sense of purpose, direction, significance, and achievement. The mission statement acts as an "invisible hand" which guides widely scattered staff members to work independently and yet collectively toward the realization of the organization's goals. The statement should serve the organization for many years and not be something that changes every few years in response to environmental changes or new unrelated opportunities.

OBJECTIVES.   The mission of an organization suggests more about where that organization "is coming from" than where "it is going to." It describes what the organization is about rather than the specific objectives and goals it will pursue in the coming period. Each organization should develop major objectives for the coming period separate from but consistent with its mission statement.

For every type of organization, there is always a potential set of relevant objectives, and the organization's task is to make a choice among them. For example, the objectives of interest to a group dental practice might include: *more total patients, increased efficiency in handling patients, higher profits, improved interaction with patients, better oral health for patients,* and so on. A practice cannot successfully pursue all of these objectives simultaneously because of a limited budget and because some of them are incompatible, such as increased efficiency in handling patients and improved interaction with patients. In any given year, therefore, organizations will choose to emphasize certain objectives and either ignore others or treat them as constraints. For example, if a dental practice finds it is losing patients, it might make having more patients its paramount objective subject to the constraint of having an adequate amount of interaction with patients and, of course, helping them to achieve the best possible oral health. Thus, an organization's major objectives can vary from year to year, depending on management's perception of the major problems that the organization must address at that time.

GOALS.   The chosen objectives should be restated in a operational and measurable form called goals. The objective "increased revenues" should be turned into a specific goal. For example, Coopers & Lybrand, the big accounting firm, has established goals of "8 percent annual growth in chargeable hours" and "13 percent increase in revenues."[2] A goal statement permits the organization to think about the planning, programming, and control aspects of pursuing that objective. Such questions arise as: Is an 8 percent increase in chargeable hours feasible? What strategy would be used? What resources would it take? What activities would have to be carried out? Who would be responsible and accountable? All of these critical questions must be answered when deciding whether to adopt a proposed goal.

Typically, the organization will be evaluating a large set of potential goals at the same time and examining their consistency. The organization may discover that it cannot simultaneously achieve goals such as "a 10 percent increase in number of clients" and "having 90 percent of our billings be for work in our favorite areas" at the same time. In situations of goal conflict, adjustments and compromises are required to arrive at a meaningful and achievable set of goals. Once the set of goals are agreed upon in the goal formulation stage, the organization is ready to move on to the detailed work of strategy formulation.

STRATEGY FORMULATION

When a professional service organization has clarified its goals, it knows where it wants to go. The question then becomes how best to get there. The organization needs a "grand design" for achieving its goals.

That is called strategy. Strategy involves the choice of major directions for pursuing goals and the allocation of supporting resources. Strategy should not be confused with tactics, which are derived activities designed to allow the organization to complete individual "steps" along its "strategic path." Strategies and goals interact closely and planners may have to move back and forth in determining a final set of realistic goals and feasible strategies.

In seeking a basic overall organizational strategy—as opposed to the more specific marketing strategies the firm must develop for each market it chooses to serve (see the next section)—the organization should proceed in two stages. First, it should develop a *service portfolio strategy*, that is, decide what to do with each of its current major services. Second, it should develop a *service/market expansion strategy*, that is, decide what new services and markets to add.

Service Portfolio Strategy

Most professional service organizations are multiservice operations. They consist of either a group of generalist professionals, who each provide a variety of different types of services, or a group of specialist professionals, who support and complement each other by providing different but related types of services. Regardless of the format, the different services offered will surely vary in their importance and contribution to the organization's mission. It therefore becomes prudent to do periodic evaluations of this "portfolio" of services—as one would do with an investment portfolio—to make hard decisions about the future of its various services.

The first step in portfolio analysis is to identify the key business, programs, or services of the organization. For example, a management consulting firm might choose government contracts, expert legal testimony, corporate strategy consulting, and new product feasibility studies as its key businesses or services. The firm then has to determine which services should be given increased support (*build*), maintained at the present level (*hold*), phased down (*harvest*), and terminated (*divest*). The principle is that the firm's resources should be allocated in accordance with the "attractiveness" of each service rather than equally to all services. The task is to identify appropriate criteria for evaluating the attractiveness of various services. And, here, different schemes have been proposed. We shall examine three of them.

BOSTON CONSULTING GROUP PORTFOLIO APPROACH. One of the earliest and most popular portfolio evaluation approaches was developed by the Boston Consulting Group (BCG), a management consulting group. Its scheme called for rating all of the organization's products or services along two dimensions, namely, *market growth* and *market share* (see

Figure 3–5). Market growth is the annual rate of growth of the relevant market in which the product or service is sold. Market share is the organization's revenues as a ratio to the leading firm's revenues.[3] By dividing market growth into high growth and low growth, and market share into high share and low share, four types of products (services, businesses, programs) emerge:

1. An organization's *stars* are those services for which the organization enjoys a high share in fast-growing markets. The organization will pour increasing resources into its stars in order to keep up with the market's growth and maintain its share leadership.

2. An organization's *cash cows* are those services for which the organization enjoys a high share in slow-growth markets. Cash cows typically yield strong cash flows to an organization which pay the bills for those other

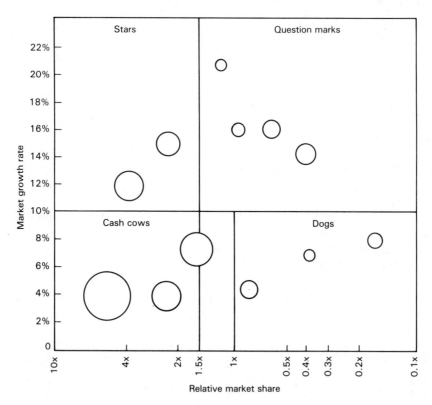

Source: Reprinted with permission from *Long-Range Planning,* February 1977, B. Hedley, "Strategy and the Business Portfolio," p. 12, copyright 1977, Pergamon Press, Ltd.

FIGURE 3–5.   Boston Consulting Group portfolio approach

services that lose money. Without cash cows, an organization would need continuous subsidy.

3. An organization's *question marks* are those services for which the organization has only a small share in a fast-growing market. The organization faces the decision of whether to increase its investment in its question-mark services, hoping to make them stars, or to reduce or terminate its investment, on the grounds that the funds could find better use elsewhere in the business.

4. An organization's *dogs* are those services that have a small market share in slow-growth or declining markets. Dogs usually make little money or lose money for the organization. Organizations often consider shrinking or dropping dogs unless they are necessary to offer for other reasons.

Applying this scheme, a law firm might find that its negligence law practice was a star, its marital law practice was a cash cow, its tax law practice was a question mark, and its real estate law practice was a dog. The BCG evaluation is useful for organizations interested in tracing the cash implications of their portfolios. High revenues generate cash and high growth consumes cash.

GENERAL ELECTRIC PORTFOLIO APPROACH. General Electric (GE) has formulated another approach to portfolio evaluation that has received considerable attention. They call it the *strategic business planning grid* (see Figure 3–6). It uses two basic dimensions, *market attractiveness* and *organizational strength.* The best services to offer are those which serve attractive markets and for which the organization has high organizational strength.

Market attractiveness is a composite index made up of the factors listed at the left side of the figure. More attractive markets would tend to have large size, rapid growth rates, high profit margins, little competition, little sensitivity to macroeconomic cycles, minor seasonal patterns, and ample scale economies.

Organizational strength is also a composite index made up of the factors listed at the top of the figure. A firm could capitalize on strengths such as a strong presence in a market, low cost and fees, high-quality services, considerable market knowledge, good selling skills, and prime location.

To implement the GE approach, the factors making up each dimension are scaled and weighted so that each current service receives a number indicating its market attractiveness and organizational strength, and therefore can be plotted in the grid.

The grid is divided into three zones. The green zone consists of the three cells at the upper left, indicating those services in which the organization should "invest and grow." The yellow zone consists of the diagonal cells stretching from the lower left to the upper right, indicating

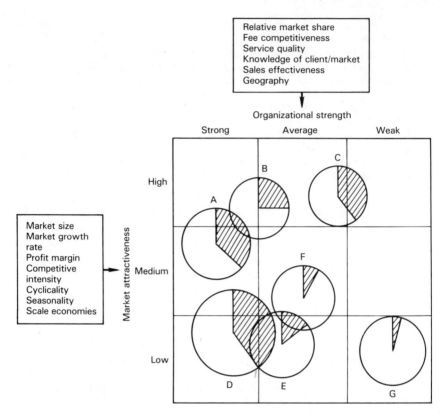

FIGURE 3–6.   General Electric portfolio approach (called the strategic business planning grid)

services that are medium in overall investment merit. The red zone consists of the three cells on the lower right, indicating those services that should be given serious consideration for harvesting or divesting.

A firm which finds itself with most of its services looking like, for example, service A in Figure 3–6 would be in particularly good shape. Service A is in a large market (indicated by the circle size) of which the firm has a large share (indicated by the shaded wedge). One could expect this service to be generating large profits by allowing the firm to achieve scale economies through obtaining the type of "leverage" we talked about in Chapter 2. That is, it is probably the type of service that can be performed primarily by junior people who can be billed out at relatively higher "multiples" of their hourly salaries than can be done with senior people. It is also probably a service for which high quality control can be maintained in spite of the reliance on junior people. Of course, the drawback to emphasizing services like these is the need they produce for having a constant supply of talented junior people. And to keep such a supply necessitates either (1) being very selective in awarding promotions (which may make it hard to recruit), (2) encouraging senior people to leave (to make room for promoted junior people), or (3) having the firm grow continuously in overall size.

TAILORED PORTFOLIO APPROACHES.   Professional service organizations may want to build their own portfolio evaluation models, using the preceding ones as suggestive. The task calls for identifying appropriate criteria for judging the services offered by the organization. For example, one management consulting firm recently used the criteria "sophistication of client" and "size of project" to help it categorize and evaluate its portfolio of services. The firm divided its portfolio into services provided for:

1. *Tigers.*   Big companies with sophisticated, well-trained managers who hire outside experts to conduct large-scale projects in well-defined problem areas.
2. *Elephants.*   Big companies with less sophisticated managers who hire less specialized outside consultants to conduct large-scale projects in loosely defined areas.
3. *Pussycats.*   Smaller companies with less sophisticated managers who hire less specialized outside consultants to conduct smaller-scale projects in loosely defined areas.
4. *Bulldogs.*   Smaller companies with sophisticated managers who hire outside experts to conduct smaller-scale projects in well-defined problem areas.

The firm then evaluated each category using criteria such as "profit margin," "competitive intensity," and "market knowledge." A decision was made to continue to pursue pussycats—among whom the firm had a strong track record and good referral networks—and to put more resources into seeking elephants, who presented great profit opportunities. Tigers were decided against because the firm lacked the specialized experts that these clients seek and because the competition for these clients is intense. Moreover, bulldogs were written off because, with their attention to detail and cost-consciousness, they seemed like more trouble than they were worth.

Other tailored portfolio approaches are clearly possible to develop. Regardless of the approach used, however, management must go into the analysis prepared to make some tough decisions and to drop services and markets, if called for. The dropping of services or clients, while often traumatic, can be surprisingly profitable. For example, the New York CPA firm of Siegel and Mendlowitz recently reported a one-year, 30 percent increase in revenues after dropping 15 percent of its clients and also simultaneously raising its fees.[4]

Service/Market Expansion Strategy

As a result of examining its current portfolio of services, a professional service organization might discover that it does not have enough stars or cash cows and that it must become more aggressive in searching for new services and markets. Needed is a systematic approach to identifying growth opportunities that can supplement the opportunity analysis discussed earlier in the chapter. A useful device for doing this is known as the service/market opportunity matrix (see Figure 3–7). Originally a 2-by-2 matrix proposed by Ansoff,[5] here it is expanded into a 3-by-3 matrix. Markets are listed at the left and services along the top.

Each cell in Figure 3–7 has a name. Management should first consider cell 1, called *market penetration.* This cell raises the question of whether the organization can maintain or expand its revenues by deepening its penetration into its existing markets with its existing services. Clients may not be utilizing the organization's services as frequently or in as large amounts as they could or should. For example, dental patients may be missing their regular checkups; or the clients of a CPA may be obtaining only a portion of the consulting advice they need on financial control procedures. Market penetration could also be called for when clients could be providing many more referrals of others like themselves to the organization.

Market penetration can generally be accomplished more efficiently

| | | SERVICES | | |
		Existing	Modified	New
MARKETS	Existing	1. Market penetration	4. Service modification	7. Service innovation
	Geographic	2. Geographic expansion	5. Modification for dispersed markets	8. Geographic innovation
	New	3. New markets	6. Modification for new markets	9. Total innovation

FIGURE 3–7. Service/market opportunity matrix

and effectively than other expansion strategies. Reminder notices and telephone calls to existing clients, or simple requests of clients to let their friends know about the organization's good services, can often accomplish much more at a lower cost than going after new markets and/or offering new services. But if penetration opportunities have clearly been exhausted, then the other cells in the matrix may provide useful guidance.

Cell 2 raises the question of whether the organization should try to expand by offering existing services to similar types of clients in new geographic markets. A *geographic expansion* strategy could involve opening branch offices in new localities or simply increasing the organization's travel and communications budgets. The biggest risk associated with this strategy is the threat to quality control presented by having services provided where they cannot be monitored as easily. Also, clients in different geographic locations may differ in subtle ways that could make existing services undesirable to new geographic markets.

A *new markets* strategy (cell 3) involves trying to expand by offering existing services to new types of clients. For example, the slump in constuction has led architects to search for new markets and clients. Some firms have contracted with cities to redesign closed school buildings for alternative community uses; others are looking for clients interested in interior design or historic preservation; one firm is specializing in the redesign of crowded prisons. The major risk here is that existing services will not appeal to the new target markets.

Next, management can consider whether it should modify some of its current services to attract more of the existing market. A *service modification* strategy (cell 4) could involve making important changes in the actual services provided and/or giving a more appealing and descriptive label to those services. For instance, several of the Big Eight CPA firms have been touting their audit services using labels like TFA ("transaction flow auditing" by Arthur Andersen), CAAG ("computer audit assistance group" by Coopers & Lybrand), and TRAP ("Touche Ross audit process").[6] Service modification may help an organization attract a larger proportion of a certain category of clients or obtain larger fees from existing clients. The strategy can backfire if existing clients liked the old services just the way they were.

Cell 5 is named *modification for dispersed markets* and cell 6 is *modification for new markets.* The organization would try to modify and tailor its existing services to the tastes and desires of new geographic or other target markets. Although these strategies are market oriented, they require dealing with totally new markets and entertaining considerable risk and difficulty.

Service innovation (cell 7) involves developing totally new services for existing clients. An engineering firm may start to offer architectural services for its clients, hoping that they will find it more convenient to commission engineering and architectural services in one package. Similarly, a CPA firm may start to offer computer system consulting services for its audit clients. This is a sound strategy as long as the people who supply the new services are experienced in that particular area and can maintain high standards of quality and professionalism. The organization must also be careful not to dilute the quality of the old, established services in its enthusiasm for building up the new services.

Finally, *geographic innovation* (cell 8) and *total innovation* (cell 9) would have the organization offer totally new services to new geographic or other target markets. Needless to say, these are the riskiest strategies of all. They require acquisition of *both* substantial knowledge of the new markets and experienced professionals to provide the new services to those markets.

The service/market opportunity matrix helps the organization imagine new opportunities in a systematic way. These opportunities are evaluated and the better ones pursued. The results of the service/market analysis and the previous portfolio analysis allow the organization to formulate more focused and effective strategic marketing plans.

FORMULATING MARKETING STRATEGIES

Once a basic organizational strategy has been formulated, marketing strategies are needed. The professional service organization must develop a marketing strategy for each service market it chooses to compete in. We define marketing strategy as follows:

> **Marketing strategy** is the selection of *target markets,* the choice of a *competitive position,* and the development of an effective *marketing mix* to reach and serve the chosen clients.

We shall examine the three basic components of marketing strategy—*target market strategy, competitive positioning strategy,* and *marketing mix strategy*—in the following sections. We elaborate much further on targeting and positioning in Chapter 5 and on the marketing mix in Chapters 8 to 13.

Target Market Strategy

The first step in preparing a marketing strategy is to understand the market thoroughly. We define a market in this way:

> A **market** is the set of all people and organizations who have an actual or potential interest in a service and the ability to pay for it.

When looked at closely, every market is heterogeneous, that is, it is made up of quite different types of buyers, or *market segments.* Therefore, managers find it helpful to construct a market segmentation scheme that can reveal the major groups making up the market. Then they can decide whether to serve all of these segments (*mass marketing*) or concentrate on a few of the more promising ones (*target marketing*).

There are many ways to segment a market (see Chapter 5). Segmentation can be done based on the type of industry, size, location, service needs, or other characteristics of potential clients. The market analyst tries different segmentation approaches until a useful one is found. For example, an architectural firm might find the most useful way to segment the business firm market is by service needs (e.g., corporate headquarters design, renovation design, etc.) and by location (e.g., Sunbelt, Northeast, etc.). Thus the firm might identify a needs/market segmentation scheme containing 9 different segments it could serve (3 needs × 3 markets). The firm would then have to decide whether to pursue target marketing and, if so, what pattern of target marketing to choose.

There are five basic patterns of market coverage possible with a given needs/market segmentation scheme. They are shown in Figure 3–8 and are described below:

1. *Need/market concentration* consists of an organization concentrating on only one market segment, such as Sunbelt corporations seeking corporate headquarters designs.

2. *Need specialization* consists of the organization deciding to serve a single need for all markets, such as the need for renovation designs.

3. *Market specialization* consists of the organization deciding to serve all the needs of a single market, such as Northeast corporations.

4. *Selective specialization* consists of the organization deciding to serve several market segments that have no relation to each other except that each constitutes an individual attractive opportunity.

5. *Full coverage* consists of the organization deciding to serve all the market segments.

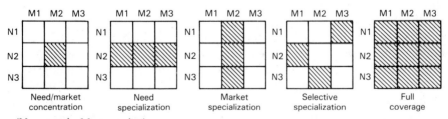

(N = needs, M = market)

Source: Adapted from Derek F. Abell, *Defining the Business: The Starting Point of Strategic Planning* (Englewood Cliffs, N.J.: Prentice-Hall, 1980), Chapter 8.

FIGURE 3–8. Five patterns of market coverage

Of course, decisions concerning type of coverage can involve an evaluation of many more potential segments defined in much more complex ways. For example, the markets dimension in Figure 3–8 could reflect firm size *and* location (creating perhaps six groups) instead of just location. However, it is best to keep the number of segments evaluated reasonably small to start out. Then, after choosing a desired coverage, *subsegmentation* can be done to evaluate whether the desired market coverage—or target market strategy—should be defined in narrower terms. Thus, upon selection of a need/market concentration of serving the corporate headquarters design needs of Sunbelt corporations, a firm may want to subsegment by project size and type of industry, eventually deciding that it wants to target high-technology companies with opportunities offering greater than $100,000 in fees.

Competitive Positioning Strategy

The selection of a target market must be followed by the development of a competitive positioning strategy that will help the organization compete against others who have targeted the same market. We define competitive positioning as follows:

> **Competitive positioning** is the art of developing and communicating meaningful differences between one's services and those of competitors serving the same target market.

The key to competitive positioning is to identify the major attributes used by the target market to evaluate and choose among competitive organizations. Suppose research conducted with auditor selection committees and chief financial officers of large corporations revealed that the attributes considered most carefully in selecting a CPA firm are (1) the amount of extra advice and service provided during audit engagements and (2) the aggressiveness of the CPA firm in seeking new business. Further, suppose that the research revealed that these people perceived four major CPA firms as having the competitive positions shown in Figure 3–9 on these attributes. In this case, firms A and B are competing head-on against one another for clients who prefer moderately aggressive firms providing much extra service. Firm C is positioned to obtain clients seeking unaggressive firms which, nevertheless, provide much extra service. Firm D is in the unenviable position of being perceived to be both unaggressive and weak on providing extra service. Management of firm A will want to consider repositioning their firm to differentiate it from firm B. They may see the open "niche" for highly aggressive firms with much extra service as one the firm could occupy with profitable results. At the same time, firm D will want to embark on a repositioning program of major proportions.

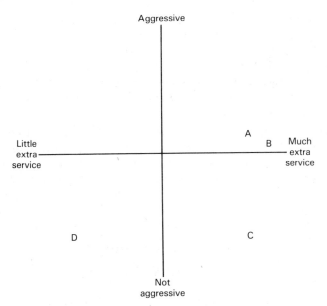

FIGURE 3–9.　Perceived positions of four CPA firms

Repositioning can be difficult because it involves trying to change people's long-standing images or impressions of an organization. Successful repositioning requires a well-formulated and executed marketing mix.

Marketing Mix Strategy

The next step in marketing strategy is to develop a *marketing mix* and a *marketing expenditure level* that supports the organization's ability to compete in its target market. By marketing mix, we mean:

> **Marketing mix** is the particular blend of controllable market-ing variables that the organization uses to achieve its goal in the target market.

Although many variables make up the marketing mix, they can be classified into a few major groups. McCarthy formulated a popular classi-fication called the "four P's": *product, price, place,* and *promotion.*[7] In the professions, the corresponding variables might be labeled: *service, fee, location,* and *communication.*

The organization chooses a marketing mix that will support and reinforce its chosen competitive position. An organization that wants to be perceived as aggressive and service-minded will have to hire aggres-sive, hungry professionals and train them extensively in how to communicate and offer the organization's services. It will also have to charge highly competitive fees and have a large-scale communications program that tells clients their business is eagerly sought. In other words, the chosen competitive position dictates the elements of the marketing mix that will be emphasized.

As for the marketing expenditure level, this depends on how much money is needed to accomplish the organization's goals. Here, past experience can provide guidance, suggesting what it cost to accomplish certain goals under similar circumstances. Experience must, of course, be adjusted for developments such as increased promotional activity or severe fee cutting by a competitor, which would tend to raise the needed marketing expenditure level. We shall say more about establishing the marketing budget in Chapter 14.

ORGANIZATIONAL STRUCTURE
AND SYSTEMS

The purpose of strategy formulation is to develop strategies that will help the organization achieve its goals. But the existing organization must be capable of carrying out these strategies. It must have the *structure, people,* and *culture* to implement the strategy successfully. A responsive organization of the type described in Chapter 2 should be in place, with the chosen strategy providing guidance concerning the finer points of the organization design.

Most organization theorists believe that "structure should follow strategy," rather than the other way around. Thus, a strategy that places emphasis on a large public relations effort would require the hiring of staff and, perhaps, the establishment of a new department to handle this effort. Similarly, a strategy that calls for the organization to provide highly specialized services to clients or patients would require a modification of an old organizational "culture" that encouraged all professionals to be generalists.

The successful implementation of strategy also requires the support of certain systems. A *marketing information system* is needed to provide accurate, timely, and comprehensive information about clients, referral sources, suppliers, competitors, and others. A *marketing planning system* is needed to provide discipline to the planning effort, supplying staff, resources, and other support to make sure that plans are developed and used. Finally, a *marketing control system* is needed to measure the ongoing results of a plan against the plan's goals and to take corrective action before it is too late. These three systems are treated in detail in Chapters 7 and 14.

SUMMARY

Strategic planning is the major tool for adapting to a changing environment, and it consists of several steps. The first step is environmental analysis, in which the organization researches its five environments: internal environment, market environment, public environment, competitive environment, and macroenvironment. Each environment component is subdivided into factors, the major trends are identified for each factor, and then the implied opportunities and threats are identified. The organization prepares plans for its most important opportunities and threats, and monitors the others that might have some eventual significance.

Following the environmental analysis, the organization proceeds to identify its major strengths and weaknesses in personnel, funds, facilities, systems, and market assets. It will favor those opportunities where it has distinctive competences and differential advantages in relation to competitors.

The environmental and resources analyses are followed by goal formulation, in which the organization establishes what it wants to achieve. It formulates its basic mission, its major objectives (qualitative variables to pursue), and its specific goals (quantified objectives with respect to magnitude, time, and who is responsible).

Strategy formulation is the organization's effort to figure out its broad strategy for achieving its goals. First, the organization analyzes its current service portfolio to determine which businesses it should build, maintain, harvest, and terminate. Second, it seeks ideas for new or modified services and markets by using a service/market expansion matrix.

Following the choice of particular service/market targets, the organization proceeds to develop marketing strategies for each service market. Marketing strategy is the selection of a target market segment(s), the choice of a competitive position, and the development of an effective marketing mix to reach and serve the chosen customers. Marketing mix consists of the particular blend of product, price, place, and promotion that the organization uses to achieve its objectives in the target market.

The organization's strategy is likely to call for changes in the organization's structure, people, and culture. Organizational structure should not dictate strategy, but an organization's strategy should shape its structure.

Finally, the organization reviews its systems of information, planning, and control to be sure that they are adequate to carry out the strategy successfully.

NOTES

1. See Derek F. Abell, "Strategic Windows," *Journal of Marketing,* July 1978, pp. 21–26.

2. Bob Tamarkin, "The New Champion: Coopers and Lybrand," *Forbes,* November 27, 1978, pp. 37–38.

3. This definition of market share is called "relative market share." Thus, a relative market share of 10 means that the organization sells 10 times as much as the next largest organization. It should not be confused with absolute market share, which measures the organization's sales as a percentage of the total market size.

4. Sanford L. Jacobs, "CPA Firm Grows Prosperous by Heeding its Own Advice," *Wall Street Journal,* May 18, 1981, p. 27.

5. H. Igor Ansoff, "Strategies for Diversification," *Harvard Business Review,* September–October 1957, pp. 113–24.

6. See Peter W. Bernstein, "Competition Comes to Accounting," *Fortune,* July 17, 1978, p. 92.

7. E. Jerome McCarthy, *Basic Marketing: A Managerial Approach,* 6th ed. (Homewood, Ill.: Irwin, 1978), p. 39 (1st ed., 1960).

4

MARKET ANALYSIS:
Understanding Client Behavior

"After more than a decade in this business, I've learned an awful lot about the way clients think and operate—and it has really helped us. But I feel you can always learn more about clients and, so, my assistant and I spend a substantial portion of our time gathering information about them."

Dave Hirzel had these comments to make during a session he was teaching to a group of architects and engineers attending a marketing course offered by the Continuing Education Program of the Harvard Graduate School of Design. Dave was reflecting on his experience as principal and marketing director with Sasaki Associates, a large architectural firm based in the Boston suburb of Watertown, Massachusetts.

"We always do our homework before meeting with a potential client for the first time. We talk to everyone we can possibly find who knows something about the organization—its key people, their problems, their personalities, their past experiences with architects, and so on—and we read everything about the client we can get our hands on, using libraries and a good clipping service to great advantage. In all our contacts with potential clients, we are constantly seeking information about their needs and concerns, their perceptions of our firm, and, most importantly, their procedures and criteria for selecting an architect. All this information allows us to tailor proposals and presentations that appeal to the unique interests and tastes of each client. I think our very high 'hit rate'—or our ability to obtain commissions once we're on the 'short lists' of clients—provides strong testimony to the value of all this information gathering.

"But I should stress that our information gathering doesn't stop once we've obtained a commission. We are constantly seeking data on the needs and attitudes of current clients so we can offer them more functional and pleasing designs and so we can identify additional, profitable services we might be able to provide them. We also seek feedback from current and past clients on their satisfaction with all aspects of how we perform our services, including their feelings about our fees, our friendliness, and our ability to stick to time schedules. On top of this, we find current and past clients to be excellent sources of leads about potential work and of ideas on how to best approach and appeal to those leads."

Dave then went on to review in more detail the types of information that he has found helpful to gather about clients. As he proceeded, he passed out examples of news articles and library information they had utilized, questionnaires they had employed for telephone surveys and personal interviews, and feedback forms they had sent to past clients. A lively session developed, as the participants offered their diverse views about client decision making and behavior.

Highly skilled professional service marketers like Dave Hirzel have learned that doing market analysis is the cornerstone of a successful marketing program. Market analysis provides the information on needs and wants of clients required to make an organization responsive and marketing oriented. Market analysis also provides information to guide strategic planning, since opportunities, threats, strengths, and weaknesses can be revealed by studying the desires, beliefs, images, attitudes, and satisfaction levels of clients. Furthermore, market analysis supplies information to guide all the finer points of a marketing program, from decisions about fee arrangements to decisions about the best appeals to use in personal communications. It allows a firm to avoid costly marketing mistakes like the one recently described by architect Charles Thomsen:

> Back in the days when I was practicing architecture in New York, I went to Maryland to give a presentation to a community college board. It started well. Heads were nodding in agreement. But late in the presentation, when I spoke about working with the college faculty, the heads stopped nodding. What was wrong?
>
> It was our standard pitch. We liked working with faculties because it helped us design good schools. But it was always a good buyer influence. School boards and faculties wanted architects that would work with them and do things the way they wanted. I figured that they had missed the point so I repeated it. More blank looks, so I really hit hard: "Your faculty knows what a good college is, not your architect! We just can't do the job without your faculty!"
>
> Finally there was a response from the board's president. "I'm sorry to hear that, Mr. Thomsen. We don't plan to hire faculty until construction is nearly complete." We didn't get the job.[1]

Market analysis involves the study of *buyer behavior.* In professional service organizations, this analysis consists of studies of how and why various clients elect, hire, contract, retain, commission, or engage certain professionals. (Each profession tends to use a different term to describe the act of "buying" its services.) For professional service organizations that serve primarily other organizations, studies must be done of *organizational buyer behavior.* For those that serve primarily individuals, studies must be done of *individual buyer behavior.* Many professional service organizations will have to study both types of behavior, either because they serve both types of buyers or because they serve organizations that place authority over certain decisions in the hands of a single individual.

In this chapter, we cover the subjects of organizational buyer behavior and individual buyer behavior in separate sections. We review the major aspects of organizational and individual buyer behavior that a professional service organization should seek to understand in mounting a serious marketing effort. In addition, we offer a few suggestions on research methods to use in studying buyer behavior. (We treat the topic of marketing research in much greater depth in Chapter 7.) For both categories of behavior, the major questions we recommend investigating are:

1. What buying decisions do buyers make?
2. Who participates in the buying process?
3. What are the major influences on the buying process?
4. What are the main steps and features of the decision process of buyers?

ORGANIZATIONAL BUYER BEHAVIOR

The organizations which professional service organizations seek as clients are extremely diverse. Big businesses, small businesses, government agencies, trade associations, hospitals, educational institutions, charities, and others exhibit numerous different ways of buying professional services. No general, comprehensive description of how organizations buy professional services can therefore be offered. Nevertheless, it is possible to offer a framework for studying organizational buying of professional services that can be used to guide the analysis of diverse types of buyers. Such a framework is described below.

Types of Decisions

The first issue to consider in examining the buying behavior of organizational clients is the type of buying decision being investigated. The *market analyst*—the label we will use here to refer to the person primarily responsible for obtaining an understanding of buyer behavior (who could be the marketing director, marketing coordinator, marketing researcher, etc.)—must recognize that some decisions are more complex, risky, or important than others, and that the number of people involved with a decision and the steps taken to make a decision will vary depending on the characteristics of that decision. One useful way of categorizing organizational buying decisions has been suggested by Robinson et al.[2] They distinguished among the following three types of buying situations called *buyclasses:*

1. *Straight rebuy.* This occurs when the organization buys something identical or very similar to what it has bought before. Decisions on who should conduct a business firm's financial audits or who should perform a land developer's land surveys are typically straight rebuy situations. These decisions do not usually require the involvement of many individuals, nor do they require an extensive decision process characterized by much information gathering.

2. *Modified rebuy.* Here the organization considers buying services with somewhat different features than the services it has bought previously. A business firm's decision about engaging a CPA firm for an audit *plus* some specialized tax work could fit this situation, as could a university's decision to commission an architect to design a dormitory. Compared to a straight rebuy, more people will generally be involved in making this type of decision and a more complex decision process, with more information gathering, will usually be undergone.

3. *New task.* This situation faces organizations buying unfamiliar services from unfamiliar professionals. A large corporation needing a product liability attorney for the first time would be in this situation. So would a hospital needing the services of a marketing research firm to do its first survey of community residents. These decisions frequently involve several people and a complex, search-intensive, decision process.

The market analyst will want to identify the types of decisions being made by the organizations within the firm's target markets. Existing clients in straight-rebuy situations should be studied to see how their past behavior can be reinforced so that they will automatically reorder services and refrain from considering other suppliers. These clients could also be studied to uncover ways to shift them tactfully to modified-rebuy or new-task situations where they will buy more from the firm. The risk in this, of course, is that buyers shifted to these situations may expand their set of considered suppliers. The analyst would want to evaluate whether reminder notices, follow-up visits, training seminars, and other forms of communications could help in accomplishing these objectives at minimal risk.

For clients in a firm's target markets who are in straight-rebuy situations, but who buy from competitors, the analyst will want to evaluate the probabilities of getting them to discontinue their loyal behavior.

TABLE 4-1
ANSWERS TO QUESTION: HOW LONG HAS YOUR COMPANY
RETAINED ITS PRINCIPAL CPA FIRM?

	500 LARGEST INDUSTRIALS	SECOND 500 LARGEST INDUSTRIALS	TOP NONINDUSTRIAL COMPANIES	COMPANIES WITH SALES OF $50–100 MILLION
Less than 1 year	2.0%	1.4%	0.5%	0.7%
1 to 4 years	4.6	4.2	8.9	16.0
5 to 9 years	9.9	12.5	20.2	26.0
10 to 14 years	11.3	23.6	14.3	12.7
15 years or longer	70.2	58.3	55.7	44.7
No answer	2.0	—	0.5	—
Total respondents*	100.0% (151)	100.0% (144)	100.0% (203)	100.0% (150)

Source: "The Balance Sheet: Top Executives Speak Out About CPA Firms," 1978 © Dow Jones and Co., Inc., p. 6.

*A four-page questionnaire and cover letter were sent to 1,050 chief executive officers or presidents of leading companies. The sample consisted of executives from the following groups: every other name selected from the *Fortune* Top 1,000 Industrials; every CEO or president in the 300 companies which comprise *Fortune's* "Top Non-Industrial Companies"; and a random sample of 250 names from companies with sales between $50 and $100 million. When the survey was closed, replies totaled 648, a response rate of 61.8%.

These probabilities might be estimated with the help of knowledgeable informants such as the professionals from other fields who service those clients. Needless to say, the organizations with high probabilities of switching should be studied intensively, while those with low switching probabilities should be studied sparingly. Unfortunately, the analyst will typically identify many buyers with low switching probabilities. The great uncertainty—and consequent tension and anxiety—many clients experience in buying professional services discourages "shopping around" and encourages loyalty. For example, the data presented in Table 4-1 provide evidence on the degree of loyalty that exists among clients of CPAs.

Intensive study should also be done of organizations in target markets that are already in modified-rebuy or new-task situations. These are the buyers that represent "live leads" and they should be investigated thoroughly to identify the participants in their buying decisions, the influences on their decisions, and the nature of their decision processes.

Decision Participants

The market analyst must attempt to identify the people in the target clients' organizations who are likely to get involved in the buying process. In many organizations, a *buying center* can be considered to exist, something Webster and Wind have defined as "all individuals and groups who participate in the purchasing decision-making process, who share some common goals and the risks arising from the decisions."[3] A buying center would include all members of the organization (including outside consultants and advisers) who play any of five roles in the buying process:

1. *Users.*   Users are the members of the organization who will make most direct use of the services. In many cases, the users initiate the buying project and play an important role in defining the buying specifications.

2. *Influencers.*   Influencers are individuals who directly or indirectly influence the buying decision. They often help develop specifications and also provide information for evaluating alternatives. Expert personnel or outside advisers are particularly important as influencers.

3. *Buyers.*   Buyers are organizational members with formal authority for selecting among competitive suppliers and negotiating terms.

4. *Deciders.*   Deciders are organizational members who have either formal or informal power to select or approve the final suppliers. In more complex buying, the officers of the buying organization are often the deciders.

5. *Gatekeepers.*   Gatekeepers are members of the organization who control the flow of information to others.

Whether it is an auditor selection committee, a facilities planning committee, or some other complex entity, the buying center and the power relationships among its members deserve close attention. The great uncertainty associated with buying professional services will tend to allow certain individuals with special knowledge, information, or expertise—who can reduce buying uncertainty—to dominate the decision process within many buying centers. The analyst's task is to identify the members of the buying center and try to figure out (1) in what decisions they exercise influence, (2) what is their relative degree of influence, and (3) what evaluation criteria does each decision participant use.

Influences on Decisions

Studying the buying center's power relationships and the decision criteria of its key people amounts to recognizing the influence of *organizational factors* and *individual factors* on organizational buying. Other organizational factors that could influence buying greatly include the organization's degree of innovativeness, the source of its funds (public or private), the competition it faces, and other aspects of its "organizational climate."[4] Other individual factors that could influence organizational buying, such as people's social backgrounds and personalities, are essentially reviewed in a later section on influences on individual buying decisions.

Organizational buying decisions can also be influenced by *interpersonal factors.* "Chemistry" between the people of a buying organization and the professionals seeking to serve them, produced by things like old-school ties or common employment experiences, can affect buying. For example, "alumni" of Big Eight CPA firms have been known to favor their past employers when they are in a position to choose or recommend a CPA firm. Not surprisingly, several of these firms devote considerable resources toward maintaining frequent and favorable contact with past employees.

Finally, organizational buying can be influenced greatly by *environmental factors.* Economic, political, legal, technological, and social/cultural forces and trends can have a substantial effect on what, where, when, and how organizations buy. Changes in tax laws, major court decisions, new communications technologies, and numerous other environmental developments can have a big impact on the buying of professional services.

Decision Process

The steps taken by an organization in buying professional services will vary depending on the type of decision, the decision participants, the type of service, and several other factors. The decision process can consist of only a step or two or of numerous steps and substeps. However, buyers of professional services today are generally becoming more systematic and elaborate about selecting professionals. The story reprinted in Exhibit 4–1 illustrates how this trend has been progressing in the design professions.

A rather elaborate, 12-step decision process is presented in Figure 4–1. These steps were identified by Wind in a study of the purchasing of scientific and technical information services.[5] Although many buying organizations will not go through such an elaborate sequence, and will combine or skip some of these steps (particularly in straight-rebuy or modified-rebuy situations), the market analyst should check how close targeted clients come to this model. We will review what the analyst should attempt to learn about each of these steps.

IDENTIFICATION OF NEEDS. The buying process begins when an organization realizes that it has a problem or situation that requires the services of outside professionals. The market analyst will want to determine how target clients typically come to such a realization. Do overworked professionals inside client organizations make a request for help? Do managers in client organizations read or hear about certain professional services through their everyday activities and then have their curiosity aroused? Do external forces, such as legal and regulatory developments or natural disasters, literally force organizations to obtain

EXHIBIT 4-1.   An illustration of changing patterns of client decision making

When William Pereira entered architecture in 1930, the old saw—"It's not what you know, it's who you know"—described the way architects usually found business. Today that's no longer true, as more corporations establish rigorous procedures for selecting architects.

Rather than a corporate mogul giving the design commission to an architect who belongs to his church or country club, committees of top executives are screening many architects before selecting one.

As a result, marketing is playing an integral role in the fortunes of the larger architectural firms. Many architects devise early warning systems alerting them to developers and companies that are likely to build soon, and they try to develop rapport with companies long before a decision on whether to build is made.

Mr. Pereira, who founded a Los Angeles architectural firm bearing his name, says people used to pick architects much the same way they would choose a doctor or lawyer. Times have changed, he says, "You can't wait for projects to come in the door."

The lengths to which Exxon Research and Engineering Co., a subsidiary of Exxon Corp., went in selecting an architect for its new 850,000-square-foot headquarters and research center in Clinton Township, N.J., illustrate the complexities of today's more sophisticated process.

The $160 million center, which will be completed in 1983, is a novel experience for the Exxon subsidiary's employees, most of whom are used to designing refineries but not research laboratories.

William Goryl, assistant project executive, says the subsidiary knew it was venturing into a new area. "Designing a research laboratory is not like designing a refinery where there are only one or two good ways of doing things," Mr. Goryl says. "You need the talent of a designer to give you the best compromises between competing needs."

Through a variety of sources, Mr. Goryl and John Leibold, assistant manager of contracts engineering, compiled a list of 38 architectural firms to be considered.

The selection committee asked the 38 firms to submit information about their capabilities and similar work they had done. Based on that information, the committee narrowed the list to 12 firms, which it then visited. Those 12 were pared down to three finalists that were required to divulge their finances, specify the employees who would be assigned to the project and give a tour of other research labs they had designed.

The prime criterion was experience in designing large labs, but architectural and engineering excellence, management capability and the personality of the firm also counted.

Hellmuth, Obata & Kassabaum, a St. Louis architectural firm with 850 employees, won the competition. Figuring heavily in Exxon's decision was a headquarters and research facility that HOK had designed for E.R. Squibb & Sons, a subsidiary of the Squibb Corp., about a decade earlier. Mr. Goryl says the tour showed that the Squibb people were happy with the work that Gyo Obata, HOK's chief designer, had done.

As a result, Exxon specified in its contract that Mr. Obata would spend 60% of his time on the Exxon headquarters and lab.

Going into the process, Gerard Gilmore, senior vice president for marketing at HOK, figured his firm had a one in 10 chance of getting the job, despite its experience with research labs. For one thing, Mr. Gilmore worried that Exxon would be swayed by the fact that competing firms had greater engineering capability. HOK was proposing to hire an outside engineering consultant, a common practice but one which was unfamiliar to Exxon.

"One of our marketing challenges was to convince them that they'd get a better job that way," Mr. Gilmore says. "This way, we told them, you'll get the best research designers and engineers."

A second hurdle for HOK was geography. Although it has a New York office, HOK's designers with expertise in research centers were in the St. Louis headquarters. The two other finalists were in New York City and Philadelphia, within an easy commute of the site.

To counter this, HOK agreed to move about a dozen design people to New York for the critical months of the design phase.

Mr. Gilmore says, "The amount of effort we spent to get that job was tremendous. It was the most rigorous selection process that we've gone through." He estimates that HOK spent at least $40,000 on the screening process. If it hadn't won the competition, HOK would have had to make it up somewhere else. But that prospect didn't deter Mr. Gilmore, because the Exxon job "was terribly attractive to us."

In its final decision, fees didn't matter much in Exxon's decision. Exxon decided that it didn't want to lock the architect into a set fee, because the architect would be more likely to resist requests for design changes from Exxon. Instead, it reimbursed HOK for its costs and overhead plus a profit margin.

Says Mr. Goryl: "Our philosophy was that this really isn't the place where you want a big incentive to minimize design costs. This should be the finest building Exxon has ever built."

HOK isn't the only architectural firm for whom this story has a happy ending. Though it lost the contract for the headquarters and research center, The Kling Partnership of Philadelphia impressed Exxon officials sufficiently that when the time came for Exxon Research and Engineering to build a new building for its computers Kling was picked to design it.

Source: Robert Guenther, "Process of Picking Architects Is Getting More Sophisticated," *The Wall Street Journal,* January 13, 1982. Reprinted by permission of *The Wall Street Journal,* © Dow Jones & Company, Inc., 1982. All Rights Reserved.

professional help? Do organizations have their need for services pointed out to them by professionals seeking to provide those services?

Decisions on how to promote and publicize professional services can receive considerable guidance from what is learned about how organizations identify their needs. For example, if it is determined that most target clients discover their need for a certain service through everyday reading or listening, then an intensified public relations effort,

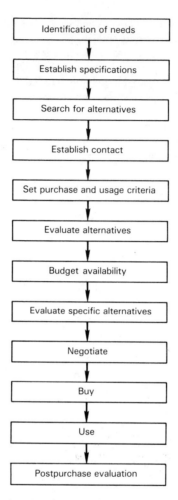

Source: Yoram Wind and Robert J. Thomas, "Conceptual and Methodological Issues in Organisational Buying Behavior," *European Journal of Marketing,* Vol. 14, No. 5/6 (1981), p. 243.

FIGURE 4-1.   Model of the organizational buying process

containing many news releases and speeches, might be effective. On the other hand, if most target clients discover their need for a service through recommendations by professionals themselves, then a promotional program involving a substantial amount of "cold calling" might be in order.

Besides examining how needs are identified, the market analyst should seek to understand how needs vary in composition and intensity across different clients. Some clients may need nonspecific assistance and require a "generalist" professional. Others may need very well-defined assistance and require a "specialist" professional. Some needs must be satisfied with great urgency, while others can wait. Information about the specific nature of needs can be extremely valuable in making targeting, positioning, and marketing mix decisions.

ESTABLISH SPECIFICATIONS.   Once an organization has identified a need for professional help, it may then develop criteria to use to determine a set of professionals who will receive some consideration. Many organizations will only consider using professionals who have served them previously—at least for projects of moderate size or greater (where the risks of choosing the wrong professional are perceived as highest). Other organizations will only consider using the biggest, oldest, closest, or cheapest professionals available. Determining the criteria used by organizations to identify candidate professionals is an essential task for the market analyst. Professional service firms need to know what minimal attributes are required to put themselves in the running for targeted opportunities.

SEARCH FOR ALTERNATIVES.   The buying organization will then search for professional service firms that qualify under the specifications that have been established. The market analyst will want to research who target clients tend to contact when they do this search. For example, the CPA firm of Deloitte Haskins & Sells found out that clients tend to go to the referral sources listed in Table 4–2 to identify candidate CPAs.

TABLE 4–2
METHODS OF OBTAINING INFORMATION ABOUT CPA FIRMS

	CORPORATE FINANCIAL OFFICERS* (%)
From business acquaintances	33
Talking to other CPA firms	24
Talking to clients of other CPA firms	13
Friends/personal contacts	10
Professional articles/position papers of firm	6
Talking to bankers	4
Never had to do it	18
Any other mentions	8
Don't know	5

Source: "An Opinion Survey of the Public Accounting Profession," sponsored by Deloitte Haskins & Sells. Conducted by Reichman Research Inc., May 1978. Reprinted with permission.

Note: Multiple response permitted.

*In total, 956 personal interviews were conducted: 464 corporate financial officers of a cross-section of U.S. companies; 76 members of accounting faculty at colleges and universities; 63 members of audit committees of corporate boards of directors; 83 outside attorneys serving on corporate boards; 79 members of the investment community; 191 members of the American Institute of Certified Public Accountants who were not involved in public accounting practice.

ESTABLISH CONTACT.   The set of candidate professionals identified during the search will then be approached by the buying organization to obtain more detailed information. Some organizations will make this contact informal and merely seek short conversations and general descriptive materials from several professional service firms. Other organizations will be extremely formal at this stage and seek specific "statements of qualifications" from professionals. The marketing analyst must attempt to figure out exactly what is sought by target clients from the initial contact. A proper response to this initial overture—showing polite eagerness and enthusiasm, but without supplying more information than the client really wants—can do much to enhance the chances of getting the desired work.

SET PURCHASE AND USAGE CRITERIA.   Once the buying organization knows more about the available professionals, it can then set out the specific features it desires and the specific criteria it will use to select a professional. Often this step will involve the issuance of a formal "request for proposals." The market analyst will want to study how purchase and usage criteria are determined and evaluate whether it is possible to somehow help shape these criteria or the content of requests for proposals. The professional service firm will generally want to take advantage of any opportunities it can obtain to advise target clients about selection criteria or proposal requests.

EVALUATE ALTERNATIVES.   The professionals who express a sincere interest in serving the identified needs of the buying organization, either by submitting a formal proposal or some equivalent sales document, will then be evaluated to see which ones deserve to be "finalists" or "short list" members. The market analyst will want to discover exactly which criteria are used at this stage (and during the remaining stages) to determine the most favored professionals. Studies such as those reported in Tables 4–3, 4–4, and 4–5 could be done to identify whether the criteria specified in proposal requests or some other criteria have determined who gets favored. Studies of this type can be extremely helpful to professional service firms in formulating their "positioning" strategy (i.e., deciding how they want to be seen by target clients). We provide guidance on how to conduct studies like these in Chapter 7.

BUDGET AVAILABILITY.   A check by the buying organization on whether it can really afford the professional services it wants often does not take place until late in the decision process, when more realistic estimates of fees have finally been offered in proposals or other sales documents. The buying organization may find that it has to rethink its plans and settle for services of a more limited scope. Needless to say, the market analyst will want to identify clients who are seeking services they cannot really afford as early as possible, so as to redirect discussion

TABLE 4–3
FACTORS INFLUENCING THE SELECTION OF A CPA FIRM

Q: How important do you consider each of the factors listed below in the selection of a CPA firm?

Summary: Factors Considered "Critical" or "Very Important"

	500 Largest Industrials	Second 500 Largest Industrials	Top Nonindustrial Companies	Companies with Sales of $50–100 Million
General reputation of the firm	97.4%	97.2%	98.5%	95.3%
Familiarity with the firm's partners	35.8	35.4	34.0	39.3
Location and number of U.S. offices	54.3	44.5	36.9	39.3
Location and number of offices outside U.S.	45.7	27.8	16.7	11.3
General and/or technical literature provided by the firm	13.9	20.8	18.2	21.3
Experience with government regulatory matters	67.5	71.6	74.9	74.0
Fee structure	49.7	61.8	58.1	60.7
Experience with litigation on controversial issues	35.1	40.3	44.3	48.0
Experience with companies in your industry/specialization	35.1	34.7	83.7	66.0
Total respondents	100.0% (151)	100.0% (144)	100.0% (203)	100.0% (150)

Source: "The Balance Sheet: Top Executives Speak Out About CPA Firms," 1978, © Dow Jones and Co., Inc., p. 18.

Note: Columns add to more than the base due to multiple answers.

toward a scope of work that meets the needs of clients without straining their financial resources. In some cases, clients may even have to be redirected toward other, less expensive professionals. Working with clients in this way is helpful for avoiding bitter conflicts over fees and for building lasting relationships and a good reputation.

EVALUATE SPECIFIC ALTERNATIVES. This is when the buying organization evaluates the finalists or the members of the short list. The

evaluation of written proposals, interviews, or formal presentations may
be an important part of this step. Among other things, the market analyst
will want to study what seems to make proposals, interviews, and presentations successful with particular target clients. How "slick" should the
firm be with its use of audio-visuals? How important is it to have the
professionals who will be providing the services actively participating in

TABLE 4–4
CHARACTERISTICS CONSIDERED MOST IMPORTANT IN
SELECTING/EVALUATING A CPA FIRM

	Corporate Financial Officers (%)	Audit Committee (%)	Attorneys (%)	Nonparticipating AICPA (%)
Technical competence	70	77	76	73
Overall reputation of firm	60	61	43	58
Quality of work performed	50	57	73	60
Experience in our industry	47	48	39	60
Provides a full range of auditing and related services	42	39	47	43
The overall quality of service provided	42	27	51	30
The level of experience assigned to the audit team	39	30	43	39
Depth of their personnel	37	48	45	43
Quality of their SEC, tax, and consulting services	32	21	16	21
World-wide coverage	27	23	22	18
Their fee structure	26	21	22	26
Their commitment to ethics	26	43	47	22
Accessibility of the partner in charge of the engagement	22	32	29	19
Their reputation within the profession	20	25	18	21
Meeting deadlines on work	20	11	31	20
Overall ease of working with them	20	23	24	23
Convenient domestic offices	17	11	14	13
Reputation of top partners	12	21	10	11

Source: "An Opinion Survey of the Public Accounting Profession," sponsored by
Deloitte Haskins & Sells. Conducted by Reichman Research Inc., May 1978. Reprinted
with permission.

TABLE 4–5
RELATIVE IMPORTANCE OF DIFFERENT FACTORS IN
CHOOSING A MARKETING RESEARCH FIRM

RANK	FACTOR	MEAN SCORE
1	Quality of work	4.57
2	Understanding of the client's problem	4.43
3	Reputation	4.37
4	Professional integrity	4.31
5	Experience	4.13
6	Referrals from satisfied clients	3.91
7	Personality of key personnel	3.27
8	Individuals who will work on project	3.19
9	Firm specialization	2.61
10	Personal contact (solicitation)	2.52
11	Price	2.24
12	Advertising	1.17

Source: Joel B. Haynes and James T. Rothe, "Competitive Bidding for Marketing Research Services: Fact or Fiction?" *Journal of Marketing,* Vol. 38, No. 3 (July 1974), p. 71. Reprinted with permission.

interviews and presentations? What are some of the personal likes and dislikes of the most influential people? We will be discussing how to obtain this kind of information in Chapter 7 and how to use it in preparing proposals and presentations in Chapter 11.

NEGOTIATE.   Buying organizations will often seek fee cuts or added services before finalizing arrangements with professionals. And sometimes competing professionals are played off against one another by clients. The market analyst can help a firm prepare for these situations by compiling information from knowledgeable sources on how clients and competitors have negotiated in the past. We provide some additional ideas on how to negotiate in Chapters 9 and 11.

BUY.   Eventually, a decision is made by the buying organization. The market analyst of a selected firm will want to find out what were perceived to be the firm's strong attributes. Such information will help the firm position and promote itself better in the future. Similarly, the market analyst of a rejected firm will want to conduct "exit" interviews to find out the firm's weak attributes. Techniques for measuring what attributes a firm is perceived to have are discussed later in this chapter and in Chapter 7.

USE.   The buying organization then makes use of the professional services. For this step, the market analyst will want to study whether clients follow the advice and instructions given to them by the firm. Ideas for improving communications with clients can be obtained in this way.

POSTPURCHASE EVALUATION.   The buying organization eventually reaches certain conclusions about the quality, timeliness, and other attributes of the professional services it has bought. The market analyst can therefore study what clients think of the way services have been provided. This satisfaction information can guide the improvement of services and this information can also reveal something about how word-of-mouth promotion might be refined. Chapter 7 contains some thoughts on how to monitor client satisfaction.

INDIVIDUAL BUYER BEHAVIOR

For those professional service organizations which serve individuals, the analysis of individual buyer behavior is essential. Moreover, those professional service organizations which serve only other organizations can also benefit greatly from studying aspects of individual buyer behavior—it can help them obtain a better understanding of how influential members of buying centers make buying recommendations. In the remainder of this chapter, we present a framework for studying how individual clients buy professional services. We address the same basic questions that we did for organizational buyer behavior.

Types of Decisions

The manner in which a person buys a professional service varies with the type of decision being made. Some buying decisions are more important, more complex, and more risky, and, consequently, tend to involve more buying participants and more deliberation. One way of categorizing individual buying decisions has been suggested by Howard and Sheth:[6]

1. *Routinized response behavior.* The simplest type of buying behavior occurs in the purchase of relatively low-cost, frequently purchased goods and services. The buyer typically is well acquainted with the available offerings and has definite preferences among them. The buying of routine health checkups, treatment for minor health problems, and other regularly bought professional services can often fit in this category. Individuals do not give much thought, search, or time to these purchases but merely go to the professionals they always use for these services (e.g., the "family" doctor).

2. *Limited problem solving.* Buying is more complex when buyers are purchasing familiar offerings but have little familiarity with the available sellers of those offerings. This situation occurs when a person moves to a new locality and must select dentists, doctors, accountants, lawyers, and so on. It can also occur when a person decides to discontinue buying from a professional who has been used for a long period of time. People in this situation generally undergo much search and deliberation.

3. *Extensive problem solving.* Buying reaches its greatest complexity when buyers are purchasing unfamiliar offerings from unfamiliar sellers. The unhappily married person seeking a divorce lawyer is probably in this situation (unless a previous divorce has been experienced). Likewise, a person seeking professional guidance to deal with serious financial or health problems would be in this situation. A lack of understanding of even the criteria to use to evaluate alternatives will lead these buyers to engage in considerable search and deliberation.

The market analyst will want to evaluate the people within each target market to identify the buying situations in which they tend to fall. Existing clients exhibiting routinized response behavior should be studied to see how their loyalty can be reinforced and how they might be convinced to purchase more services. The effectiveness of various types of reminder notices and other printed communications could be evaluated. On the other hand, people who exhibit routinized response behavior, but who buy from competitors, should probably receive minimal attention from the marketing analyst. Nevertheless, the analyst might want to devote some effort toward discovering what makes or could make these people switch professionals.

In addition, limited and extensive problem solvers deserve careful examination by the market analyst. Learning more about how these people eventually select certain professionals can be quite useful for developing strategies to improve referral networks, communications, fee structures, and so on. A portion of the necessary information can be obtained by having people fill out questionnaires on this subject during one of the first times they receive services. These questionnaires should ask more than "Who referred you?" They should seek data on who was consulted during the person's search, the criteria that were employed in making the decision, and other factors that may have been influential.

Decision Participants

In an effort to reduce the great uncertainty experienced in buying professional services, people tend to seek large amounts of information from others before making a decision. Family members, friends, co-workers, and other trusted sources will often become involved with a person's decision. The market analyst must therefore attempt to identify the kinds of people who might be playing each of the following roles in the decision making of the individuals in the firm's target markets:

1. *Initiator.* The initiator is the person who first suggests or thinks of the idea of buying the particular service.
2. *Influencer.* An influencer is a person whose views or advice carries some weight in making the final decision.

3. *Decider.* The decider is a person who ultimately determines any part of or the entire buying decision: whether to buy, what to buy, how to buy, or where to buy.

4. *Buyer.* The buyer is the person who makes the actual purchase.

5. *User.* The user is the person(s) who receives the services.

Discovering who plays these roles can guide the design of services, the creation of promotional messages, and the allocation of promotional budgets. If it is discovered, for example, that wives tend to be the deciders on where their husbands go for dental work, then a dental clinic will want to direct most of its advertising toward wives instead of husbands. Similarly, if it is determined that insurance companies, through their variations in coverage, influence the types of mental health services people will seek, then a mental health clinic will want to aim its promotional efforts and services at people who would be insured for services provided by the clinic. Knowing the main participants and the roles they play helps an organization fine-tune its marketing program.

Influences on Decisions

An enormous number of factors can influence how individuals buy professional services. The market analyst will want to identify the most important factors and judge their relative impact on decision making. This information can be used to guide all aspects of marketing planning, particularly the formulation of service and promotion strategies. Figure 4–2 shows several of the major influential buyer characteristics. We will comment briefly on each of these characteristics.

Cultural characteristics have the broadest influence on the buyer. The buyer's *culture, subculture,* and *social class* can have subtle but extremely important effects on decision making. These characteristics

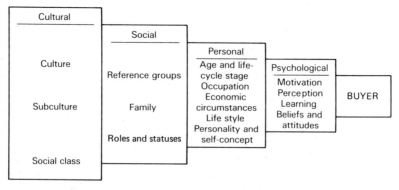

FIGURE 4–2. Detailed model of influential buyer characteristics

affect the socialization process people go through. The values, attitudes, and behaviors a person learns through the years from others of similar religious, ethnic, geographic, and financial backgrounds will certainly affect his or her approach to buying professional services. For instance, people of upper-class backgrounds may never feel comfortable walking into dentists' or lawyers' offices located in shopping centers, while people of lower-class backgrounds may feel more comfortable entering this type of office than they would entering offices in imposing office buildings or private homes.

Social characteristics also influence buying behavior. A person's *social groups, reference groups, family,* and *social roles and statuses* can all shape the buying process. A desire to please, impress, or upstage family members, friends, co-workers, or others can lead to the selection of certain types of professionals over others. For example, many people feel obliged to use the professional services of a family member or friend. And others seek to improve their social status by using professionals who have been used by celebrities or other high-status individuals.

Personal characteristics like a person's *age, life-cycle stage, occupation, economic circumstances, life style, personality,* and *self-concept* can also affect buying. Thus, older people require different services from health care professionals than the average person, as do people with physically demanding occupations, exercise-oriented life styles, or hard-driving personalities.

Finally, individual *psychological characteristics* will affect the buying process. People vary in their *motivations, perceptions, learning patterns,* and *beliefs and attitudes,* and this will impact their decisions. The analyst will want to examine these characteristics, recognizing that even though people may have identical cultural, social, and personal characteristics, their differing psychological characteristics could lead them to exhibit different behavior patterns. The analyst will want to study issues like whether people retain tax lawyers to either help them save money or "get even with the IRS." Or attention might be paid to the attitudes people have toward fee-for-service practices versus prepaid practices in either law or health care.

Decision Process

As with organizational buyers, the decision process of individual buyers of professional services will vary depending on the type of decision, the decision participants, the type of service, and several other factors. We will review what can be learned by examining the five-step decision process presented in Figure 4–3. Of course, market analysts will want to probe modifications of this model which seem to describe with greater accuracy the buying of their particular professional services.

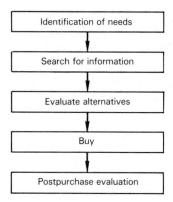

FIGURE 4–3. Model of the individual buying decision process

IDENTIFICATION OF NEEDS.   The buying process starts with the buyer recognizing a need or problem. The need can be triggered by *internal or external cues.* An internal cue consists of the person beginning to feel a need for, or readiness to do, something. The cue might take the form of a physiological stimulus, such as illness or injury, or a psychological stimulus, such as loneliness or anxiety. An external cue consists of something from the outside coming to the person's attention and stimulating interest in a professional service. The external cue can be *personal* (a friend, co-worker, or salesperson) or *nonpersonal* (a magazine article or advertisement).

The market analyst will want to give considerable attention to the types of cues that trigger interest in the relevant professional service. Research studies employing group discussions, personal interviews, telephone surveys, or mail surveys could be conducted to ask people to recall what set their interest in motion. These studies could also seek specific information about the nature of needs, such as details on the extent of financial or emotional problems. Naturally, obtaining information about sensitive or personal subjects will be difficult, requiring the use of very carefully prepared questions. Chapter 7 contains some material on how to formulate research questions.

SEARCH FOR INFORMATION.   Once a need has been identified, an individual buyer may or may not search for more information about ways to satisfy the need. Further search may be avoided if the buyer either perceives the need as relatively trivial or sees no plausible services available. If search goes forward, it may take a limited form called *heightened attention* or a more extensive form called *active information search.*

Heightened attention would be when a person becomes more receptive to messages about a service, noting them among the numerous messages a person is exposed to in a normal day. Active information search involves purposive data gathering from sources that can be characterized as *personal* (family, friends, neighbors), *commercial* (advertising, salespersons, professional societies, professionals in related fields), *public* (mass media), and *experiential* (trying a little of the service). The extent of a person's search depends on the intensity of the need, the amount of information available to start out, and the costs and benefits he or she perceives to be associated with searching.

The market analyst can clearly benefit from studying how and where individual buyers search for information. Data on this activity can help the professional service firm design and place more effective communications.

EVALUATE ALTERNATIVES.   The search for information will usually allow the individual buyer to narrow available professionals down to a *choice set*. The next step therefore involves an evaluation of the set members. In attempting to understand how buyers conduct these evaluations, the market analyst will find it useful to obtain information on the following:

1. The *attributes* buyers consider in looking at alternative providers of the professional service. This information could be obtained from group or personal interviews with buyers. For example, Table 4–6 contains information obtained from interviews on the attributes people seek in a lawyer.

2. The *relative importance* buyers assign to the considered attributes. Which attributes have the greatest importance in forming an overall judgment of a provider, and which attributes have lesser importance? Buyers could be asked to fill out rating scales to indicate the importance or weight they give different attributes in their decision making. (See Chapter 7 for an example.)

3. The *beliefs* buyers have about how much of each important attribute the alternative providers have. Measures could be obtained of where buyers see providers as standing along the attributes. The set of beliefs a person has about a provider make up the person's *image* of that provider. Exhibit 4–2 contains material on how to measure beliefs or images. We also cover belief measurement in Chapter 7.

4. The *ideal levels* for each attribute. As shown in Exhibit 4–2, measures can be taken of what levels of each attribute are considered most desirable or ideal to buyers.

5. The *evaluation procedures* used by buyers in arriving at an overall judgment about alternative providers. Many possible procedures exist. Some buyers will simply arrive at a judgment that favors the provider who is believed to be closest to having the ideal level of the single most important attribute. Thus, the provider perceived to be the oldest, biggest, or closest may be favored without consideration of other attributes. Other buyers will go through a more complex procedure in which consideration will be given to multiple attributes and the perceived location of each provider on those attributes. A buyer may identify minimum desired levels of several attributes and, by process of elimination, find only one provider who is acceptable. Or a buyer may go through a more complex evaluation

which will lead to preference of the provider who comes closest to having the ideal levels of the several most important attributes.

Obtaining information on all of the above can pay great dividends in formulating an effective marketing program. A firm can find out where it is currently positioned in the minds of target buyers by looking

TABLE 4-6

KEY QUALITIES SOUGHT IN A LAWYER

	Percent of Total Mentions*		
Comment Related to:	Favorable Attribute Sought in Lawyer Chosen (% of total favorable mentions)	Unfavorable Attribute Sought To Be Avoided in Lawyer Chosen (% of total unfavorable mentions)	Favorable Plus Unfavorable Attributes (% of aggregate mentions)
Personal relations with client			
Lawyer's interest in respondent/ respondent's problem	10.5	14.9	12.5
Lawyer's communication with client	7.2	7.6	7.4
	17.7	22.5	19.9
General reputation	19.2	16.8	18.1
Ethical standards, honesty, integrity	16.2	16.2	16.2
Lawyer's professional skill			
Competence, experience	7.7	4.3	6.2
Expert in subject area	7.4	2.6	5.2
Won–lost record	4.3	3.1	3.8
	19.4	10.9	15.2
Lawyer's personal characteristics			
Personality	9.5	10.1	9.8
Personal appearance, demographic characteristics	3.9	5.1	4.5
	13.5	15.2	14.3
Lawyer's fees			
Amount, reasonableness	7.9	11.2	9.4
Lawyer's preoccupation with fee	0.6	2.9	1.6
	8.5	14.1	11.0
Lawyer's work habits	2.9	2.9	2.9
Other	2.4	2.0	2.3

Source: Survey reported in *Alternatives,* January 1976, p. 15. Reproduced with permission of Legal Services Division, American Bar Association.

*Some respondents mentioned two or more attributes.

EXHIBIT 4–2. Image assessment

No fruitful image work can be done with an organization until research is conducted to determine how the organization is seen by its various key publics. The *set of beliefs that a person or group holds of an object* is called its *image.* The organization might be quite pleased with its measured image and simply want to do the work necessary to maintain it. Or the organization might discover that it has some serious image problems, in which case its interest lies in correcting and improving its image.

Image assessment calls for developing a survey instrument to measure the organization's image among its major publics. One part of the survey will establish the visibility–favorability position of the organization's image, and the other part will measure the content of the organization's image.

Figure 4–4A shows the results of measuring the visibility–favorability images of five management consulting firms. The two management consulting firms in quadrant I are in the best position. Firm 1 in particular is highly visible and enjoys the highest repute. Firm 3 in quadrant II also has high repute but is less well known. Its marketing need is to increase its visibility so that more people will know how good it is. Firm 4 in quadrant III is less well regarded than the preceding firms, but fortunately not many people know about it. This firm should maintain a low profile and introduce improvements in its management consulting practice designed to attract more approval. If effective, firm 4 will move to quadrant II, from which it can then seek more publicity. Finally, firm 5 in quadrant IV is in the worst situation in that it is seen as a poor service provider *and* everyone knows about this. This is sometimes called the "Amtrak syndrome." The firm's best course of action is to try to reduce its visibility (which would move it to quadrant III) and then plan to move successively to quadrants II and I. Of course this would take several years—if the firm ever accomplished it at all. Thus it should be clear that a firm's initial position in the visibility–favorability space defines the basic type of strategy it should pursue.

The second part of the image study is designed to reveal the content of the organization's image. One of the major tools for measuring the content of an image is

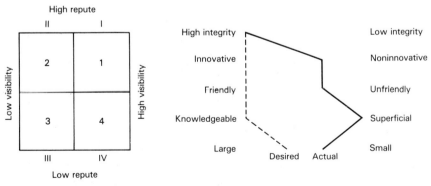

A. Visibility-favorability image space

B. Content image space

FIGURE 4–4. Image assessment tools

EXHIBIT 4-2   (*cont.*)

---

the *semantic differential.* The semantic differential involves identifying a set of appropriate object attributes and stating each attribute in bipolar terms. Respondents are asked to place a mark on each scale according to their impression of the degree to which the object possesses that attribute. The image researcher then averages the responses on each scale and represents this by a point. The points of the various scales are connected vertically, forming an image profile of the object.

Suppose firm 4 in Figure 4-4A finds its image profile to be that shown by the solid line in Figure 4-4B. Firm 4 is regarded as being high in integrity but not particularly innovative, friendly, knowledgeable, or large. The firm will either be surprised to learn this or recognize its validity. In either case the firm knows that these image weaknesses handicap its growth and profitability.

The firm should recognize that its "average" image as shown in Figure 4-4 (A and B) is probably not its image among every key public and even within each key public. The organization's image should be separately examined for each key public, and where it is acceptable, little marketing effort need be directed toward that public. The image consistency should also be examined within each key public. The firm may want its image to be highly specific or may prefer it to be somewhat varied.

Source: Philip Kotler, *Principles of Marketing,* 2nd ed. (Englewood Cliffs, N.J.: Prentice-Hall, 1983), pp. 597–98.

at beliefs information. It can then identify new potential positions by examining the most important attributes and the ideal levels of those attributes. The firm can evaluate whether it is capable of providing services that are perceived to have the ideal levels of the most important attributes. If this looks too difficult to accomplish, the firm may attempt, through various communications, to alter what buyers see as important or ideal to persuade them to prefer providers with attributes the firm *can* be perceived to provide.

Additionally, a firm may consider whether it is possible to persuade buyers to change their evaluation procedures to an approach that favors the firm. For example, a small firm that would stand to lose if buyers merely selected the biggest or oldest provider might try to convince buyers that they should weigh numerous attributes when making a decision.

BUY.   The evaluation of alternatives leads to the identification of a favored provider. But this provider may not necessarily be the one from whom a purchase is made. The *attitudes of others,* such as respected family members or friends, or *unanticipated situational factors,* such as the loss of a job or a sudden illness, may discourage or prevent purchase from the favored provider. Buying could also be delayed or prevented if the buyer sees high *perceived risk* associated with the purchase. People cope with high perceived risk in many different ways, including the gathering of more information or the complete avoidance of making a decision.

Knowing the kinds of obstacles that can prevent favored services from actually being bought can be helpful to the marketing effort. Arguments can be prepared to offset any last-minute anxiety that arises. And people can be assigned to "hand-hold" or communicate frequently with buyers to remind them of how much their business is desired.

POSTPURCHASE EVALUATION.   After buying and using a particular service, the buyer will revise beliefs about the service providers and form some overall judgment about satisfaction or dissatisfaction. Obtaining information about the satisfaction levels of individual buyers can be extremely helpful in planning service improvements and communications programs. For example, if it is found that past clients or patients have been highly satisfied with the services they have received, then this information can be featured in promotional materials and presentations. Exhibit 4–2 contains material on how to measure buyer satisfaction. We will have more to say about how to measure satisfaction and dissatisfaction in Chapter 7.

SUMMARY

Market analysis is the cornerstone of a successful marketing program. Understanding the needs, wants, and buying behavior of target clients and patients allows more effective marketing programs to be formulated. Both organizational buyers and individual buyers can be studied and analyzed for guidance.

Organizational buyers proceed differently, depending on whether they are making a straight-rebuy, modified-rebuy, or new-task decision. In many organizations, a buying center will purchase professional services, with several people becoming involved filling roles as users, influencers, buyers, deciders, and gatekeepers. Their decisions tend to be influenced by organizational, individual, interpersonal, and environmental factors. A complex decision process—containing steps in which needs are identified, information is sought, criteria are set, alternatives are evaluated, suppliers are selected, and satisfaction is determined—often takes place.

Individual buyers proceed differently, depending on whether they are engaged in routinized response behavior, limited problem solving, or extensive problem solving. An individual will often draw others into the buying of professional services and allow them to serve as influencers or even deciders of needed decisions. Numerous cultural, social, personal, and psychological characteristics can influence a person's buying of professional services. An individual's decision process can often be complicated, involving identification of needs, search for information, evaluation of alternatives, buying, and postpurchase evaluation.

NOTES

1. Charles Thomsen, "Marketing is Everybody's Business," *SMPS News*, Vol. 7 (October–November 1982), p. 2. Reprinted with permission.

2. Patrick J. Robinson, Charles W. Faris, and Yoram Wind, *Industrial Buying and Creative Marketing* (Boston: Allyn & Bacon, 1967).

3. Frederick E. Webster, Jr., and Yoram Wind, *Organizational Buying Behavior* (Englewood Cliffs, N.J.: Prentice-Hall, 1972), p. 6.

4. Yoram Wind and Robert J. Thomas, "Conceptual and Methodological Issues in Organisational Buying Behavior," *European Journal of Marketing*, Vol. 14, No. 5/6 (1981), pp. 239–47.

5. Ibid.

6. See John A. Howard and Jagdish N. Sheth, *The Theory of Buyer Behavior* (New York: Wiley, 1969).

5

FOCUSING THE BUSINESS DEVELOPMENT EFFORT:

Market Segmentation, Targeting, and Positioning

Joel Zylberberg was an ambitious, hustling Clevelander. A determined promoter, possessed of intelligence and wit. By the age of 25, just a few years ago, he had bootstrapped himself into the Ivy League (Dartmouth College, Yale Law School), worked for one of the best Wall Street law firms just long enough to pump up his résumé, married a millionaire senator's daughter he met on a blind date, managed his father-in-law's successful election campaign, and changed his name to the more euphonious Joel Z. Hyatt.

An opportunist? Let's just say that here was a man who knew how to package himself. A success story waiting to happen. Clearly, we would be hearing more.

And so we have. Joel Hyatt has finally arrived. On any given day you're likely to see him, in a half-minute of pinstriped kitsch, earnestly hyping his very own nationwide discount law firm. The firm is called Hyatt Legal Services. Remember that: someday it may be to law what H&R Block is to taxes.

Hyatt is using television ads to attract a new kind of legal client: the middle-income American who seldom, if ever, has been to a lawyer. "We're filling a need," Hyatt says. "We're growing by leaps and bounds." The market is wide open—over two-thirds of the adult population don't use lawyers—and Hyatt wants to corner it. If he succeeds, the result will be a revolution in our legal system. And it might even be a bonanza for lawyers themselves.

In a survey a few years back, the American Bar Association found that most people didn't consult a lawyer when they really needed one. The reasons were simple enough: some people were afraid of them or thought they would charge too much; others just didn't know how to go about finding a lawyer, short of throwing darts at the Yellow Pages. With his nationwide chain of cut-rate law offices—they're in sixteen major cities so far, with more being added monthly—Hyatt has been changing the trend, giving the legally deprived middle-class the kind of lawyerly attention it has never had before. Worried about high legal fees? Hyatt's young lawyers (average age: about 30) quote a flat fee in advance and stick to it. Can't drive downtown to see a lawyer? Hyatt's offices are in suburban shopping centers, open evenings and Saturdays. Perplexed about finding the right lawyer? Anyone who sees those simple television spots will come to know and trust Joel Hyatt, a darkly handsome 32-year-old who projects the guilelessness of an Eagle Scout.

There are an estimated 600 self-styled legal clinics around the country—all claiming to give cut rates for everyday legal services, many using radio, television, and newspaper ads of greatly varying sophistication. But Hyatt Legal Services is the biggest, the best, and the most aggressive. Only this year it moved into the top spot, ahead of Jacoby & Meyers, which has offices in Los Angeles and New York.

Source: Excerpted from John A. Jenkins, "Chain Gang," *TWA Ambassador,* October 1982, p. 1, with the permission of author and publisher. Copyright © 1982, Trans World Airlines, Inc.

Joel Hyatt is practicing *target marketing.* He is not trying to be everything to everyone, but seeks instead to position his offerings to appeal to a narrowly defined market segment. He is willing to let other law practices serve persons who do not fall within the targeted segment.

Although a "chain-store" strategy might not be right for most professional service organizations, the practice of target marketing certainly deserves close consideration from all organizations. Target marketing has several advantages over marketing approaches that involve trying to appeal to all clients either with a single service ("mass marketing") or with an assortment of services ("product-differentiated marketing"). Target marketing helps organizations identify marketing opportunities better. They can develop the right services for each target. They can adjust their fees, distribution channels, and promotional activity to reach the target market efficiently. Instead of scattering their marketing effort ("shotgun approach"), they can focus it on the buyers who have the greater purchase interest ("rifle approach").

Target marketing calls for three major steps (see Figure 5–1). The first is *market segmentation,* the act of dividing a market into distinct groups of clients who might require separate services and/or marketing mixes. The organization identifies different ways to segment the market, develops profiles of the resulting segments, and evaluates each segment's attractiveness. The second step is *market targeting,* the act of evaluating and selecting one or more of the market segments to serve. The third

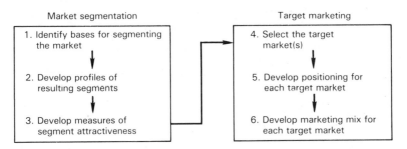

FIGURE 5–1. Steps in market segmentation and target marketing

step is *market positioning,* the act of formulating a competitive positioning for the service and a complementary detailed marketing mix. In this chapter, we will build on the material introduced at the end of Chapter 3 and describe the principles of market segmentation, market targeting, and market positioning.

MARKET SEGMENTATION

Markets consist of clients, and clients differ in one or more respects. They may differ in their wants, resources, geographic locations, attitudes, and practices. Any of these variables can be used to segment a market.

The General Approach to Segmenting a Market

Figure 5–2A shows a market of six clients. Each client is potentially a separate market because of unique needs and wants. Ideally, a professional service organization might design a separate marketing program for each client. Where there are only a few clients, this may be feasible. For example, a therapist tailors a different treatment to each patient, depending on what each patient needs. This ultimate degree of market segmentation is illustrated in Figure 5–2B.

But most professional service organizations will not find it worthwhile to "customize" their services totally. By providing similar services to similar clients, certain efficiencies may be obtained that can boost profitability considerably. The organization will want to identify broad classes of clients who differ in their service requirements and/or marketing responses. For example, the organization may discover that clients from different geographic locations differ in their wants. In Figure 5–2C, a number (1, 2, or 3) is used to identify each client's location. Lines are drawn around clients in the same location. Segmentation by location results in three segments, the most numerous segment being location 1.

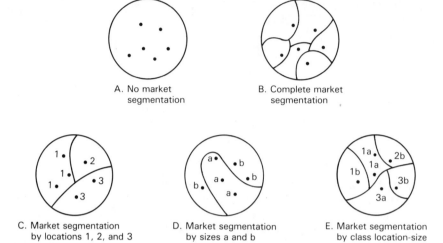

FIGURE 5–2.   Different approaches to segmentations of a market

On the other hand, the organization may find pronounced differences between large clients and small clients. In Figure 5–2D, a letter (a or b) is used to indicate each client's size. Segmentation by size results in two segments, each with three clients.

Now location and size may both count heavily in influencing the client's behavior toward the services. In this case, the market can be divided into five segments: 1a, 1b, 2b, 3a, and 3b. Figure 5–2E shows that segment 1a contains two clients and the other segments contain one client. As a market is segmented using more characteristics, the organization achieves finer precision, but at the price of multiplying the number of segments and thinning out the populations in the segments.

Bases for Segmenting Markets

There is no single way to segment a market. An organization has to try different segmentation variables, singly and in combination, hoping to find an insightful way to view the market structure. Table 5–1 contains a listing of the major bases or variables that can be used to segment markets. The variables listed under the geographic and behavioristic sections of the table could be used to segment markets consisting of either organizations or individuals. However, the demographic section is divided up to show variables that apply to markets of organizations and variables that apply to markets of individuals. In addition, the psychographic section applies only to markets of individuals. A discussion of several of these variables follows.

TABLE 5-1
MAJOR SEGMENTATION VARIABLES

Variable	Typical Breakdowns
Geographic	
• Region	Pacific, Mountain, West North Central, West South Central, East North Central, East South Central, South Atlantic, Middle Atlantic, New England
• County size	A, B, C, D
• City or SMSA size	Under 5,000; 5,000–19,999; 20,000–49,999; 50,000–99,999; 100,000–249,999; 250,000–499,999, 500,000–999,999; 1,000,000–3,999,99; 4,000,000 or over
• Density	Urban, suburban, rural
• Climate	Northern, southern
Demographic—Organizational Characteristics	
• Age	Under 6; 6–11; 12–19; 20–34; 35–49; 50–64; 65+
• Life-cycle stage	New; growth; maturity; decline
• Size	Dollar categories for assets or billings; or number of employees
• Industry	SIC codes
Demographic—Individual Characteristics	
• Age	Under 6; 6–11, 12–19; 20–34; 35–49; 50–64; 65+
• Family life-cycle stage	Young, single; young, married, no children; young, married, youngest child under 6; young, married, youngest child 6 or over; older, married, with children; older, married, no children under 18; older, single; other
• Sex	Male, female
• Family size	1–2, 3–4, 5+
• Resources	Income under $3,000; $3,000–$5,000; $5,000–$7,000; $7,000–$10,000; $10,000–$15,000; $15,000–$25,000; $25,000 and over
• Occupation	Professional and technical; managers, officials, and proprietors; clerical, sales; craftsmen, foremen; operatives; farmers; retired; students; housewives; unemployed
• Education	Grade school or less; some high school; graduated high school; some college; graduated college
• Religion	Catholic, Protestant, Jewish, other
• Race	White, black, oriental
• Nationality	American, British, French, German, Scandinavian, Italian, Latin American, Middle Eastern, Japanese

TABLE 5–1 (*cont.*)

Variable	Typical Breakdowns
Psychographic	
• Social class	Lower lowers, upper lowers, lower middles, upper middles, lower uppers, upper uppers
• Life style	Straights, swingers, longhairs
• Personality	Compulsive, gregarious, authoritarian, ambitious
Behavioristic	
• Purchase occasion	Regular occasion, special occasion
• Benefits sought	Quality, service, economy
• Type of problem	Variety of financial, legal, design, or health problems
• User status	Nonuser, ex-user, potential user, first-time user, regular user
• Usage rate	Light user, medium user, heavy user
• Loyalty status	None, medium, strong, absolute
• Buying structure	Informal, formal
• Decision process stage	Unaware, aware, informed, interested, desirous, intending to buy
• Primary referral agent	Lawyers, bankers, old clients, alumni, professors, etc.
• Attitude toward service	Enthusiastic, positive, indifferent, negative, hostile
• Marketing factor sensitivity	React to advertising, do not react to advertising

Geographic segmentation. Geographic segmentation calls for dividing the market into different geographic units such as nations, states, regions, counties, cities, or neighborhoods. The organization must decide whether to (1) operate in one or a few geographic areas or (2) operate in all but pay attention to variations in geographic needs and preferences. Thus, some law firms restrict their practices to a particular state, while other firms will develop practices in multiple states, taking account of the unique needs created by the laws of each state.

Demographic segmentation. Demographic segmentation consists of dividing the market into groups on the basis of demographic variables such as age, sex, size (of a family or an organization), life cycle, occupation, industry, education, religion, race, and nationality. Demographic variables are the most popular bases for distinguishing buying groups. One reason is that buyer wants, preferences, and usage rates are often highly associated with demographic variables. Another is that demographic variables are easier to measure than most other types of variables. Even when the target market is described in nondemographic terms (say, a life-style type), the link back to demographic characteristics is necessary in order to know the size of the target market and how to reach it efficiently. For example, knowing the demographic profile of hypochondriacs can help an organization determine the size of this life-style segment as well as the media most likely to reach it (since newspapers and other media often provide demographic profiles—but not necessarily life-style profiles—of their audiences).

Here we will illustrate how certain demographic variables might be used for market segmentation.

AGE AND LIFE-CYCLE STAGE. Client wants and capacities change with age. Thus, children, middle-aged adults, and elderly people all have vastly different health care requirements. And the types of legal services generally needed by individuals will vary greatly across age and life-cycle groupings. Obviously, pediatric and geriatric health care specialists make use of age as a segmentation variable, as do attorneys who specialize in juvenile criminal law or estate law. Less obvious is the use of age or life cycle as a segmentation variable when organizational clients are served. Yet there are law and accounting firms which offer special expertise in dealing with the problems of newly incorporated firms, and there are consulting firms which offer expertise in areas like launching new products or extending the life cycle of old products.

SEX. Males and females differ in their needs for professional services and in their approach to buying those services. Men and women have different health care problems, and they often have different financial and legal problems. Moreover, there are organizations and institutions that have aligned themselves with particular sexes—such as women's colleges, hospitals, and banks—which often have somewhat unique needs. Consequently, many doctors, lawyers, consultants, and other professionals have formed practices that emphasize the service of one sex over another. And other professionals have used sex as a segmentation variable (without choosing to serve only a single sex) in the way they have focused on reaching members of only one sex with their promotional messages. Thus a law firm that aims its advertising at males may do so out of a belief, which a research study by Humphreys and Kasulis supports,[1] that males are likely to be more receptive to attorney advertising.

INCOME OR WEALTH. Professionals who attempt to serve only individuals within certain income brackets are quite common, as are professionals who attempt to serve only organizations in particular types of financial situations. Carriage-trade lawyers, tax-shelter accountants, investment counselors, legal aid clinics, and bankruptcy lawyers all aim to serve segments with well-defined levels of financial resources.

INDUSTRY.   An increasing number of professional service firms are choosing to specialize in serving certain industries. Many law firms, for example, are focusing on one or a few industries—real estate, banking, high technology, and so on—to ply their craft.

MULTIVARIABLE SEGMENTATION.   Very often an organization will segment a market by combining two or more variables. For example, a combination of the variables age, wealth, size, and industry might lead a public accounting firm to evaluate the relative merits of (1) the segment containing young, marginally profitable, small firms in high-technology industries versus (2) the segment made up of old, highly profitable, large firms in consumer package goods industries. Breaking down a market more finely can make it easier to identify attractive opportunities.

Psychographic segmentation.   In psychographic segmentation, clients are divided into different groups on the basis of their social class, life style, and/or personality characteristics. People within the same demographic group can exhibit very different psychographic profiles.

SOCIAL CLASS.   Social classes are relatively homogeneous and enduring divisions in a society which are hierarchically ordered and whose members share similar values, interests, and behavior. Social scientists have distinguished six social classes: (1) upper uppers (less than 1%); (2) lower uppers (about 2%); (3) upper middles (12%); (4) lower middles (30%); (5) upper lowers (35%); and (6) lower lowers (20%), using variables such as income, occupation, education, and type of residence.[2] Social classes tend to show distinct consumption preferences. Most upper-class people would not want to be seen walking into an H & R Block office for tax advice or a Sterling Dental Center for dental work. At the same time, most lower-class people will shy away from professionals with fancy offices in high-rent locations.

LIFE STYLE.   Different consumer life styles are found within and even between social classes. Researchers have found that they can identify life-style segments by clustering people into groups sharing common *activities*, *interests*, and *opinions*. For instance, research done by the advertising agency Needham, Harper and Steers has suggested that men can generally be broken down into the following life-style groups:

1. Ben, the self-made businessman (17%)
2. Scott, the successful professional (21%)
3. Dale, the devoted family man (17%)
4. Fred, the frustrated factory worker (19%)
5. Herman, the retiring homebody (26%)[3]

Each life-style group may have specific service preferences and media preferences. Dale may prefer to use an accountant who is a family friend and who advertises by giving donations to the high school yearbook; while Scott will only use a CPA from a national firm which runs advertisements in major business magazines.

More service-specific life-style studies can also be done. For example, Ziff studied life styles related to drug purchases, discovering four groups that could conceivably be used by health care professionals to segment markets:

> 1. *Realists* (35%) are not health fatalists, or excessively concerned with protection or germs. They view remedies positively, want something that is convenient and works, and do not feel the need of a doctor-recommended medicine.
>
> 2. *Authority seekers* (31%) are doctor and prescription oriented, are neither fatalists nor stoics concerning health, but they prefer the stamp of authority on what they do take.
>
> 3. *Skeptics* (23%) have a low health concern, are least likely to resort to medication, and are highly skeptical of cold remedies.
>
> 4. *Hypochondriacs* (11%) have high health concern, regard themselves as prone to any bug going around, and tend to take medication at the first symptom. They do not look for strength in what they take, but need some mild authority reassurance.[4]

PERSONALITY. Personality variables can also be used to segment markets. An organization can try to match its *organizational personality* (or image) to the *individual personalities* (or self-images) of the clients it seeks to serve. Thus, a CPA firm might want to portray itself in promotional materials and personal communications as aggressive and competitive in order to appeal to aggressive, competitive clients.

Behavioristic segmentation. In behavioristic segmentation, clients are divided into groups on the basis of their knowledge, attitude, use, or response to an actual service or its attributes. Many marketers believe that behavioristic variables are the best starting point for constructing meaningful market segments.

PURCHASE OCCASION. Clients can be distinguished according to occasions when they purchase a service. Individuals may buy preventive or emergency health care services. Organizations may buy preventive (proactive) or emergency (reactive) management consulting services. Different sets of resources are required to serve preventive versus emergency clients. Serving the emergency segment requires an ability to provide help very quickly. A larger professional staff will probably be needed to insure that someone is always "on call." The ability to respond quickly will also need to be stressed in promotional materials.

BENEFITS SOUGHT. Clients can be segmented according to the particular benefit(s) that they are seeking from a service. Some clients look for one dominant benefit from a service and others seek a particular *benefit bundle*.[5] Many markets are made up of three core benefit segments: *quality buyers, value buyers,* and *economy buyers.* Quality buyers seek out professionals with the best reputations and credentials and have little concern for cost. They will go after big-name firms and talent. Value buyers look for the best value for the money and expect the service to match the fee or price. They are content with less prestigious professionals, but insist on getting considerable attention and satisfactory performance for what they can afford to pay. Economy buyers are primarily interested in minimizing their cost and favor the least expensive market offer. They are willing to go to paraprofessionals and unlicensed or uncertified practitioners to obtain the lowest cost services.

In addition to general benefits, each service should be evaluated for the specific benefits that different clients might seek. Some clients of CPA audit services may seek "management letters" with much "free" consulting advice in them, while other clients will not even think about this. Some clients of architectural services may seek unusual, high-style designs, while others may seek only functional designs. A separate marketing strategy can be worked out for each segment, based on the unique benefits sought and the associated characteristics of the segment members.

Benefit segmentation, it should be added, works best when people's preferences are correlated with demographic and media characteristics, making it easier to reach them efficiently.

USER STATUS.   Many markets can be segmented into nonusers, ex-users, potential users, first-time users, and regular users of a service. Many of the new clinic-type professional service practices have been designed to attract nonusers and turn them into first-time or regular users. Other, more traditional, professional service organizations target their efforts exclusively toward regular users, seeing the payoff from attracting this segment as being substantially greater. An overlooked segment is often the ex-users (of, for example, consulting or engineering services), who may really be potential users but who need to be contacted occasionally to determine their interest in becoming a user again (perhaps to take advantage of a new service).

USAGE RATE.   Markets can also be segmented into light-, medium-, and heavy-user groups of a service (called volume segmentation). Heavy users are often a small percentage of the market but account for a high percentage of total consumption. For example, the federal government is only one of many buyers in several markets, but it consumes an extremely large amount of consulting, engineering, accounting, and other professional services. Targeting the heavy users of certain services, such as the government, is a strategy pursued by many professional service organizations. Needless to say, the competition for the heavy users in most markets is intense, since obtaining just a few heavy users as clients can keep an organization profitable.

LOYALTY STATUS.   A market can also be segmented by client loyalty patterns. An organization should research its own and its competitors' clients to determine their degree of loyalty. Four groups can generally be distinguished: (1) *hard-core loyals*, who are exclusively devoted to one organization; (2) *soft-core loyals*, who are devoted to two or three organizations; (3) *shifting loyals*, who are gradually moving from favoring one organization to favoring another organization; and (4) *switchers*, who show no loyalty to any organization. If most of an organization's clients are hard-core loyals, or even soft-core loyals, the organization is basically healthy. It might study its loyals to find out the basic satisfactions they derive from their affiliation, and then attempt to attract the shifting loyals of competing organizations who are seeking the same satisfactions.

BUYING STRUCTURE.   Organizations and family units vary greatly in the formal procedures and structures they use in buying. Governments, for example, typically have extremely rigorous procedures involving numerous committees, competitive bidding, and much red tape. Some families are reasonably formal about large purchases, having family meetings to determine budgets and spending plans. At the other end of the spectrum are organizations and families with no formal procedures whatsoever.

Segmentation by buying structure is used frequently by professional service organizations. Many firms choose not to go after business from clients who have certain types of buying structures. Thus, there are architectural firms that refuse to enter design competitions; CPA firms that avoid competitive bidding situations; law firms that do not seek work from clients who request written proposals from prospective attorneys; and consulting firms that avoid government work unless available on a "sole-source" basis.

DECISION PROCESS STAGE.   Markets can be segmented based on the stage of the buying decision process that different clients occupy. The two decision processes discussed in Chapter 4 could be used to guide the segmentation process. The professional service organization may want to design different promotional programs for reaching segments at different stages. For example, communications aimed at organizations or individuals in the very early stages of their decision processes should emphasize creating a favorable image for the professional service firm, attempting to keep the firm in the choice set that receives more serious consideration. On the other hand, personal or written communications aimed at clients in the latter stages of the decision processes should contain more specific information about how the firm can uniquely meet the clients' needs.

PRIMARY REFERRAL AGENT. Segmentation by primary referral agent involves recognizing that clients vary in the types of people they rely on for advice on where to obtain professional services. Some clients, because of a desire for privacy or fear of being misunderstood, make buying decisions by themselves. But most clients rely heavily on others for guidance. Depending on the service to be bought and their own unique circumstances, clients may turn to trusted sources such as lawyers, bankers, doctors, local college faculty, competitors, club and association acquaintances, and so forth. Professional service organizations that segment by referral agent include CPA and law firms that target the clients of certain banks, professionals of all types who target those who receive advice from certain college professors, or specialized physicians who target the patients of certain general practitioners. Of course, when segments such as these are targeted, considerable effort must be devoted toward maintaining excellent relationships with the chosen referral agents.

ATTITUDE. The clients in a market can be classified by their degree of enthusiasm for a professional service. Five attitude classes can be distinguished: enthusiastic, positive, indifferent, negative, and hostile. In most cases, professional service organizations will want to target the enthusiastic and positive clients, recognizing that the other three segments can be difficult and expensive to attract. But some professional service organizations may find their best opportunities for growth lying within segments that are indifferent, negative, or even hostile. An ability to turn lawyer-haters, dentist-haters, doctor-haters, and other negative individuals—who may seriously need professional services—into satisfied clients can prove to be very profitable for some firms.

MARKETING FACTORS. Markets can also be segmented into groups who respond differently to marketing factors such as personal selling, advertising, and price. For example, there are clients who are turned off by advertising of professional services; and there are clients who see such advertising as legitimate and useful. Knowing the marketing factor sensitivities of different segments can be very helpful in allocating marketing resources.

Requirements for Effective Segmentation

Clearly, there are many ways to segment a market. However, not all segmentations are effective. To be useful, the market segments that emerge should have the following characteristics:

1. *Measurability.* The degree to which the size and purchasing power of the segments can be measured. Certain segmentation variables provide difficult measurement problems, such as life style, loyalty status, and attitude. It is often hard to measure the size and purchasing power of groups like hypochondriacs, "switchers," or "hostiles."

2. *Accessibility.* The degree to which the segments can be effectively reached and served. If it becomes too expensive to reach and serve segments with relatively unique communications and services, then it is not worth breaking down the market into those segments. Segments such as hypochondriacs, "switchers," or "hostiles" may also have difficulty meeting this requirement, since it may be hard to find efficient ways of reaching these groups.

3. *Substantiality.* The degree to which the segments are large and/or profitable enough. A segment should be the largest possible homogeneous group worth going after with a tailored marketing program. It would not pay, for example, for a veterinarian to specialize in the care of a rare breed of dogs.

4. *Actionability.* The degree to which effective programs can be formulated for attracting and serving the segments. The identification of segments that a firm has neither the expertise nor resources to serve adequately is not very helpful.

MARKET TARGETING

Market segmentation reveals the market segment opportunities facing the organization. The organization now has to decide on (1) how many segments to cover and (2) how to identify the best segments. The first decision involves choosing among three possible market coverage strategies, known as undifferentiated marketing, differentiated marketing, and concentrated marketing. We shall discuss each of these strategies below.

Undifferentiated Marketing

In undifferentiated marketing, the organization chooses not to recognize the different market segments making up the market. It treats the market as an aggregate, focusing on what is common in the needs of clients rather than on what is different. It tries to design services and a marketing program that appeal to the broadest number of clients. It would be exemplified by the consulting firm that offers the same training program or computer software to everyone, the law firm that offers the same uncontested divorce settlement to everyone, or the plastic surgeon who gives the same shaped nose to everyone.

Undifferentiated marketing is typically defended on the grounds of cost economies. It is "the marketing counterpart to standardization and mass production in manufacturing."[6] Service costs, research costs, promotion costs, and training costs are all kept low by offering a limited line of services. The lower cost, however, is usually accompanied by reduced client satisfaction through failure of the organization to meet individually varying needs. Competitors have an incentive to reach and serve the neglected segments, and become strongly entrenched in these segments.

Differentiated Marketing

Under differentiated marketing, an organization decides to operate in two or more segments of the market but designs separate services and/or marketing programs for each. By offering service and marketing variations, it hopes to attain higher sales and a deeper position within each market segment. It hopes that a deep position in several segments will strengthen the client's overall identification of the organization with its professional field. Furthermore, it hopes for greater loyalty and repeat purchasing, because the organization's services have been bent to the desires of clients rather than the other way around.

The net effect of differentiated marketing is to create more total revenues for the organization than undifferentiated marketing. However, it also tends to create higher costs of doing business. The organization has to spend more in service design, marketing research, communication materials, and training. Since differentiated marketing leads to higher sales and higher costs, nothing can be said in advance about the optimality of this strategy. Some professional service organizations push differentiated marketing too far in that they run more segmented programs than are economically feasible; some should be pruned. But other organizations probably err in not pushing differentiated marketing far enough in light of the varying needs of their clients.

Concentrated Marketing

Concentrated marketing occurs when an organization decides to divide the market into meaningful segments and devote its major marketing effort to one segment. Instead of spreading itself thin in many parts of the market, it concentrates on serving a particular market segment well. Through concentrated marketing, the organization usually achieves a strong following and standing in a particular market segment. It enjoys greater knowledge of the market segment's needs and behavior and it also achieves operating economies through specialization in service provision and promotion. This type of marketing is done, for example, by law firms that specialize in handling particular types of litigation or by consultants who specialize in the management problems of a single industry. Other examples include interior designers who specialize in certain types of offices (e.g., banks), CPAs who specialize in formulating tax shelters, or surgeons who specialize in certain types of surgery.

Concentrated marketing does involve higher than normal risk, in that the market may suddenly decline or disappear. Becoming dependent on only one segment also holds the risk of being bad for an organization's reputation, as clients and competitors may begin to question the independence and integrity of a firm that appears beholden to a specific set of clients. This last problem developed in the following situation:

> A two-person Minneapolis law partnership was doing extremely well specializing in handling liability suits filed against A. H. Robins Co., the manufacturers of the ill-fated Dalkon shield intrauterine birth control device. After handling over nine hundred cases, the firm found itself the target of considerable adverse publicity and several investigations about the way it was handling the Dalkon cases. It was charged that a "cozy" relationship between the firm and an insurance adjuster allowed the firm to obtain rapid, but allegedly inferior, cash settlements in its cases. The firm became so bogged down with handling all the charges against it that it was forced to withdraw from over four hundred pending Dalkon cases at a time when the charges against the firm had not really been substantiated.[7]

Choosing a Market Coverage Strategy

The actual choice of a marketing strategy depends on specific factors facing the organization. If the organization has *limited resources*, it will probably choose concentrated marketing because it does not have enough resources to relate to the whole market and/or tailor special services for each segment. If the market is fairly *homogeneous* in its needs and desires, the organization will probably choose undifferentiated marketing because little would be gained by differentiated offerings. If the organization aspires to be a leader in several segments of the market, it will choose differentiated marketing. If *competitors* have already established dominance in all but a few segments of the market, the organization might try to concentrate its marketing in one of the remaining segments. Many organizations start out with a strategy of undifferentiated or concentrated marketing and, if they are successful, evolve into a strategy of differentiated marketing.

If the organization elects to use a concentrated or diffentiated marketing strategy, it has to evaluate carefully the best segment(s) to serve. The best way to do this is to apply the General Electric strategic business planning grid discussed in Chapter 3 (pp. 53–55). Each segment should be rated on its market attractiveness and the organization's strengths. The organization should focus on those market segments which have intrinsic attractiveness and which it has a differential advantage in serving. In Chapter 6, we review several techniques that can be used to quantify the potential of different segments.

MARKET POSITIONING

Once a professional service organization decides on a segment to target, it must then decide how to best compete for that segment. If it is an established segment, competitors already operate in this segment. The competitors have furthermore taken "positions" in this segment. That is, they have each developed a standing on the set of attributes considered most important to the clients in that segment. The organization has to undertake a competitive analysis to identify the positions of existing competitors as a prelude to deciding on what should be done about its own positioning.

Using the techniques for measuring beliefs or images introduced in Chapter 4 in Exhibit 4–2 (pp. 87–88), the organization should be able to develop a *perceptual space map* that indicates where clients in a segment perceive the different competitors to be positioned along specific attributes. Such a map was presented in Chapter 3 (Exhibit 3–9 on p. 61) when we first introduced the concept of positioning. Another example of a perceptual space map is presented in Figure 5–3. This example represents how the clients in a targeted segment tend to see a group of competing law firms on the attributes of prestige and friendliness. Firm

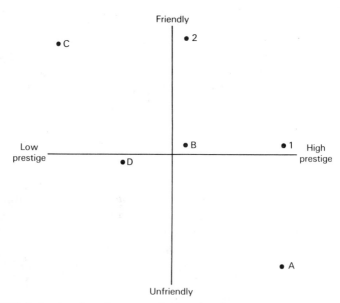

FIGURE 5–3.   Product space map for four law firms

A is seen as highly prestigious and very unfriendly, firm B as moderately prestigious and moderately friendly, and so forth.

Formulating a positioning strategy for a firm like B would next involve researching what clients in the segment view as the most desirable configuration of attributes for a law firm to have. Clients could be asked to indicate "ideal" levels of attributes on rating scales. It might be discovered that most clients in the segment prefer to retain highly prestigious and moderately friendly firms (those near point 1), with a substantial minority preferring moderately prestigious and very friendly firms (those near point 2). Management of firm B would then have to choose among the following positioning approaches:

1. Seeking to improve the firm's prestige to position itself near point 1. This might be done by hiring a well-known political figure or by taking on a highly publicized *pro bono* case.
2. Seeking to improve the firm's friendliness to position itself closer to point 2. This might be done by staff training or by a revision of hiring and promotion policies.
3. Some combination of the above in order to try to position itself to be attractive to all clients in the segment.

Choosing a positioning strategy essentially becomes a market targeting task, as a decision must be made on which *subsegment*—using "benefits sought" as the subsegmentation variable—to target: those that prefer prestige or those that prefer friendliness. As was just discussed, market targeting (and therefore positioning) should be based on the attractiveness of the segments and on the strengths of the organization.

Positioning and Differentiation

The selection of a positioning strategy amounts to choosing a distinctive image or "personality" for an organization that can help it overcome the "limited differentiability" problem cited in Chapter 1. The entire marketing program of the organization should be set up to be consistent with the chosen positioning. As Keane states in talking about the importance of this task for CPA firms:

Clients should be able to distinguish one firm from another. This means that each firm must have an individual "personality." This will give the firm identity and visibility, and people will remember it. For instance, a firm might be noted for its research accomplishments, its public interest role, its government expertise, its innovativeness or its industry specialization.

Each firm must critically assess its strengths and weaknesses when it considers the image it wants to project. When a decision is made on which special characteristics it wants to emphasize, the accounting firm should

TABLE 5–2
"POSITIONING" OF THE "BIG EIGHT" CPA FIRMS

Firm	Worldwide Revenues (fiscal 1977, in millions)	U.S. Revenues (fiscal 1977, in millions)	Number of Fortune 500 Clients (1977)	How They See Themselves	How Competitors See Them
Peat, Marwick, Mitchell & Co.	$516	$365	67	Aggressive but not in an unprofessional way. We have the best people. Biggest weakness: too decentralized.	Trying to recover from past problems with SEC. Very aggressive. Price cutter. Expanding scope of practice.
Coopers & Lybrand	$490	$256	50	Tough. We work harder. We've got a winner's kind of feeling. Our real strength is in the management team.	Has changed a lot. Most aggressive of the eight in hustling business. Price cutter.
Price Waterhouse & Co.	$479	$245	99	The premier accounting firm. We are to accounting what sterling is to silver. Our clients are the cream.	Not very aggressive. Stuffy. Arrogant. Getting steamed up after losing some clients.
Arthur Andersen & Co.	$471	$351	72	Tough. Aggressive. We speak with one voice everywhere. Not well known outside the U.S.	Aggressive. Likes publicity. First firm to emphasize growth. No room for individual thought.

				What they say about themselves	What others say
Deloitte Haskins & Sells	$410	$220	53	Not as aggressive as most of the Big Eight. Technical leader in the profession. The auditor's auditor.	Not very aggressive. Narrow in scope of services. Getting their act together. Strong auditors.
Arthur Young & Company	$390	$210	52	Tend to be less aggressive than others. Heavy emphasis on client service. We do not want to be the biggest.	Not as aggressive as other Big Eight firms. Widely respected. Super-professional.
Ernst & Ernst	$385	$285	61	A practical firm. Pragmatic. We put strong emphasis on quality service to our existing clients.	Sleepy. Not growing fast except in certain industries. Not on the competitive edge. Loosest organization overseas.
Touche Ross & Co.	$350	$185	24	We want to be the best. We're not as big as we want to be. We're not price cutters, but we are price competitors.	Very aggressive in hustling business. Enamored of size. Price cutter. Weak overseas.

Source: Peter W. Bernstein, "Competiton Comes to Accounting," FORTUNE, July 17, 1978, p. 92. FORTUNE Art Dept./Carolyn Mazzello; © 1978 Times Inc. Reprinted with permission.

Note: The data on FORTUNE 500 clients were prepared by Deloitte Haskins & Sells and Price Waterhouse. The big accounting firms are private partnerships, and they have only recently begun releasing financial information about their own operations. Arthur Andersen was the first to issue an annual report, five years ago. Last year, Peat, Marwick, Mitchell and Price Waterhouse also published annual reports. Touche Ross has disclosed only its revenues. The other four firms released their revenue figures to *Fortune*—the first time they have let this information out. The Peat, Marwick figure for U.S. revenues is an estimate. The Touche Ross numbers do not reflect the firm's 1977 merger with J.K. Lasser.

ensure that they are highlighted and communicated consistently through every medium available—for example, newsletters, speeches, client meetings, business proposals, news releases, interviews and recruiting literature.[8]

Some of the positions that Big Eight CPA firms have apparently sought to occupy are reflected in Table 5–2 in the left-hand column. These self-descriptions were reported in a 1978 article in *Fortune* on competition in the accounting profession.[9] A more accurate picture of how they were actually positioned may be provided by the right-hand "how competitors see them" column. But the best way to determine actual positions would have been to obtain data on *client* perceptions.

Maister has pointed out that professional service organizations have historically tended to position themselves—consciously or unconsciously—as having one of three distinctive attributes: (1) more "brains," (2) more "grey hair," or (3) superior procedures.[10] These positioning approaches may still have considerable value today—but they should only be pursued if research results suggest that targeted clients are seeking these attributes.

Difficult decisions about targeting and positioning can be made easier by having good data on the buying potential and probable purchase rates of various segments. Some tools for doing market measurement and forecasting are described in the next chapter.

SUMMARY

Target marketing involves distinguishing the different groups that make up a market and developing appropriate services and marketing mixes for each target market. The key steps in target marketing are market segmentation, market targeting, and market positioning. Market segmentation is the act of dividing a market into distinct groups of clients who might merit separate services and/or marketing mixes. The organization tries different variables to see which reveal the best segmentation opportunities. Segmentation variables can be classified as geographic, demographic, psychographic, and behavioristic. The effectiveness of the segmentation analysis depends upon arriving at segments that are measurable, accessible, substantial, and actionable.

Next, the organization has to select the best market segment(s). The first decision is how many segments to cover. The organization can ignore segment differences (undifferentiated marketing), develop different market offers for several segments (differentiated marketing), or go after one or a few market segments (concentrated marketing). The attractiveness of each segment must be weighed against the organization's strengths in deciding on which segments to target.

Market targeting then defines the organization's competitors and positioning possibilities. The organization should research the competitors' positions and decide whether to take a position similar to some competitor or go after an unoccupied position. The organization can then build an entire marketing program around the position or image that has been chosen.

NOTES

1. Marie A. Humphreys and Jack J. Kasulis, "Attorney Advertising," *Journal of Advertising Research*, December 1981, pp. 31–37.

2. See James F. Engel, Roger D. Blackwell, and David T. Kollat, *Consumer Behavior*, 3rd ed. (New York: Holt, Rinehart & Winston, 1978), pp. 127–28.

3. See Peter W. Bernstein, "Psychographics Is Still an Issue on Madison Avenue," *Fortune*, January 1978, pp. 78–84.

4. Ruth Ziff, "Psychographics for Market Segmentation," *Journal of Advertising Research*, April 1971, pp. 3–9.

5. See Paul E. Green, Yoram Wind, and Arkun K. Jain, "Benefit Bundle Analysis," *Journal of Advertising Research*, April 1972, pp. 31–36.

6. Wendell R. Smith, "Product Differentiation and Market Segmentation as Alternative Marketing Strategies," *Journal of Marketing*, July 1956, p. 4.

7. See Paul Blustein, "How 2 Young Lawyers Got Rich by Settling IUD Liability Claims," *Wall Street Journal*, February 24, 1982, p. 1.

8. John G. Keane, "The Marketing Perspective: The CPA's New Image," *Journal of Accountancy*, January 1980, p. 64.

9. Peter W. Bernstein, "Competition Comes to Accounting," *Fortune*, July 17, 1978, p. 92.

10. David H. Maister, "Balancing the Professional Service Firm," *Sloan Management Review*, Fall 1982, pp. 15–29.

6

MARKET MEASUREMENT AND FORECASTING

California Family Dental Centers, Inc., was the invention of a San Francisco dentist, Joel Rosenbloom. Rosenbloom had been very successful in his private practice over the previous ten years. Prior to that he had worked at a dental clinic as an associate dentist. He had always wondered about the inconsistencies in attitudes regarding dental care in the United States. In his private practice, located in a suburban area of San Francisco, he saw only middle-upper- and upper-income patients. At the dental clinic, he used to see more middle- or lower-income patients, but only if the lower-income families belonged to a dental insurance plan, or if supplemental payment was made by the government.

Rosenbloom felt that there was a need for a new type of dental care facility and he came up with the idea of California Family Dental Centers. He felt that it was possible to offer dental care to lower-middle- and middle-income households at significantly reduced cost, but in surroundings similar to a private practice. He thought he could do this in two ways. First, he would have to generate sufficient consumer demand for the dental center's services. Through tight scheduling and other cost-efficient measures adopted from his clinic experience, he could minimize unused time and the total amount of time each patient would actually be with a dentist. Supplies could be purchased in bulk to cut costs, and laboratory work and other services could be performed on the site by dental center employees rather than being acquired externally. Volume, he reasoned, if efficiently managed, would generate economies of scale. This, in turn, could yield lower fees but, not coincidentally, high profits.

Second, Rosenbloom thought that it would be best to have the dental center office operate in such a way as to closely resemble a private practice. He planned to set up each center with one other dentist as his professional associate. Rosenbloom would arrange financing, the facility, supplies, and promotion under the California Family Dental Centers name. The associate dentist would operate the center and take a share of the profits. Other dentists would be hired on salary plus a limited profit-sharing plan.

The overall objective of the concept would be to establish many individual dental centers, with Rosenbloom at the head of the entire organization and in charge of procurement, management methods, and marketing. The day-to-day operation of the centers would be managed by his associate dentists.

The time had come to test his concept. Rosenbloom needed to select a site for the location of the first California Family Dental Centers office. He knew that he wanted to locate in metropolitan areas with high growth rates, and he did some preliminary analysis on a number of areas in California. Of interest to him were population and income figures as well as present competition. Rosenbloom personally knew a dentist in Detroit, Ben Turner, who wanted to move to the San Diego area, so Rosenbloom paid particular attention to that location. Turner had expressed interest in the dental center concept and was potentially an ideal candidate to open the first office.

Preliminary research using data from the American Dental Association showed that the San Diego area was growing rapidly, but was already moderately saturated in terms of existing dentists. Rosenbloom collected more information about the San Diego area since it appeared to suit his criteria and because of Turner's interest in moving there. This included data on income levels, race, age, and housing obtained from the U. S. Census Bureau and the San Diego City Planning Department. He was troubled, however, that some of the data were more recent than others, and that some data were for the entire county while the rest were for only the city of San Diego.

From the San Diego Dental Society he obtained a directory which showed the number of dentists in each geographic area in the county. Rosenbloom compared these to population figures for a few areas in which he had initial interest. He eventually found a suitable location to set up his trial office.

Source: Excerpted from Donald Sciglimpaglia, "California Family Dental Centers," in William G. Zikmund, William J. Lundstrom, and Donald Sciglimpaglia, eds., *Cases in Marketing Research* (Chicago: Dryden Press, 1982), pp. 19–30.

Dr. Rosenbloom did not try to operate intuitively in selecting a geographic market to serve with his first center. He based his decision on data he had obtained that allowed him to develop reasonably good estimates of the potential demand levels associated with different locations. This chapter contains a discussion of methods for assessing the current and future demand levels of markets or market segments. These methods can be used to support the task of market targeting covered in the last chapter. They can also be useful in doing personnel planning and budgeting. We review methods for measuring current market demand first, followed by a review of methods for forecasting future market demand.

MEASURING
CURRENT MARKET DEMAND

There are four types of estimates that an organization will want to make to gain an understanding of its current market demand situation: *total market potential, total market size, organization market share*, and *market expansibility*. The estimation of each is treated separately below.

Estimating Total Market Potential

The total market potential of a market (or market segment) represents the maximum number of hours per time period of a specific service that all the clients in a market could conceivably buy under current prices and current economic, social, political, and technological conditions. In other words, it is the upper limit in total billable hours that all the firms providing a given service to a market can hope to reach under current conditions, no matter how much marketing effort is put forth. Total market potential can only change if underlying environmental conditions change. If the national economy improves or if a market's population grows or if fee levels fall, then total market potential can increase. But more spending on marketing will not increase potential— this will only allow a market's demand to be expanded closer to its potential.

The estimation of total market potential is an essential first step in evaluating the current demand situation of a market (or market segment). In fact, in cases where potential is determined to be very small, this step may be the only one needed before reaching a (negative) decision about targeting a market. However, the estimation of total markct potential typically proves to be a difficult task for professional service organizations. They are often unsure as to what calculations to make to arrive at an estimate and what data to use in making these calculations. We offer a few suggestions for dealing with these problems in the following paragraphs.

A useful technique for calculating an estimate of total market potential is the *chain ratio method*. Use of this technique requires the market analyst—the label we will use to refer to the person assigned to do market measurement and forecasting—to make a set of assumptions about (1) environmental conditions and (2) the values of various descriptors (mostly in the form of ratios or percentages) of market characteristics. A calculation of market potential is essentially made by multiplying all of the descriptors together. An illustration of how this technique works follows:

> A CPA firm with experience and expertise in counseling individuals undergoing tax audits by the Internal Revenue Service would like to bill 800 hours per year in this area. The firm's market analyst assumes that during the coming year there will be no major shifts in IRS policies or in the socioeconomic conditions of its metropolitan area. The analyst can then calculate total market potential in this way:

Total number of individual taxpayers in the firm's metropolitan area	250,000
Percentage of taxpayers (with profiles like those in the area) who are audited annually	× .01
Percentage of those audited who seek outside help	× .20
Percentage of those seeking outside help who prefer CPAs over lawyers	× .50
Number of potential clients	250
Average number of billable hours for tax-audit cases	× 6
Total market potential	1,500 hours

The analyst would then want to perform a *sensitivity analysis* on the results. This would involve examining the effects on the estimate of varying the assumptions about any of the descriptors or any of the underlying conditions. If after trying out many different ratios and figures all the estimates of market potential remained low relative to the desired goals, then the market would not be targeted (as would probably happen in this example). On the other hand, if the potential estimates all came out considerably higher than the desired goals, then further examination of market demand could be called for.

Of course, different descriptors will have to be used in estimating the potential of different markets. Where can the data be obtained to guide the market analyst in estimating different descriptors? Helpful data are often available from secondary sources such as government documents, professional and trade association reports, or business magazines. Other useful data may be extracted from an organization's own records on its existing or former clients. Surveys of experts and clients may also be helpful for developing descriptors. We provide an extended discussion on how to obtain and organize market information in our next chapter.

Estimating Total Market Size

Besides measuring potential demand, an organization will usually want to know the actual total size, in billable hours and revenues, of a market (or market segment). How much of the market's potential is actually being captured? How much money is being brought in from this market? Answering these questions requires identifying the other organizations serving the market. This is not as simple as it may sound because of the many definitions of a market. For example, a consulting firm specializing in giving strategic planning advice to medium-sized businesses would have to identify other firms and individuals which offer similar advice to this category of buyers. Should CPA firms that sometimes offer this advice through their management services divisions be included? How about college professors who provide this advice as private consultants? The organization must carefully define its real competition as the first step in developing estimates of total billable hours and total revenues.

Then the organization has to estimate the hours billed and revenues of each competitor. How is this information to be obtained? The easiest way is to contact each competitor and offer to exchange information. In this way, each organization can measure its performance against every other organization and against the total hours and revenues for the industry. However, this solution frequently is not available. Trading information of this type is illegal in many industries. In other cases, particular competitors are not willing to divulge this information. In the latter case, the organization can still compare its figures to those of the cooperating organizations and find this useful.

Another solution calls for professional associations to collect the data and publish the hours and revenues of each organization and/or the total hours and revenues. In this way, each organization can evaluate its performance against specific competitors or against the industry as a whole.

If this solution is not available, the organization will have to estimate the hours and revenues of one or more competitors through indirect methods. A competitor's figures might be inferred from information about the size of its staff, the extent of its office space, the amount of certain raw materials it orders from common suppliers (e.g., paper, office machines), and other indicators.

Estimating Organization Market Share

With data on total market size, an organization can proceed to estimate its share of a market's billable hours or revenues. Organizations can estimate at least three types of market share figures. Ideally, the organization should know its (1) share of the total market, (2) share of the subsegment(s) of the market it is most interested in serving, and (3) share relative to the leading competitor or leading three competitors. Each of these measures yields useful information about the organization's market performance and potential.

Estimating Market Expansibility

Data on market potential, market size, and market share allow an organization to determine where there may be room to grow. A large gap between total market size (in hours) and total market potential might be perceived as a growth opportunity by firms willing to mount an aggressive marketing effort. A small market share in a large market might also be perceived as a growth opportunity by certain firms. However, a firm should attempt to determine how *expansible* market size and market share might be before targeting a given market.

Markets are expansible if additional revenues can be obtained in them without an equivalent addition to expenses. High expansibility would exist if considerable additional revenues could be obtained in the market with only small additional marketing expenses. For example, many people believe that the lower-middle-class market for dental care fits this description (see this chapter's opening story). Low expansibility would exist if the only ways to capture more potential or share were to lower fees and/or raise marketing expenditures to unprofitable levels—because of the need to counter either market resistance or competitive reactions.

Estimating the expansibility of a market requires an understanding of how the clients in it react to changes in fees and marketing expenditures. If data are available, one can examine how the market (or markets similar to it) reacted to changes in fees and marketing expenditures in the past. But if a market is being considered that has never been targeted before, relevant data probably are not available. Consequently, the market analyst may have to turn to some of the forecasting techniques discussed in the next section (i.e., client intentions surveys, intermediary estimates, market tests) for estimating expansibility. Essentially, people could be asked to reveal whether usage of a particular service would be affected by changes in fees, the frequency of "sales" calls from professionals, the amount of advertising they see, and so forth. We provide additional guidance on how to conduct good interviews, surveys, and experimental studies in the next chapter.

FORECASTING
FUTURE MARKET DEMAND

Having looked at ways to estimate current demand, we are now ready to examine the problem of forecasting future demand. How might an organization forecast what will happen to market potential, market size, market share, and market expansibility? Unfortunately, few services lend themselves to easy forecasting. The few cases generally involve a service whose absolute level or trend is fairly constant and whose competition is nonexistent or stable. In the vast majority of markets, total market demand and specific organization demand are not stable from year to year and good forecasting becomes a key factor in effective performance. Poor forecasting can lead to excess personnel and supplies or, on the other hand, to insufficient personnel and supplies. The more unstable the demand, the more critical is forecast accuracy and the more elaborate is forecasting procedure.

In approaching forecasting, one should list all the factors that might affect future demand and predict each factor's likely future level and effect on demand. The factors affecting demand might be classified into three categories: (1) *noncontrollable macroenvironmental factors* such as the state of the economy, new technologies, and legal developments; (2) *competitive factors* such as competitors' fees, new services, and promotional expenditures; and (3) *organizational factors* such as the organization's fees, new services, and promotional expenditures.

In view of the many factors that might be involved, organizations have turned to various approximation methods to forecast future demand. Five major methods are discussed below. They arise out of three information bases for building a forecast. A forecast can be based on *what people say, what people do,* or *what people have done.*

The first basis—what people say—involves systematic determination of the opinions of clients or of those close to them, such as salespersons or outside experts. It encompasses two methods: (1) client intentions surveys, and (2) intermediary estimates. Building a forecast on what people do involves another method: (3) market tests. The final basis—what people have done—involves using statistical tools to analyze records of past buying behavior, using either (4) time-series analysis or (5) statistical demand analysis. Each of these methods is described and illustrated below.

Client Intentions Surveys

One way to form an estimate of future demand is to ask a sample of target clients to state their buying intentions for the forthcoming period. Suppose an architectural firm is trying to estimate the number of apartment and/or condominium projects that will be started (and that it might obtain commissions for) during the next two years in a given region. Among other things, the firm might want this information to guide it in making decisions concerning staffing needs. A small sample of developers and contractors can be asked to indicate their building plans for the upcoming years. If 20 percent say that they intend to start projects, the firm can multiply this against the total number of developers and contractors in the region and infer the number of actual projects that would be commenced.

The reliability of client intentions forecasts depends on (1) clients having clear intentions, (2) clients being likely to carry out their intentions, and (3) clients being willing to describe their intentions to interviewers. To the extent that these assumptions are weak, then the results must be used with caution. Suppose that during the middle of an audit a CPA firm asked its clients about their intention to engage the firm for the following year. The problem is that the clients may not have thought about renewal and may want to finish the audit before forming their intention. Client intentions data in this case would be weak.

Client intentions could be asked about in a number of ways. A "yes-or-no" form of the question would be: "Do you intend to use outside consulting engineers to help you refine your manufacturing process during the next year?" This requires the respondent to make a definite choice. Some researchers prefer the following form of question: "Will you (a) definitely use, (b) probably use, (c) probably not use, or (d) definitely not use outside consulting engineers next year?" These researchers feel that the "definite users" would be fairly dependable as a minimum estimate and some fraction of the "probable users" could be added to arrive at a forecast.

Intermediary Estimates

Another way of developing a forecast is to ask people who are close to the clients what those clients are likely to do. For example, a law firm that is trying to anticipate billings for different clients might ask its partners to estimate the amount of activity that can be anticipated from the clients under their charge. The partners will examine past data and what they have recently heard and prepare a forecast. Some partners will overestimate (the optimists) and some will underestimate (the pessimists).

If individual partners are fairly consistent overestimators or underestimators, their forecasts can be adjusted by top management for their known bias before using the forecasts for planning purposes.

When business firms use this method, they ask for estimates from their sales force, distributors, and dealers, since all of these are presumably closer to the customers and can render an opinion about likely demand. Professional service organizations can also find similar "experts," such as staff members, bankers, consultants, lawyers, professors, and trade association personnel. Asking people who come in contact with the clients for their estimates is called "grassroots forecasting." In using the method, the grassroots forecasters should be given a set of basic assumptions about the coming year, such as the state of the economy, the organization's tentative marketing plans, and so on. This is preferable to allowing each expert to make personal assumptions about major demand influences that will operate next year.

Market Tests

In cases where clients do not plan their purchases carefully or are very erratic in carrying out their intentions or where experts are not very good guessers, a more direct market test of likely behavior is desirable. A direct market test is especially desirable in forecasting the demand for a new service or the likely demand for an established service in a new market. Small-scale market tests could be set up for professional services aimed at *individuals* by establishing marketing programs in isolated communities or neighborhoods. For example, a prepaid legal service program might see how it is received in a small neighborhood before trying to obtain enrollees from an entire city.

Establishing market tests to forecast demand for professional services aimed at *organizations* is a more difficult task. But by choosing very narrowly defined segments to target in the initial stages of a marketing program, and assessing the success of the program in that small segment, one can approximate what is accomplished by a market test.

Time-Series Analysis

As an alternative to costly surveys or market tests, many organizations prepare their forecasts on the basis of a statistical analysis of past data. The underlying logic is that past time series reflect causal relations that can be uncovered through statistical analysis. The findings can be used to predict future revenues.

A time series of past revenues of a service can be analyzed into four major components.

The first component, *trend*, reflects the basic level and rate of change in the size of the market. It is found by fitting a straight or curved line through the time-series data. The past trend can be extrapolated to estimate next year's trend level.

A second component, *cycle*, might also be observed in a time series. The revenues of many organizations are affected by periodic swings in general economic activity. If the stage of the business cycle can be predicted for the next period, this would be used to adjust the trend value up or down.

A third component, *season*, would capture any consistent pattern of revenue movements within the year. The term "season" is used to describe any recurrent hourly, daily, weekly, monthly, or quarterly revenue pattern. The seasonal component may be related to weather factors, holidays, and so on. The researcher would adjust the estimate for, say, a particular month by the known seasonal level for that month.

The fourth component, *erratic events*, includes strikes, blizzards, fads, riots, fires, war scares, price wars, and other disturbances. This erratic component has the effect of obscuring the more systematic components. It represents everything that remains unanalyzed in the time series and cannot be predicted in the future. It shows the average size of the error that is likely to characterize time-series forecasting.

Here is an example of how time-series forecasting works:

A small consulting firm billed 12,000 hours this year. It wants to predict next summer's billings in order to know how many summer interns it should hire from nearby MBA programs. The long-term trend shows a 5 percent growth rate per year in number of hours billed. This implies billings next year of 12,600 (= 12,000 × 1.05). However, a business recession is expected next year, and this generally depresses billings to 90 percent of the expected trend level. This means the number of hours billed next year will more likely be 11,340 (= 12,000 × .90). If billings are the same each month, this would mean monthly billings of 945 (= 11,340/12). However, July and August are below-average months with seasonal indexes standing at .80. Therefore, billings during the summer may be as low as 756 (= 945 × .80). No erratic events, such as major competitive initiatives, are expected.

Statistical Demand Analysis

Numerous real factors affect the demand for any offering. *Statistical demand analysis* is a set of statistical procedures designed to discover the most important real factors affecting demand and their relative influence. The factors most commonly analyzed are prices or fees, income, population, and promotion expenditures.

Statistical demand analysis consists of expressing number of hours billed (H) as a dependent variable and trying to explain historical variation in this variable as a result of variation in a number of independent variables $X1, X2, \ldots, XN$; that is,

$$H = f(X1, X2, \ldots, XN)$$

This says that the level of activity, H, is a function of the levels of the independent factors $X1, X2, \ldots, XN$. Using a technique called multiple regression analysis, various equation forms can be statistically fitted to data on past market occurrences in the search for the best predicting factors and equations.[1]

Here is an example:

A CPA firm sought to forecast the number of hours it might bill from audit clients during the coming year. The following equation was fitted to past data using regression techniques:

$$H = 20{,}000 - 20X1 - 10{,}000X2 + .01X3$$

where:

$X1$ = average hourly fee charged to audit clients
$X2$ = annual growth rate in GNP
$X3$ = dollar expenditures on business development
(e.g., advertising and other tools)

Thus, the firm found that (1) charging higher average fees has brought them less billable hours, (2) having the overall economy healthy has brought them less hours (or vice versa), and (3) spending on business development has brought them more hours. If next year the firm expected fees to average $100, GNP to fall 3 percent, and business development spending to reach $80,000, then its forecast of number of hours it would bill would be:

$$H = 20{,}000 - 20(100) - 10{,}000(.03) + .01(80{,}000) = 18{,}500$$

Marketing researchers are constantly improving the available tools for producing reliable market size estimates and sales forecasts. The great demand by marketers for market measures and forecasts on which to base their marketing decisions is being matched on the supply side by an encouraging increase in data and tools to aid marketers in their marketing planning, execution, and control.

SUMMARY

In order to carry out their responsibilities for marketing planning, execution, and control, marketing personnel in professional service organizations need measures of current and future market demand. Total current market potential can be estimated through the chain ratio method, which involves multiplying a base number by a succession of appropriate percentages. Estimating total market size requires identifying the relevant competitors and using some method of estimating the billable hours and revenues of each. Additionally, the organization should compare its revenues to industry revenues to find whether its market share is improving or declining. Finally, the expansibility of considered markets should be estimated.

For estimating future demand, the organization can use one or any combination of five forecasting methods: client intentions surveys, intermediary estimates, market tests, time-series analysis, or statistical demand analysis. The methods vary in their appropriateness with the purpose of the forecast, the type of service, and the availability of data.

NOTES

1. See David A. Aaker, ed., *Multivariate Analysis in Marketing*, 2nd ed. (Palo Alto, Calif.: Scientific Press, 1981).

7

ESTABLISHING A MARKETING INFORMATION SYSTEM

At 6:30 on a Friday evening during the winter of 1981, his midtown office was the last place that Steve Whitter wanted to be. Steve was the managing partner of the Grover Stanton Group, a 47-person architectural firm in New York City. An hour earlier he had received from Bill Lyle, the firm's marketing manager, a summary of their active leads and the principal responsible for each. He also had on his desk the information on potential target markets presented a day earlier by Rebecca Halston, their marketing coordinator. Steve had felt the need to focus on markets and clients whom they really wanted to serve rather than merely to respond to the varied opportunities that came to them on referral or through Lyle's friends in the construction industry. With this in mind, he had asked Halston to research several markets to facilitate the partners' decision making. A meeting of all the partners was planned for Monday morning to arrive at several important marketing decisions.

Lyle's summary divided the leads into three categories, A, B, or C. The basis of the categorization was the estimated timing of a real project coming to the surface. The closer the likelihood, the more frequently the lead should be called on. Thus, "As" were to be contacted monthly, "Bs" once every three months, and "Cs" annually.

Halston's report contained an assortment of information, including data on a variety of geographic and building-type markets. She had been instructed to examine the following seven markets: corporate office buildings (national), manufacturing facilities (Midwest), sports facilities (national), convention centers (national), federal office buildings, airline terminal buildings (national), and "high-design" shopping centers (East and Midwest). The firm had done at least one major project in each of these areas during the last ten years, except for the last area. The report's contents included (1) extensive economic and demographic information for each geographic area being considered; (2) a local economic forecast prepared by a major bank for each of 21 cities; (3) summaries of discussions with economic development agency people in 12 states; (4) 45 interviews with sample clients; and (5) numerous clippings from *Engineering News Record, Fortune,* and the *A/E Marketing Journal.*

It bothered Steve that, even with the 45 interviews, the partners didn't seem to know what the firm's image was. He wasn't clear on how important it was to have this knowledge, and was less clear on how to acquire it. A friendly competitor had given him an interview guide that had been used by that firm to learn how it was seen by past clients, and he wondered how to use it and whether it was the answer to helping the firm gear itself to any markets it might elect to address.

With reports and papers piled all over his desk, Steve pondered his next moves. He knew prompt action was required on several matters, particularly if he was going to be able to find more time for practicing architecture.

Source: Excerpted from Hugh Hochberg and Paul N. Bloom, "The Grover Stanton Group," Case #9-582-502 (Cambridge, MA: President and Fellows of Harvard College, 1982). Reprinted with permission of the Harvard Graduate School of Design.

Information is an essential resource in making marketing decisions. Throughout the last few chapters, we have been pointing out various forms of information that can support a professional service organization's marketing effort. Generally speaking, the more information an organization has available about its markets, competitors, referral sources, and others, the better it will be able to design an effective marketing program. But information has to be timely, accurate, and easy to use if it is to serve an organization well. And information "overload" must be avoided, so that marketing decision makers are not forced into inactivity while trying to cope with mountains of data. An information *system* is needed to aid marketing decision making, not a group of uncoordinated and voluminous reports like Steve Whitter had to deal with. Our definition of a marketing information system (MIS) is:

> A **marketing information system** is a continuing and inter-
> acting structure of people, equipment, and procedures de-
> signed to gather, sort, analyze, evaluate, and distribute
> pertinent, timely, and accurate information for use by market-
> ing decision makers to improve their marketing planning, exe-
> cution, and control.

The role and major subsystems of an MIS are illustrated in Figure 7-1. At the left is shown the marketing environment that marketing decision makers must monitor—specifically target markets, intermediaries, competitors, publics, and macroenvironmental forces. Developments and trends in the marketing environment are picked up in the organization through one of three subsystems making up the marketing information system—namely, the internal records system, the marketing intelligence system, and the marketing research system. The information then flows to the appropriate marketing personnel to help them in their marketing planning, execution, and control. The resulting decisions and communications then flow back to the marketing environment.

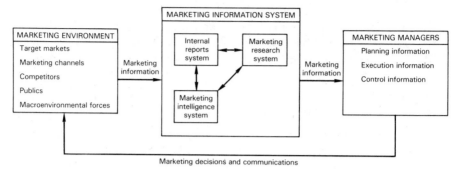

FIGURE 7–1. The marketing information system

INTERNAL RECORDS SYSTEM

Valuable information for guiding marketing decisions can be obtained by simply doing conscientious record-keeping. The recording and careful filing of information about a wide range of everyday events and developments can provide data that can be used to evaluate and refine marketing strategies and programs. The following quote, provided by a management consultant who recently entered a solo practice, illustrates the kind of valuable information that internal records can supply:

> Over the first six months, 110 letters were sent out, 680 phone calls made, 28 appointments were developed, 7 people stood me up, 21 people were interviewed, 15 proposals were solicited, and 3 new clients were obtained that subsequently generated over $175,000 in billings. That worked out to a value of $237.35 per phone call, despite the low "hit" rate.[1]

The internal records system should provide information on the extent of the marketing effort being put forth by the organization—the number of phone calls, mailings, advertisements, meetings, proposals, presentations, and so on. Information should also be available about the responses to marketing actions such as:

1. The number of inquiries received
2. The number of "short lists" made
3. The number of new clients obtained
4. The amount of new work obtained from old clients
5. The number of communications received that express satisfaction or dissatisfaction with services.
6. The amount of billings generated

Of course, all of these data can be organized by type of client, supplying information that can be useful for deciding how to segment markets and how to choose targets. Moreover, additional information can be retained about existing clients—their past history, the way they came to your organization, the club and association memberships they have,

TABLE 7–1
QUESTIONNAIRE FOR DETERMINING MARKETING
INFORMATION NEEDS OF MANAGERS

1. What types of decisions are you regularly called upon to make?
2. What types of information do you need to make these decisions?
3. What types of information do you regularly get?
4. What types of special studies do you periodically request?
5. What types of information would you like to get that you are not now getting?
6. What information would you want daily? weekly? monthly? yearly?
7. What magazines and reports would you like to see routed to you on a regular basis?
8. What specific topics would you like to be kept informed of?
9. What types of data analysis programs would you like to see made available?
10. What do you think would be the four most helpful improvements that could be made in the present marketing information system?

the names of other professionals they use, their long-run and current problems—that can prove valuable in trying to maintain their loyalty, in designing new services for them, and in deciding how to market toward others just like them.

We will have more to say about the indices or measures that could be a part of a good internal records system in our final chapter (Chapter 14), as we cover the issue of controlling the marketing effort. But regardless of what measures are utilized in this system, it must be a system which does not overload marketing decision makers with difficult-to-interpret or rarely useful data. A marketing manager does not need to be told every week how many weekly phone calls have been made to prospective clients; nor does he or she need to have weekly figures on inquiries, billings, or other indices. The internal records system—as well as the other components of the MIS—must be designed to serve the information needs of decision makers in a timely and cost-effective way. One way to help design a more needs-oriented MIS is to conduct periodic surveys of decision makers to ascertain their perceived information needs. Table 7–1 shows the types of questions that can be asked of them. Once their opinions are gathered, the information system designers can design a system that reconciles (1) what decision makers think they need, (2) what decision makers really need, and (3) what is economically feasible.

MARKETING INTELLIGENCE SYSTEM

Whereas the internal records system supplies decision makers with *results data,* the marketing intelligence system supplies them with *hap-*

penings data. Our definition of a marketing intelligence system is:

> The **marketing intelligence system** is the set of sources and procedures by which marketing decision makers obtain their everyday information about developments in the external marketing environment.

Most professional service organizations collect marketing intelligence in an informal way through having high-level people read various trade and other publications and through having them carry on regular discussions with well-informed intermediaries, experts, and clients themselves. Important developments are frequently identified through these procedures. However, an informal approach to intelligence gathering can also lead to missing, or learning too late of, some important developments, such as a new business opportunity with a large client or a pending shift in competitive strategy by a rival firm.

An organization can take some concrete steps to improve the quality of marketing intelligence available to its top people. First, the organization must "sell" its entire professional staff on the importance of gathering marketing intelligence and passing it on to others in the organization. Intelligence-gathering responsibilities can be facilitated by designing information forms that are easy to fill out and circulate. Examples of the kinds of forms certain individuals could be assigned to fill out and keep updated are found in Exhibits 7–1 to 7–3. Forms could be regularly filled out and circulated on key existing clients, key prospective clients, key intermediaries (or contacts or informants), and key competitors.

Intelligence gathering can also be improved by setting up an individual or an office to coordinate and manage the activity. The coordinator of marketing intelligence would have the responsibility for tasks like (1) "tickling" other people in the organization to make sure that all intelligence forms are updated regularly, (2) scanning major publications, with perhaps the help of a clipping service or one of the computer search services, for news about competitors, clients, relevant government actions, and so on, (3) soliciting suggestions and complaints about marketing from staff members, and (4) organizing a filing system for intelligence that will make the retrieval of past and current information relatively easy. The performance of these and other tasks would greatly enhance the quality of information available to marketing decision makers.

MARKETING RESEARCH SYSTEM

From time to time, professional service organizations need to commission specific marketing research studies in order to have adequate information to make pending decisions. Marketing research studies can be done to obtain many different forms of information, such as the potential of certain market segments (see Chapter 6), the image or positioning the organization has with prospective clients (see Chapters 4

EXHIBIT 7–1.   Prospective client data form

BACKGROUND:

Name of Prospect: _____

Address and Telephone: _____
                                           _____

Classification code for
       industry, etc.
       (SIC or other):   _____

Growth potential of
       industry: _____

Major products/Services: _____
                                           _____

Sales: _____

Number of employees: _____

Financial condition: _____

Major strengths: _____

Major weaknesses: _____

Major competitors: _____

Other key developments: _____
                                           _____

DECISION MAKERS:

Names	Title	Club/Association Affiliations	Our Contact
Managers:			
_____	_____	_____	_____
_____	_____	_____	_____
_____	_____	_____	_____
_____	_____	_____	_____
Board Members/Major Stockholders:			
_____	_____	_____	_____
_____	_____	_____	_____
Bankers/Professionals Used:			
_____	_____	_____	_____
_____	_____	_____	_____
_____	_____	_____	_____

POTENTIAL:

Volume of Service Currently Being Used:

Type of Service	Yearly Hours	Professionals Used	Satisfaction
_____	_____	_____	_____
_____	_____	_____	_____
_____	_____	_____	

Potential Volume of Service per Year:

Type of Service	Yearly Hours
_____	_____
_____	_____
_____	_____

Competitors for This Work: _____

OUR MARKETING PROGRAM:

Our Person-in-Charge: _____

Needed Frequency
       of Contact: _____
                                           _____

Core Marketing Strategy: _____
                                           _____

EXHIBIT 7–2. Key intermediary data form

Name of Intermediary: _____

Address and Telephone: _____
                        _____

Profession/Position: _____
                      _____

Our Previous Experience
        with Person:

Situation   Our Contact   Outcome

_____   _____   _____

_____   _____   _____

_____   _____   _____

Ties to Prospective Clients:

Client   Nature of Relation

_____   _____

_____   _____

_____   _____

_____   _____

_____   _____

Club/Association Affiliations:

Club/Association   Our Contact

_____   _____

_____   _____

_____   _____

Needed Frequency of Contact: _____

Our Person-in-Charge: _____

---

and 5), the satisfaction levels of existing clients or patients (see Chapter
4), and the reach and recall achieved by marketing communications (see
Chapters 11 to 13). Many studies could prove worthwhile to an organization but, in the face of a limited budget, the organization must have
know-how to choose marketing research projects carefully, design them
efficiently, and implement the results effectively.

First, we define marketing research:

> **Marketing research** is the systematic design, collection,
> analysis, and reporting of data and findings relevant to a
> specific marketing situation or problem facing an organization.

The key idea is that management initiates or commissions a study to
develop information on a subject by a certain date. There are numerous
types of studies that qualify as marketing research projects. Studies can
be done that involve the use and analysis of previously collected data
(secondary data) or the collection and analysis of new data (primary data).
Studies can seek information on the characteristics and potential of
certain markets, the activities of competitors, the best ways to price or
distribute services, the effectiveness of different communications, and a
host of other subjects.

EXHIBIT 7–3.   Competitor data form

Name of Competitor: _____

Address and Telephone: _____

_____

Number Partners/Staff: _____

Strongest Markets:

Market   Major Clients

_____   _____

_____   _____

_____

Directly Competing
         Services: _____

_____

New Services or Areas
        Being Developed: _____

_____

Reputation/Image: _____

_____

Key Personnel:

Name   Title

_____   _____

_____   _____

_____   _____

Key Club/Association
        Memberships: _____

_____

Major Strengths: _____

_____

Major Weaknesses: _____

_____

Fee Strategy and
        Hourly Rates: _____

_____

Major Marketing and
        Promotion Activities: _____

_____

Other Developments: _____

Our Person-in-Charge of Monitor-
        ing: _____

Who does these studies for an organization? Larger organizations with full-time marketing professionals on their staff can have these people conduct selected marketing research studies. Having marketing research done internally has several advantages—data is less likely to be "leaked" to competitors; valuable information is not "lost" or forgotten when data is transmitted from the outside source to the inside personnel. But using outside research resources has several advantages. External research firms may have expertise that is not available within the organization, and they may be better able to maintain necessary objectivity in conducting research studies. The expertise and objectivity these firms possess can lead to higher response rates in surveys, more valid findings, and more creative interpretation of results. Thus, even organizations that can afford to do their own studies may find it more efficient to use outside marketing research firms to conduct complete studies or portions of studies.

Information about outside marketing research firms can be obtained from a number of sources, including the annual research issue of the weekly trade journal *Advertising Age*, the *Green Book* published by the New York chapter of the American Marketing Association, the *Directory of U.S. and Canadian Marketing Surveys and Services*, [2] and *Bradford's Directory*.[3] Three major categories of research firms are listed in these sources:

> 1. *Syndicated service research firms.* These firms specialize in gathering continuous consumer and trade information which they sell in the form of standardized reports on a fee-subscription basis to all clients. A professional service firm can purchase syndicated reports on, for example, construction potentials from the F.W. Dodge Division of McGraw-Hill Information Systems Company. Similarly, information about the line of business, sales volume, number of employees, location of major buying centers, and other details of over 4,500,000 U.S. companies can be obtained from Dun and Bradstreet's *Dun's Market Identifiers*.
>
> 2. *Custom marketing research firms.* These firms can be hired to carry out one-of-a-kind research projects to provide data needed by a particular client. They participate with the client in designing the study and the report becomes the client's property.
>
> 3. *Specialty-line marketing research firms.* These firms provide specialized services to other marketing research firms and company marketing research departments. The best example is the field service firm which sells field interviewing services to other firms.

Marketing researchers have been steadily expanding and improving their techniques. Many techniques were developed outside of marketing by researchers in economics, statistics, sociology, social psychology, and psychology. They were adopted by marketing researchers who recognized opportunities for their use.

The challenge facing professionals who need marketing research is to know enough about its potentialities and limitations so that they can get the right information at a reasonable cost and use it intelligently. If they know nothing about marketing research, they might allow the wrong information to be collected, or collected too expensively, or interpreted incorrectly. One protection against this is to work with only highly experienced and credible marketing researchers and agencies because it is in their interests to do a good job and produce information that leads to correct decisions. An equally important protection is that professionals should know enough about marketing research procedures to assist in its planning and in the interpretation of results.

Figure 7–2 describes the five basic steps in good marketing re-

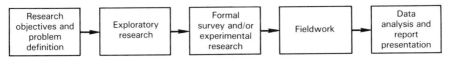

FIGURE 7–2. The marketing research process

search. We will illustrate these steps in connection with the following situation:

> The Michael Baker Corporation is a civil engineering firm which found itself in 1976 faced with the imminent completion of its two biggest jobs: the Trans-Alaska Oil Pipeline and Haul Road and the Interstate Highway. Michael Baker, III, the company's president, saw the following options available at the time: "Terminate the employment of a large number of very experienced people. Or find new markets in which their skills can continue to generate profit for this company. The first option is not acceptable to management." Baker therefore sought research and consultation help from the Hilton Agency to allow him to pursue the second option.[4]

Research Objectives and Problem
Definition

The first step in research is to define carefully the research objectives. The objective may be to learn about a market, or to find a practical idea for increasing the demand for a service, or to measure the impact of a marketing tool. The research objectives make it easier to arrive at a useful definition of the problem. If the problem is stated vaguely, if the wrong problem is defined, or if the uses of the research are not made clear, then the research results may be useless or even misleading to the professional service organization.

In the case of the Michael Baker Corporation, Mr. Baker provided the Hilton Agency with the research objectives of (1) helping to find a direction for Baker's marketing to take, (2) locating a target market, and (3) providing information to help guide the formulation and delivery of appropriate messages to the decision makers in the target market. These objectives led the Hilton people to define the following research problems that they would address for Baker:

> 1. Identify five industries with the greatest potential need for "outside" engineering consulting services.
> 2. For the industries with greatest potential, identify the specific nature of their engineering consulting needs.
> 3. Determine who within the high-potential industries makes the decisions to employ outside engineering services.
> 4. Identify the attributes these decision makers find most attractive in engineering consultants.
> 5. Determine which media will do the most effective job of reaching the targeted decision makers.

Exploratory Research

This step calls for carrying out preliminary research to learn more about the market before any formal research tasks are undertaken. Exploratory research is done to generate new ideas and hypotheses, not to reach firm estimates of the magnitude of anything or of the accuracy of any predictions or assumptions. The major procedures at this stage include collecting secondary data, doing observational research, and carrying out informal interviewing with individuals and groups.

Secondary data research.   In seeking information, a researcher should initially gather and review secondary data if any exists. *Secondary data* are relevant data that already exist somewhere, having been collected for another purpose. Secondary data are normally quicker and less expensive to obtain and will give the researcher a start on the problem. Afterward, the researcher can gather *primary data*, namely, original data to meet the problem at hand.

The following major sources of secondary data are available to the professional service organization:

1. *Internal records.*   A firm like Michael Baker could have examined data on existing or prospective clients, old proposals and reports, marketing activities, or other forms of information to help identify attractive targets and how to attract them.

2. *Government.*   The federal government publishes more marketing data than any other source in the country. Many organizations depend on data found in the *Census of Population, Census of Housing, Census of Business, Census of Manufacturers, Census of Agriculture, Census of Minerals,* and *Census of Governments,* as well as on special research reports issued at all levels of government.

3. *Trade, professional, and business associations.*   Hundreds of associations regularly collect data about their members and about topics that interest their members. A professional service organization can often obtain valuable information about target markets and competitor activities from interacting in its own associations. Additional valuable information can often be obtained by contacting and working with the associations of targeted clients. Thus, an engineering firm interested in obtaining clients from the coal industry would want to monitor and perhaps become involved with the activities of that industry's associations.

4. *Competitors and other private organizations.*   While one cannot expect direct competitors to make available marketing research studies they have completed, it might be possible to obtain valuable old studies from less direct competitors, such as firms located in other geographic regions or those serving very different market segments. Moreover, professional service organizations in other professions might be willing to share old data on markets of mutual interest. Additional data can be obtained from large banks—which often publish studies on the economic prospects of their regions—and from other large businesses.

5. *Marketing firms.* Marketing research firms, advertising agencies, and media firms may possess old studies or syndicated data having considerable value.

6. *Universities, research organizations, and foundations.* The range of issues and industries that have been examined by researchers in the more "intellectual" organizations is enormous. A check of these organizations can be worthwhile.

7. *Published sources.* Both the scholarly literature and the general business press can be helpful. Scholarly journals like the *Journal of Marketing, Journal of Marketing Research,* and *Journal of Consumer Research* are useful for obtaining general ideas about marketing strategy and marketing research methods. Trade and business periodicals like *Business Week, Advertising Age,* and *Fortune* also provide general ideas. More specialized magazines focusing on specific industries can stimulate thinking about more focused strategies and tactics.

These secondary data are likely to provide useful ideas and findings at a reasonable cost. For instance, the Michael Baker Corporation used secondary sources such as government statistics and McGraw-Hill data to select the coal industry as a potential target market. However, the marketing researcher must be careful in making inferences from secondary data, since these data were collected for a variety of purposes and under a variety of conditions that might limit their usefulness. Marketing researchers should check these data for relevance, impartiality, validity, and reliability. Often it becomes necessary to move beyond the secondary data to the collection of exploratory primary data. Typically, this is done through observational research or qualitative interviewing.

Observational research. One way to collect primary data is to carry out personal observation in various situations. Staff members can be observed when making phone contacts, visiting clients, or making presentations. The places of business of certain prospective clients (e.g., retailers) could be visited to obtain a better feeling for their problems. Brochures and other printed materials of competitors could be examined. Observational research is done to suggest issues to explore in more depth in qualitative interviews or more formal research studies.

Qualitative interviewing. In addition to gathering data through observation, researchers need to conduct some interviewing during the exploratory stage of a marketing research project. The purpose of the interviewing is to collect further ideas on the factors that play a role in the marketing problem being investigated. In the exploratory stage, the interviewing should be qualitatively rather than quantitatively oriented. Qualitative interviewing is largely open-ended. People are asked leading questions as a means of stimulating them to share their thoughts and feelings regarding specific professional service organizations or other relevant topics. The distinct uses of qualitative research are to (1) probe deeply into clients' underlying needs, perceptions, preferences, and satisfaction, (2) gain greater familiarity and understanding of marketing problems whose causes are not known, and (3) develop ideas that can be further investigated through quantitative research. On the other hand, quantitative research seeks to generate statistically reliable estimates of particular market or client characteristics. Quantitative research entails sampling a much larger number of people than qualitative research, and it assumes that one knows in advance what specific questions to ask.

Qualitative research basically takes two forms: *individual interviewing* and *group interviewing*. Individual interviewing involves obtaining data from one person at a time, either in person, over the telephone, or through the mails. Group interviewing typically involves having a trained interviewer meet for a lengthy period with six to ten persons in an informal setting (with refreshments). The interviewer—who must possess objectivity and ample knowledge of group dynamics, client behavior, and the relevant profession—encourages free and easy discussion among participants, hoping that the group dynamic will bring out real feelings and thoughts. At the same time, the interviewer "focuses" the discussion to avoid irrelevant comments. "Focus group" interviews have become one of the most widely used forms of marketing research in all industries. They would appear to be a particularly good way for professional service organizations to obtain useful information from existing clients.

Whether individual or group qualitative interviews are being conducted, respondents should be asked to participate in the study using an honest, nonthreatening appeal. They should be told that the study is being done to enable the professional service firm to become more informed about trends in an industry, about the service needs of clients, about the way services are bought, or about something similar. The questioning should then begin with a broad, interesting question that will get people talking. If a firm like Michael Baker were interviewing coal industry executives, an opening question like the following might work well: "Over the next few years, what major technological changes in the way coal is mined or transported might occur that could have a significant impact on your industry?" Such a question could be followed up with inquiries about the likelihood of certain changes occurring and the types of engineering tasks that most firms will need performed to cope with those changes. The line of questioning could slowly be shifted toward gathering more specific information about the needs of the respondents themselves and about how they tend to search for and purchase engineering consulting services.

At no time during an interview should any overt attempt be made to sell anything or to arrange a sales call. As we will discuss further in Chapter 11, it is desirable to "sell" by impressing respondents with the quality of your questions and your side comments. But doing overt selling during a research interview will only hurt the reputation of your firm and prevent you from obtaining valuable data that can be used to guide other phases of your marketing program.

Qualitative research is not only a desirable first step, it is sometimes the only step permitted by the budget of many professional service organizations. If only qualitative studies can be done, care must be exercised not to overreact to findings from these studies. It must be remembered that this type of research can only be expected to generate new insights or hypotheses. It cannot be expected to provide highly reliable estimates. A firm would be entertaining great risk by making a major change in its services, markets, communications, or anything else based on the results of a few qualitative studies. This type of research is more wisely used to make small adjustments in marketing strategies and tactics.

Formal Research

After defining the problem and doing exploratory research, the researchers may wish to carry out more formal research to measure magnitudes or test hypotheses. The Michael Baker Corporation decided to survey executives in the coal industry in a formal manner using a detailed, four-page, 100-item questionnaire. The mailing list they used was compiled by McGraw-Hill Research and had a special emphasis on operations and engineering executives, presidents, and general managers. Although they obtained a response from only 15 percent of those who were sent questionnaires, the returns represented both underground and surface-mining companies of all sizes operating in 22 states, Canada, and overseas. The information proved extremely valuable in designing a successful advertising campaign and sales program targeted at the coal industry. By 1981, Baker had grown from having near zero to having more than $5 million in billings from the coal industry.

Conducting formal research that can be as helpful as the Baker study requires attention to numerous issues. In the following discussion, we introduce some of the issues that must be addressed in conducting formal survey and experimental research.

Survey research. Many managers take an overly simplistic view of survey work. They think that it consists of writing a few obvious questions and finding an adequate number of people in the target market to answer them. The fact is that amateur research is liable to many errors that can waste anywhere from $3,000 to $50,000 of the organization's funds. Designing a reliable survey is the job of a professional marketing researcher. Here we will describe the main things that users of marketing research should know about developing the research instrument, the sampling plan, and the fieldwork.

RESEARCH INSTRUMENT. The main survey research instrument is the questionnaire. The construction of good questionnaires calls for considerable skill. Every questionnaire should be pretested on a pilot sample of persons before being used on a large scale. A professional marketing researcher can usually spot several errors in a casually prepared questionnaire.

A common type of error occurs in the *types of questions asked*: the inclusion of questions that cannot be answered, or would not be answered, or need not be answered, and the omission of other questions that should be answered. Each question should be checked to determine whether it is necessary in terms of the research objectives. Questions should be dropped that are just interesting (except for one or two to start the interview) because they lengthen the time required and try the respondent's patience.

The *form of questions* can make a substantial difference to the response. An *open-ended question* is one in which the respondent is free to answer in his or her own words. An example would be "What is your opinion of engineering consulting firms?" The problem with open-ended questions is that the answers can be quite diverse, making it difficult to aggregate results and summarize findings. This is not a problem with *closed-ended questions*. But closed-ended questions can be too leading, putting ideas for responses in people's minds that might not have arisen with an open-ended question. Closed-ended questions can also force people into responding with answers that do not truly reflect their feelings. Some examples of types of closed-ended questions follow:

- *Dichotomous question*: "Have you ever heard of the Michael Baker Corporation?" Yes ( ) No ( )
- *Multiple choice question*: "The Michael Baker Corporation is a firm that offers (a) interior design services, (b) architectural services, (c) mechanical engineering services, (d) civil engineering services, (e) all of the above."
- *Semantic differential question*: "The Michael Baker Corporation is (a) a very large firm, (b) a large firm, (c) neither large nor small, (d) a small firm, (e) a very small firm."
- *Likert scale question*: "How much do you agree with the statement: Our company currently has a need for civil engineering consulting services? (a) Strongly agree, (b) Agree, (c) Uncertain, (d) Disagree, (e) Strongly disagree."

The *choice of words* also calls for considerable care. The researcher should strive for simple, direct, unambiguous, and unbiased wording. Other "dos" and "don'ts" arise in connection with the *sequencing of questions* in the questionnaire. The lead questions should create interest, if possible. Open-ended questions are usually better here. Difficult, sensitive, or personal questions should be introduced toward the end of the interview, in order not to create an emotional reaction that may affect subsequent answers or cause the respondent to break off the interview. The questions should be asked in as logical an order as possible in order to

EXHIBIT 7–4.   Client behavior questionnaire

Hello, my name is _____ and I'm helping to conduct a research project for _____ on the way _____ professional services are searched for and used by people like yourself. This is purely a research study designed to obtain the kind of information about client decision making that will allow _____ to continue serving its clients well in the future. We are sampling only a small, randomly selected group of persons and pledge to keep all their responses strictly confidential. If I could have no more than 10 minutes of your time to ask a few short questions, it could make a valuable contribution to our study. Most people find our questions to be interesting and enjoyable to answer. Would this be a convenient time?

I. GENERAL OPINIONS

1. In general, what is your opinion of _____ (lawyers, CPAs, etc.)?

2. Please tell me how much you agree with each of the several statements I will read to you. Do you STRONGLY AGREE, AGREE, NEITHER AGREE NOR DISAGREE, or STRONGLY DISAGREE with each of the following statements:

   a. _____ (Lawyers, CPAs, etc.) vary greatly in their skills.
   STRONGLY AGREE   AGREE   NEITHER   DISAGREE
   STRONGLY DISAGREE
   b. It is difficult to find a good _____ .
   STRONGLY AGREE   AGREE   NEITHER   DISAGREE
   STRONGLY DISAGREE
   c. _____ generally charge too much for their services.
   STRONGLY AGREE   AGREE   NEITHER   DISAGREE
   STRONGLY DISAGREE
   d. _____ rarely finish a project by the time they have promised.
   STRONGLY AGREE   AGREE   NEITHER   DISAGREE
   STRONGLY DISAGREE
   e. _____ should be allowed to advertise.
   STRONGLY AGREE   AGREE   NEITHER   DISAGREE
   STRONGLY DISAGREE

II. PRIOR EXPERIENCES

1. Have you or your organization used the services of a _____ (lawyer, CPA, etc.) during the last 12 months?
   a. Yes
   b. No (Go to Section III.)

2. Were all the _____ you used ones you had used in previous years?
   a. Yes (go to II6.)
   b. No
3. Was this the first time you have ever used a _____?
   a. Yes
   b. No (Go to II5.)
4. What first stimulated you to seek the services of a _____?
   a. An advertisement
   b. An article you read
   c. A comment by a friend or business associate
   d. An uninvited call or visit by a _____
   e. Other (please specify)

SKIP TO II6.

5. What first led you to consider using the services of a new or different _____ during the last 12 months?
   a. A desire to pay lower fees
   b. A desire to obtain better quality services
   c. A desire to obtain more prompt services
   d. A desire to find a more friendly _____
   e. Simply a desire for a change
   f. Other (please specify)
6. How satisfied overall are you with the services you have received during the last 12 months from _____?
   a. Very Satisfied   b. Satisfied   c. Neutral   d. Dissatisfied   e. Very Dissatisfied

III. CURRENT PRACTICES

1. Please give the titles of the people in your organization who tend to (or would tend to) become involved in decisions on using _____ (lawyers, CPAs, etc.)?

2. How important would the following attributes be in any future choices you might make among _____? Please answer by stating VERY IMPORTANT, IMPORTANT, OF SLIGHT IMPORTANCE, or NOT IMPORTANT AT ALL.

a. Reputation	VI	I	OSI	NIAA
b. Fees	VI	I	OSI	NIAA
c. Location	VI	I	OSI	NIAA
d. Experience with problems similar to yours	VI	I	OSI	NIAA
e. Size of firm	VI	I	OSI	NIAA

3. How many hours of a _____'s time do you expect to require over the next 12 months?
   a. None
   b. Less than 20
   c. 21 to 50
   d. 51 to 100
   e. More than 100 (please specify amount) _____ .
4. For what types of projects are you most likely to require a _____'s services over the next 12 months? Over the next 3 years?

IV. SPECIFIC OPINIONS

1. Have you ever heard of any of the following _____ (lawyers, CPAs, etc.)?
   a. Firm A
   b. Firm B
   c. Firm C
   d. Firm D
2. How do you feel Firm A rates on the following attributes? Would you say that it rates VERY GOOD, GOOD, NEITHER GOOD NOR BAD, BAD, or VERY BAD on each attribute?
   a. Reputation   VG G N B VB
   b. Fees   VG G N B VB
   c. Location   VG G N B VB
   d. Experience with
      problems similar
      to yours   VG G N B VB
   e. Size of firm   VG G N B VB
3. How do you feel Firm B rates on the following attributes? (Repeat sequence)

V. CLASSIFICATION DATA

I'll conclude with just a few questions about you and your organization which we need answered in order to classify responses into groups. Let me remind you that all information will be kept strictly confidential.

1. Which category does your organization fall into in terms of its annual sales volume?
   a. Under $100,000
   b. $100,001 to $500,000
   c. etc.
2. Which category does your organization fall into in terms of its number of employees?
   a. Under 20
   b. etc.
3. What are the major products and services sold by your organization?
4. What is your position in the organization?
That completes the interview. Thank you very much for your help.

avoid confusing the respondent. Classificatory data on the respondents—such as the size of their firm or the number of years they have been working in their present position—are usually asked last.

Questionnaires have to be tailored to the specific research problems facing an organization. There is no single questionnaire that will obtain desired data for all professional service organizations. However, Exhibit 7–4 contains a sample questionnaire that could be adapted by many accounting, law, consulting, or architectural engineering firms to obtain valuable information about prospective clients.

SAMPLING PLAN.   The other element of research design is a sampling plan, and it calls for four decisions.

1. *Sampling unit.*   This answers the question: *Who is to be surveyed?* The proper sampling unit is not always obvious from the nature of the information sought. Should it be the usual instigator, influencer, decider, user, purchaser, or someone else?

2. *Sample size.*   This answers the question: *How many people should be surveyed?* Large samples obviously give more reliable results than small samples. However, it is not necessary to sample the entire market or even a substantial part of it to achieve satisfactory precision. Samples amounting to often less than a fraction of 1 percent of a population can often provide good reliability, given a creditable sampling procedure.

3. *Sampling procedure.*   This answers the question: *How should the respondents be chosen?* To draw valid and reliable inferences about the target market, a random probability sample of the population should be drawn. Random sampling allows the calculation of confidence limits for sampling error. But random sampling is almost always more costly than nonrandom sampling. Some marketing researchers feel that the extra expenditure for probability sampling could be put to better use. Specifically, more of the money of a fixed research budget could be spent in designing better questionnaires and hiring better interviewers to reduce response and nonsampling errors, which can be just as fatal as sampling errors.

4. *Means of contact.*   This answers the question: *How should the subjects be contacted?* The choices are telephone, mail, or personal interviews. *Telephone interviewing* stands out as the best method for gathering information quickly. It also permits the interviewer to clarify questions if they are not understood. The main drawback of telephone interviewing is that only relatively short, not too personal, interviews can be carried out. The *mail questionnaire* may be the best way to reach persons who would not give personal interviews or who might be biased by interviewers. On the other hand, mail questionnaires require simple and clearly worded questions, and the return rate is usually low and/or slow. *Personal interviewing* is the most versatile of the three methods. The personal interviewer can ask more questions and can supplement the interview with personal observations. Personal interviewing is the most expensive method and requires more technical and administrative planning and supervision.

Experimental research.   The experimental method is being increasingly recognized in marketing circles as the most rigorous and conclusive one to use if the proper controls can be exercised and the cost afforded. The method requires selecting matched groups of subjects, giving them different treatments, controlling extraneous variables from making a difference, and checking on whether observed differences are statistically significant. To the extent that the design and execution of the experiment eliminates alternative hypotheses that might explain the same results, the researcher and marketing manager can have confidence in the conclusions.

Experiments could be used by professional service organizations in many ways. For example, an organization could:

1. Test the effectiveness of different direct-mail pieces by sending them to different, matched groups of subjects.

2. Test the effectiveness of different advertisements by running them in different regional editions of the same publication.

3. Test the effectiveness of different ways of requesting cooperation with a survey by making different requests to different matched groups of subjects.

Fieldwork

The fieldwork phase of survey or experimental research follows after the research design has been finished and pretested. It is important to select and train interviewers who can be trusted, are personable, and are able to do their work in a reasonably short time. The fieldwork phase could be the most expensive and the most liable to error. Four major problems have to be dealt with in this phase:

1. *Not present.* When randomly selected respondents are not reached on the first call, the interviewer must either call them back later or substitute another respondent. Otherwise, nonresponse bias may be introduced.

2. *Refusal to cooperate.* After reaching the subjects, the interviewer must interest them in cooperating. Otherwise, nonresponse bias may be introduced.

3. *Respondent bias.* The interviewer must encourage accurate and thoughtful answers.

4. *Interviewer bias.* Interviewers are capable of introducing a variety of biases into the interviewing process, through the mere fact of their age, sex, manner, or intonation. In addition, there is the problem of conscious interviewer bias or dishonesty.

Data Analysis and Report Presentation

The final step in the marketing research process is to develop meaningful information and findings to present to the marketing decision maker. The researcher will tabulate the data and develop one-way and two-way frequency distributions. Averages and measures of dispersion will be computed for the major variables. The researcher might attempt to apply some advanced statistical techniques in the hope of discovering additional findings.

The researcher's purpose is not to overwhelm management with numbers and fancy statistical procedures. The researcher's purpose is to present major findings that will help the manager make better marketing decisions.

SUMMARY

To carry out effective marketing, the professional service organization needs timely, accurate, and adequate information. Three systems make up the organization's marketing information system.

The first, the internal records system, consists of all the information that the organization gathers in the regular course of its operations. It includes sales and cost information by service, client, territory, and so on. Many useful questions can be answered by analyzing the information in the internal records system.

The second, the marketing intelligence system, describes the set of sources and procedures by which management obtains its everyday information about developments in the marketplace. An organization can improve the quality of its marketing intelligence by motivating staff members to scan the environment and report useful information to others, and hiring intelligence specialists to find and disseminate important information.

The third, the marketing research system, consists of the systematic design, collection, analysis, and reporting of data and findings relevant to a specific marketing situation or problem facing an organization. The marketing research process consists of five steps: developing the research objectives and problem definition; exploratory research; formal survey and/or experimental research; fieldwork; and data analysis and report presentation.

NOTES

1. Larry E. Griener and Robert O. Metzger, *Consulting to Management* (Englewood Cliffs, N.J.: Prentice-Hall, 1983), p. 47.

2. *Directory of U.S. and Canadian Marketing Surveys and Services* (Fairfield, N.J.: Kline, 1979).

3. Ernest S. Bradford, *Bradford's Directory of Marketing Research Agencies and Management Consultants in the United States and the World* (Middlebury, Vt.: Bradford, 1973–74).

4. The Michael Baker Corporation's experience is described in Bergen F. Newell, "Advertising Strikes a New Vein," *Magazine Age*, December 1982, pp. 60–63. Reprinted with permission.

8
DEVELOPING
A SERVICE MIX STRATEGY

Health Systems Inc. had been founded in 1970 by Robert DeVore, an architect, and Robert Bland, a venture capitalist, who had been classmates at college. DeVore and Bland were convinced that market analysis, project and operating cost models, and elaborate forecasting could be applied to public and nonprofit health care projects as well as private sector construction. At the same time, they considered it essential to recognize the unique needs of health care facilities in design, capital construction, and financing. Originally Health Systems was organized to offer design, engineering, construction, and financial expertise in a single package; unfortunately, such broad positioning resulted in a severe competitive handicap as HSI, which was not a contractor, found itself competing against both architects and contractors for jobs. As DeVore himself later remarked, describing the company's early struggles: "We made the classical marketing error of running in 20 different directions at 20 different times."

From his present office on the 22nd floor of a downtown Boston skyscraper with a view of the harbor, DeVore could laugh as he recalled HSI's early days. Typical of these days was a project management job for a hospital in Vero Beach, Florida. The stakes were high: a $10,000 job at a time when the company's total annual income was about $40,000. HSI threw all its resources into the proposal, and came out second best. Afterward, the chairman of the board of trustees commented frankly to DeVore: "We know you boys can do a better job. But if I pick you, and you fail, I'll be killed for giving the job to a small, unknown firm. If the other guys fail, no one can blame us for choosing them."

In desperation, DeVore and Bland decided to reposition HSI. Rather than competing for projects at major medical centers across the nation, they decided in 1972–73 to concentrate on the design and construction of doctors' office buildings and ambulatory care (outpatient) centers in the Northeast, an area they knew well. Their reasoning was that a small company could defeat the "big boys" for small jobs by putting its best people into the project and assimilating more information about the client's needs, objectives, and environment than large competitors were willing to pursue for a proposal. Almost immediately the new strategy paid off, as HSI won contracts for medical office buildings in Marlborough, Massachusetts, and Rochester, New York, defeating much larger design firms.

In 1974, the company came close to disaster in an abortive attempt to develop a medical office condominium in Houston. The absence of any real roots in Texas was a significant problem in the venture; as everyone came to realize, "we weren't good old boys." As he spent more and more time trying to salvage what he could in Houston, DeVore was increasingly unavailable for other projects, and the firm's income dropped. Finally Houston was written off, and Bland later summed up the whole episode in a pungent sentence: "It costs lots of money to go to school."

HSI recovered by 1977, when professional fees more than doubled over those earned the previous year. As contracts began to flow into the firm, DeVore made another crucial decision: HSI was not in the business of architecture. Design would be subcontracted in the future, as would a few smaller services originally offered by the company. Government regulation of health care was mushrooming in the mid-1970s, especially in Massachusetts, and DeVore was convinced that the firm's future lay in management, financial planning, and construction cost control.

By 1980, HSI's revenues appeared to justify his decision: professional fees topped $900,000 in fiscal 1979—a 55 percent increase over 1978—and were projected to reach $1.4 million for the year ending July 31, 1980. By the end of its first decade of operations, the company employed 14 professionals and 9 supporting staff.

Source: From the case study "Health Systems Inc.," by Penny Pittman Merliss and Christopher H. Lovelock. Copyright © 1980 by the President and Fellows of Harvard College. Reprinted by permission of the Harvard Business School.

The most basic marketing decision organizations must make is what product/service offerings to provide to their target markets. Firms like HSI must carefully define a service mix or offering strategy for its targeted clients. Most firms will not want to provide too many services— as HSI was doing—so as to help differentiate themselves through the services they choose to emphasize. A service strategy also should be adaptable, allowing a firm to change—as HSI did—with varying environmental conditions.

Professional service organizations face a large number of decisions in developing a sound service strategy. We shall examine the following questions in this chapter:

1. What are the characteristics of services, and especially professional services?
2. How can the organization assess and improve its overall service mix? (*service mix decisions*)
3. How can the organization assess and improve individual services in its mix? (*individual service decisions*)
4. How can the organization improve its handling of its services over their life cycles? (*service life-cycle decisions*)

THE NATURE OF SERVICES

One of the major developments in America has been the phenomenal growth of service industries. Service businesses now provide 73 percent of the payroll jobs of the U.S. nonfarm work force. As a result, there is a growing interest in the special characteristics of services marketing and how to improve service productivity.

We define a service as follows:

> A **service** is any activity or benefit that one party can offer to another that is essentially intangible and does not result in the ownership of anything. Its production may or may not be tied to a physical product.

Renting a hotel room, depositing money in a bank, traveling on an airplane, visiting a psychiatrist, having a haircut, having a car repaired, seeing a movie, having clothes cleaned in a dry-cleaning establishment, getting advice from a lawyer—all involve buying a service.

Major Characteristics of Services

Services have four characteristics that must be considered when designing marketing programs.

Intangibility. Services are intangible. They cannot be seen, tasted, felt, heard, or smelled before they are bought. The woman getting a "face lift" cannot see the result before the purchase, and the patient in the psychiatrist's office cannot know the outcome in advance. The buyer has to have faith in the service provider.

Service providers can do certain things to improve the client's confidence. First, they should try to increase the service's tangibility and concreteness.[1] A plastic surgeon can make a drawing showing the patient's probable appearance after the surgery. Second, service providers can emphasize the benefits of the service rather than just describing its features. Thus a dentist can talk to the patient about the better smile she will have once her teeth are straightened, rather than the technical steps in straightening her teeth. Third, service providers can develop brand names for their service to increase confidence, such as Arthur Andersen's TFA (stands for "transaction flow auditing"). Fourth, service providers can use a celebrity to create confidence in the service, as a Washington, D.C., law firm has done by using football star John Riggins in its TV advertisements.

Inseparability. A service cannot exist separately from its providers whether they are persons or machines. A service cannot be put on a shelf and bought by the customer whenever needed. The service requires the presence of the service provider. Filling a cavity requires the presence of a dentist and his equipment; verifying the accuracy of a company's accounting records requires the work of an auditor.

Several strategies exist for relaxing this limitation. The service provider can learn to work with larger groups. Psychotherapists have moved from one-on-one therapy to small-group therapy to groups of over three hundred people in a large hotel ballroom getting "therapized." The service provider can learn to work faster—the psychotherapist can spend 30 minutes with each patient instead of 50 minutes and see more patients. The service organization can train more service providers and build up client confidence, as H & R Block has done with its national network of trained tax consultants.

Variability. Services are highly variable, as they depend on who provides them and when and where they are provided. A Dr. Christiaan Barnard heart transplant is likely to be of higher quality than one performed by a recent M.D. And Dr. Barnard's heart transplants will vary with his energy and mental set at the time of each operation. Service buyers are aware of this high variability and frequently talk to others before selecting a service provider.

Service firms can take two steps toward quality control. The first is investing in careful personnel selection and training. Law firms and accounting firms spend considerable sums in the training of their professional employees. The second step is monitoring client satisfaction through suggestion and complaint systems, customer surveys, and comparison shopping, so that poor service can be detected and corrected.

Perishability. Services cannot be stored. The reason many doctors charge patients for missed appointments is that the service value exists at the time the patient is supposed to show up. The perishability of services is not a problem when demand is steady, because it is easy to staff the services in advance. When demand fluctuates, service firms have difficult problems.

Sasser has described several strategies for producing a better match between demand and supply in a service business.[2] Professional service firms can influence the demand level in several ways:

- *Differential pricing* will shift some demand from peak to off-peak periods. For example, a public accounting firm can charge higher fees during the busy tax season to discourage nontax work during this period.
- *Nonpeak demand can be cultivated.* A public accounting firm can go after lower fee business during the summer months when business is slow.
- *Complimentary services* can be developed during peak time so that customers do not have to spend as much time waiting. The Doctors of Northbrook Court, a group medical practice in a large shopping center near Chicago, provides patients with a personal pager so they can shop or stroll around the mall until they hear the beep.
- *Reservation systems* are a way that doctors, dentists, and other professionals manage the demand level.

The supply level can also be influenced in several ways:

- *Part-time employees* can be hired to serve peak demand. Some law firms call in paralegals on a temporary basis to help meet peak demand.
- *Peak-time efficiency routines* can be introduced. Employees perform only essential tasks during peak periods. Paramedics assist physicians during busy periods.
- *Increased consumer participation* in the tasks can be encouraged, as when patients fill out their own medical records.
- *Shared services* can be developed, as when several hospitals share medical equipment purchases.
- *Facilities making potential expansion possible* can be developed, as when a law firm rents extra space in anticipation of further growth.

Improving Service Productivity

As competition increases and costs rise, professional service firms are under great pressure to increase productivity. There are five approaches to improving service productivity. The first is to have service providers work harder or more skillfully for the same pay. Working harder is not a likely solution, but working more skillfully can occur through better selection and training procedures. The second is to increase the quantity of service by surrendering some quality. Psychotherapists, for example, could give less time to each patient. The third is to add equipment to increase service capabilities. Levitt recommended that companies adopt a "manufacturing attitude" toward producing services as represented by McDonald's assembly-line approach to fast-food retailing, culminating in the "technological hamburger."[3] Automatic bank tellers and personal computers provide technological means to expand professional services. The fourth is to reduce or make obsolete the need for a service by inventing a product solution. Thus the invention of penicillin reduced the need for tuberculosis consulting. The fifth is to design a more effective service. Nonsmoking clinics and jogging may reduce the need for expensive medical services later on. Hiring paralegal workers reduces the need for expensive legal professionals.

The Nature of Professional Services

Our discussion of the nature and characteristics of service applies to all services.

Gummesson cites the following criteria for identifying professional services:

- The service should be provided by qualified personnel, be advisory, and focus on problem solving.
- The professional should have an identity, that is, be known in the market for his specialties and under a specific name such as "architect" or "management consultant."
- The service should be an assignment given from the buyer to the seller.
- The professional should be independent of suppliers of other services or goods.[4]

Gummesson goes on to indicate that professionals have specialist know-how, a standard methodology of carrying out assignments, and an interest in finding solutions and seeing them implemented.

SERVICE MIX DECISIONS

Most professional service organizations are multiservice firms. They have a "service mix" consisting of *the set of all service lines and individual services that a particular organization makes available to clients.* A "service line" can be viewed as a *group of services within a service mix that are closely related, either because they serve similar needs, are made available to the same clients, or are marketed through the same types of channels.* For example, CPA firms generally have a service mix with three basic service lines: auditing, tax advisory, and management consulting. Similarly, law firms typically offer multiple service lines in areas such as personal injury law, real estate law, family law, antitrust law, and so on.

We can describe an organization's service mix in terms of its *length*, *width*, and *depth*. These concepts are illustrated in Figure 8–1 for the service mix of a hypothetical law firm. We see that the service mix, in terms of its length, consists of three service lines: personal injury, real estate, and family law. Each line has a certain width: thus the personal injury line includes product liability, automobile accidents, and medical malpractice. Finally, each individual service has a certain depth: the firm has five attorneys who work primarily on product liability litigation.

Suppose the firm is thinking of expanding its service mix. This could be accomplished in any of three ways. The firm could lengthen its service mix by adding, say, some attorneys with expertise in tax law. Or the firm could add another personal injury area, say airline crashes, extending the width of one line. Or the firm could add a sixth attorney who does product liability litigation, deepening its service mix in this area.

Suppose, on the other hand, that the firm considered contracting its service mix either to bring down its costs or to attain a more specialized position in the marketplace. The firm could drop real estate and even family law, concentrating exclusively on personal injury. It could, alternatively, eliminate certain personal injury areas or decide to reduce the staff in certain areas.

In considering the service mix, we should recognize that the various services differ in their relative contribution to the organization. Some services constitute the *essential* services of that organization and others are *ancillary* services. Thus, auditing is the essential service of most CPA firms and management consulting is an ancillary service. Furthermore, certain *flagship services* provided by certain *superstar professionals* may

<— ———————————— Service Mix Length ———————————— —>

	Personal Injury	Real Estate	Family
Service Line Width ↑	Product liability (5)*	Commercial (3)	Divorce (2)
	Automobile accidents (3)	Residential (4)	Adoptions (1)
↓	Medical malpractice (2)		

*The numbers in parentheses indicate the number of professionals assigned primarily to provide the corresponding service.

FIGURE 8–1. Length, width, and depth of a law firm's service mix

play a major role in drawing clients to the organization. An organization can showcase these services and professionals in its literature and promotion. The high cost of acquiring a superstar may be well repaid by the public relations value it produces.

A professional service organization should periodically reassess its service mix. Its service mix establishes its position vis-à-vis competitors (i.e., it differentiates it) in the minds of buyers. But its service mix is also the source of its costs. The organization must be constantly alert to services whose costs have begun to exceed their benefits, and whose elimination would release funds for bringing in new, more worthwhile services into its service mix.

INDIVIDUAL SERVICE DECISIONS

In developing an individual service to offer to a market, the marketing strategist has to distinguish three levels of the concept of a serivce: the core, perceptible, and augmented levels.

Core Service

At the most fundamental level stands the core service, which answers the questions: What is the client really seeking? What need is the service really satisfying? A business firm that retains a tax attorney is really buying savings on its tax bill and not just tax advice. A corporate president arranging for an architect to design a corporate headquarters may be seeking a "monument" to his leadership and not just a functional building. With many professional services, clients may be really buying a "sense of security" or "peace of mind." The marketing person's job is to uncover the essential needs hiding under every professional service so that service benefits, not just service features, can be described in firm communications. The core service stands at the center of the total service, as illustrated in Figure 8–2.

Perceptible Service

The core service is always made available to the client in some perceptible form. Professional service markcters can attempt to configure the following six basic attributes—or other attributes unique to particular professions—of a service so that clients perceive the service (or see it "positioned") as providing the core benefits they are seeking:

1. *Personnel.* The people who perform the service.
2. *Quality level.* The level of professional competence in which the service is performed.

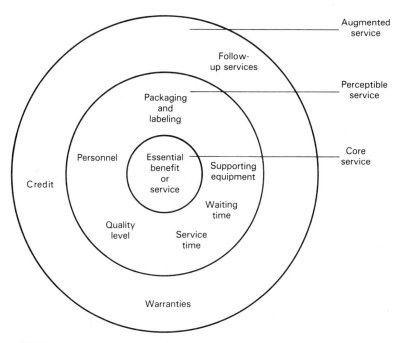

FIGURE 8–2. Three levels of a service

3. *Service time.* The amount of professionals' time required to perform the service (i.e., billable time).

4. *Waiting time.* The amount of time the client has to wait before the service is completed satisfactorily.

5. *Supporting equipment.* The machinery, instruments, and other facilities the professional uses to help deliver the service.

6. *Packaging and labeling.* The name and associated description given to the service or to the set of services.

While fee level or price could be considered another basic attribute of a professional service, we prefer to discuss this attribute separately in the next chapter. The six attributes listed above are treated in more detail below.

Personnel. The people who provide a professional service are the key attribute of that service. Clients often buy "people" rather than services and it is crucial for the professional service marketer to pay close attention to how professionals are perceived by clients. The experience levels, education levels, personalities, communication skills, and other characteristics of the professionals have to be pleasing to the clients. In particular, many clients focus intensely on experience levels, since they prefer not to take the risk of being one of the first clients to use a professional.

The selection of a highly experienced professional can provide protection from criticism if something happens to go wrong—criticism that would be likely to occur if an inexperienced professional were hired.

Reaching decisions on which personnel should provide certain services is often difficult for the professional service organization. Clients, of course, usually want the most experienced and most friendly professionals. But allowing senior partners or principals to do most of the work for every client is not feasible for several reasons. First, using mostly senior people on a job makes the job more expensive—and this would lead the organization to have to charge more than it really should to have highly satisfied clients. Having less experienced professionals working on a job allows the organization to charge more competitive fees and, as we discussed in Chapters 2 and 3, it permits greater profits to be earned. Second, using mostly senior people prevents junior professionals from obtaining the necessary experience that might help them obtain work on their own and contribute to the growth of the firm. Finally, using mostly senior people to perform services makes it more difficult to find time for these people to make their very much needed contribution to marketing the organization's services.

Developing a strong "people" attribute for an organization's services requires a number of steps. First, a strong commitment to recruiting talented personnel must be made by the organization. The firm should have enough resources to (1) recruit experienced professionals in areas where experienced staff are in short supply and/or (2) recruit "fast learners" who will be able to gain considerable experience in a short period of time. Second, the organization must make a commitment to train new professionals to accelerate their learning process. Finally, the organization must reward those professionals who exhibit "fast learning."

Quality level.   As we discussed in several earlier chapters, maintaining a high quality level for a professional service is no easy matter. Keeping track of how professionals perform services, without being too intrusive and destroying needed autonomy, is a difficult task. And making sure that clients follow professional advice, thereby insuring that they obtain a high-quality service, can also be difficult. Furthermore, trying to measure the actual quality level of a professional service can be problematical, since the ideas of different professionals and of buyers on what constitutes quality may vary widely. No simple indexes or surveys are available to tell how well a lawyer defended a client or how good the advice was of a management consultant.

In spite of the difficulties involved, professional service organizations must continually monitor their quality levels and try to keep them high. Pressures to lower quality levels, because of a need to match the lower fees of competitors, should be resisted. A lessening of quality can severely damage a firm's reputation and can leave it open to malpractice or liability suits. Careful recruiting and training can help to maintain high quality levels, as can a strong effort to educate buyers about the benefits of carefully following professional advice. Supervisor reviews, peer reviews, and self-regulation programs can also help. Finally, surveys of clients can tell much about how quality levels are *perceived*, suggesting areas where either service refinements are needed or better communication to clients of actual quality levels must be implemented.

Service time. The amount of time it takes to perform a service can have a big influence on how clients evaluate that service. Depending on how a service is being billed, clients may desire the service time to be very short or very long. The former situation would apply when hourly charges are being made, while the latter would apply when fixed fees are being charged. To avoid misunderstandings, professional service organizations should attempt to educate their clients about appropriate service times. Moreover, professionals should be discouraged from any time-wasting activities when in hourly-charge situations. On the other hand, they should be encouraged to spend time in less formal discussions with clients when in fixed-fee situations. A recent comment by author Norman Cousins, in a speech delivered at Tulane School of Medicine, is particularly relevant for professionals in fixed-fee situations: "Doctors who spend more time with their patients may have to spend less money on malpractice insurance policies."[5]

Waiting time. The shorter the time clients have to wait to begin receiving a professional service and to have that service performed satisfactorily, the more they like it. People dislike waiting in offices, waiting on the phone, waiting for proposals, or waiting for reports. The professional service organization that has enough staff to respond rapidly to client demands and that does careful scheduling of its work will be viewed more favorably by clients. Although many clients like to use professionals who are very "busy"—seeing this as an indicator that a professional is highly competent—most clients like it when a professional can "make time for them."

Supporting equipment. Another attribute of a professional service that clients evaluate is the supporting equipment used to deliver the service. Clients form impressions of professionals based, in part, on the types of computers, instruments, and office machinery they have. Thus, clients will often be favorably impressed by CPAs carrying the most modern portable microcomputers, lawyers having access to the most modern computer search facilities, land surveyors possessing the most modern photogrammetry equipment, and dentists using the most modern drilling and X-ray machines. Where research indicates that clients in the target markets are highly sensitive to the type of supporting equipment being used, efforts must be made to obtain the favored equipment.

Packaging and labeling.   Many professional service organizations have recognized the value of bundling their services in well-defined "packages" and putting "labels" or even "brand names" on them. For example, some management consulting firms provide packages of bundled services that are given the label "strategic planning." These packages will consist of component services such as environmental scanning, goal determination, strategy formulation, and so forth. These firms could also choose to put firm-specific brand names on their strategic planning packages. As mentioned in Chapter 3, the use of brand names has appeared among the Big Eight CPA firms, who have branded their packages, labeled "financial audits," with names like CAAG (for Coopers & Lybrand's "computer audit assistance group"), TRAP (for the "Touche Ross audit process"), and STAR (for Deloitte Haskins & Sells' "statistical techniques for analytical review").[6] Putting services in appropriately branded packages helps to differentiate the services in the eyes of clients and also helps clients remember the services.

Augmented Service

The professional service marketer can offer to the target markets additional services and benefits that go beyond the perceptible service, thus making up an augmented service. For example, a dentist can provide patients with easy payment plans (or accept credit cards), offer a guarantee of satisfaction with all work done, and provide free educational materials on dental care. Organizations augment their perceptible service to meet additional client wants and/or to differentiate their services from competition. Competing in terms of the "extras" is becoming more and more necessary in many professions.

In sum, we see that a professional service is not a simple thing but a complex offer consisting of a core need–satisfying service, a set of perceptible characteristics, and a set of augmented benefits. The organization should deeply examine each of its services and design them in a way that will distinguish them from competitors' offers and carry the intended qualities to the intended target market. The more the service can be taken out of the commodity class and moved toward a branded or specialized class, the more control the organization will have over the level, timing, and composition of demand for its service.

SERVICE LIFE CYCLE

It is not possible for a professional service's attributes and marketing approach to remain optimal for all time. Broad changes in the macroenvironment (population, economy, politics, technology, and culture) as well as specific changes in the market environment (buyers, competitors, referral sources) will call for major service and marketing adjustments at key points in the service's history. The nature of the appropriate adjustments can be conveyed through the concept of the *service life cycle* (or what is typically called the *product life cycle* in most marketing writings).

Many services can be viewed as having something analogous to a "biological" life cycle. They received high acceptance at one time and then moved into a period of decline later. One only has to think of the ups and downs of management consulting ideas or services such as "zero-based budgeting" or "management by objectives" to recognize that life cycles exist. The life of a typical service exhibits an S-shaped revenues curve marked by the following four stages (see Figure 8–3):

1. *Introduction* is a period of slow billings growth as the service is introduced in the market.
2. *Growth* is a period of rapid market acceptance.
3. *Maturity* is a period of leveling off in billings growth because the service has achieved acceptance by most of the potential clients.
4. *Decline* is the period when billings show a strong downward drift.

The service life-cycle (SLC) concept can be defined according to whether it describes a service class (mental health service), a service form (psychoanalysis), or a brand (Menninger Clinic). The SLC concept has a different applicability in each case. *Service classes* have the longest life cycles. The billings of many service classes can be expected to continue in the mature stage for an indefinite duration. Thus, "mental health service" began centuries ago with organized religion and can be expected to persist indefinitely. Service forms, on the other hand, tend to exhibit more standard SLC histories than service classes. Thus, mental health services are dispensed in such forms as psychoanalysis, bioenergetics,

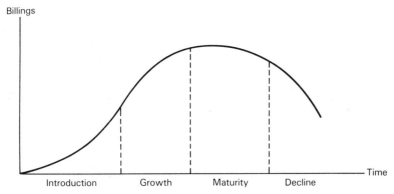

FIGURE 8–3. Typical S-shaped life-cycle curve

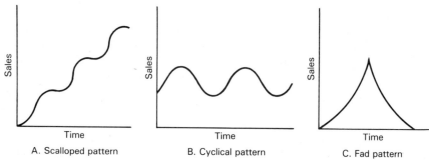

FIGURE 8–4.   Three anomalous service life-cycle patterns

group therapy, and so on, some of which are beginning to show signs of maturity. As for brands, they are the most likely to show finite histories. Thus, the Menninger Clinic is a well-known psychoanalytically oriented clinic that had a period of rapid growth and is now mature. It will pass out of existence eventually, as is the fate of most brands and institutions.

It is important to note that not all services exhibit an S-shaped life cycle. Three other common patterns are:

1. *Scalloped pattern.*   (Figure 8–4A) In this case, service billings during the mature stage suddenly break into a new life cycle. The service's new life is triggered by service modifications, new uses, new users, changing tastes, or other factors. For example, the market for psychotherapy reached maturity at one point and then the emergence of group therapy gave it a whole new market.

2. *Cyclical pattern.*   (Figure 8–4B) The billings of some services show a cyclical pattern. For example, architectural services go through alternating periods of high billings and low billings, reflecting changes in demand and supply in the construction market. The decline stage is not a time to eliminate the service but to maintain as much of it as possible, waiting for the next boom.

3. *Fad pattern.*   (Figure 8–4C) Here a new service comes on the market, attracts quick attention, is adopted with great zeal, peaks early, and declines rapidly. The acceptance cycle is short and the service tends to attract only a limited following of people who are looking for excitement or diverson. Some tax shelter deals and therapy forms exhibit the pattern of a fad.

We will now return to the S-shaped SLC and examine the characteristics and appropriate marketing strategies at each stage.

Introduction Stage

The introduction stage takes place when the professional service is first made available for purchase in the marketplace. The introduction into one or more markets takes time, and billings growth is apt to be slow. Slow growth could occur because firms often have difficulty (1) staffing up to provide a new service, (2) working out the details of the service, (3) finding ways to distribute the service, and (4) getting clients to accept the service. These situations have faced consulting firms offering new computer software packages, law firms offering prepaid legal services, CPA firms offering less expensive "reviews" instead of full-scale audits, and architectural firms offering computer-assisted design services.

In the introductory stage, costs are high because of the low adoption and the need for heavier promotion expenses. People have to be informed about the new unknown service and induced to try it. The organization should direct its selling effort to those clients who are the readiest to buy, namely, early-adopter types. Studies of early adopters of a variety of products and services have shown them to generally be younger, more educated, more cosmopolite, and more exposed to mass media.[7] (See Exhibit 8-1 for an example of the problems of starting up a new professional service business.)

Growth Stage

If the new professional service satisfies the market, billings will start climbing substantially. The early adopters will continue their purchasing and other clients will follow their lead, especially if there is favorable

EXHIBIT 8-1.   Starting up a new professional services business.

Each year, between 150 and 200 new advertising agencies are opened up either by advertising freshmen eager to run their own business or seasoned professionals who are tired of working for large agencies. Recently, Allan Kay and Lois Korey broke away from giant Needham, Harper & Steers, Inc., to form their own agency and in the process gave up cushy jobs and salaries in the $200,000 range. They had to establish a name and image for their new firm, find a suitable location and office space, establish a referral system, and set lower fees to attract clients. They named their firm Korey, Kay & Partners, moved into a one-room office in the Empire State Building, and proceeded to contact more than one thousand prospective clients, only to hear that their agency was too new or too small, or that it was too late to be considered this year. They found that starting a business was much harder than anticipated. However, they persisted and managed to pick up six clients in the first year. They were able to hire 16 employees, move into a larger office, and clear a first-year profit of $830,000. Their job isn't done yet, though. Some new agencies fold within a few years as they bump into cash-flow problems, lose key executives, or fail to find new clients to replace exiting ones.

Source: Adapted from "Pair of Ad Executives, Pampered But Restless, Set Out on Their Own," *Wall Street Journal,* June 9, 1983, p. 1.

word-of-mouth. New competitors will enter the market, attracted by the opportunity. They will introduce feature, brand, and packaging variations, and this will expand the market. During this stage the organization tries to sustain rapid growth as long as possible. This is accomplished in several ways:

1. The organization undertakes to improve service quality and add new-service features and packages.
2. It vigorously searches out new market segments to enter.
3. It keeps its eyes open for new physical locations to gain additional service exposure.
4. It shifts its communications from building service awareness to trying to bring about service conviction and purchase.

The major challenge facing professional service firms during a period of rapid growth is to maintain a high level of service quality. There is usually a shortage of experienced personnel and they are strained to work long hours to meet the demand. The firm hires new personnel as rapidly as possible but there is a "breaking-in" time. The firm should resist the temptation to take on more business than it can service at a high quality level. Otherwise it will damage its reputation and this will hurt it when demand levels off. (See Exhibit 8–2.)

Maturity Stage

At some point a professional service's rate of billings growth will slow down, and the service will enter a stage of relative maturity. This stage normally lasts much longer than the previous stages, and it poses some of the most formidable challenges to people with marketing responsibilities. *Most professional services are in the maturity stage of the life cycle, and therefore most of the marketing of professional services deals with mature services.*

The beginning of a slowdown in the rate of billings growth has the effect of producing overcapacity in a professional service area. The overcapacity leads to intensified competition. Competitors engage more frequently in fee or price cutting, and there is a strong increase in promotional budgets. Other organizations increase their research and development budgets to find better versions of the service. Still others resort to modifying their client mix or service mix. These steps result in higher costs. Some of the weaker competitors start dropping out. The area eventually consists of a set of well-entrenched competitors whose basic orientation is toward gaining competitive advantage.

EXHIBIT 8-2.   Overmarketing is possible, too!

A firm can make the mistake of overmarketing as well as undermarketing. This possibility is little recognized because so far the problem has been too little marketing, rather than too much. Overmarketing occurs when a firm invests so much in marketing that other results and values are jeopardized.

Overmarketing occurred in the case of a management consulting firm that was formed with the objective of achieving rapid billings growth. The firm's management developed a long-range plan incorporating strong marketing activity.

- Marketing was recognized as a firm-wide activity. Staff personnel were expected to work on expanding services to existing clients. Officers were expected to develop new clients and to close sales leads initiated by the staff. The entire program was under the personal direction of the president.

- There was a carefully planned and vigorous program for building referral sources. Each officer was asked to join an organization and a country club. Officers were expected to develop speaking engagements and write articles.

- Frequent meetings were held to coordinate and plan new business development activities. Training sessions were conducted to improve new business development skills.

- A public relations consultant was retained to obtain favorable newspaper and trade paper publicity. Publicity releases were prepared covering important company assignments. Seminars were sponsored from time to time to call attention to new management techniques.

- Every effort was made to motivate new business development activity. Staff personnel received bonuses for successful leads. Ability to generate new business was made a significant element in promotion. Officers' compensation was based almost entirely on the volume and rate of growth of the client assignments under their supervision.

This program initially produced outstanding results. By 1978, annual fee billings had risen to over $12 million from offices located in six major cities. However, this represented a high point from which the firm began to decline, at first slowly and then precipitously. As the billings of the firm declined, it fell into disarray. All the branch offices were closed. Several officers resigned to establish their own consulting firms. At the present time, the firm is still in existence but is no longer a major competitor.

The firm's decline was not the result of adverse conditions in the marketplace. Rather, it was paying a deferred penalty for long-term overemphasis on hard selling. Having committed itself to rapid growth, it neglected other things, specifically:

- The original objective was for a sustained growth rate of 15 percent a year. This was achieved but the effort did not leave sufficient time for the acquisition, training, and development of the professional staff. The firm was developing business at a faster rate than its capacity to deliver quality work.

- The staff perceived that high awards were given for business development but not for professional excellence. A number of staffers with great professional promise but little interest in selling left the firm to join competitors. The multiplier effect of these resignations increased the difficulty of coordinating staff development with growth.

- Because officers were selected primarily for their ability to develop new business, several lacked the technical background to properly supervise the assignments handled by their staff. Since the difference in compensation between officers and staff was substantial, this led to poor morale and increased turnover.

- The high financial rewards for new business development led to intense competition and infighting among officers and created an unhealthy atmosphere in the firm.

Thus, a firm can overemphasize the marketing task to the detriment of other important business functions. An intense passion for sales growth can come at the expense of long-run profitability. Authentic marketing should focus on achieving long-run profitability, not short-run sales growth.

Decline Stage

Many professional services eventually enter a stage of billings decline. This happens for a number of reasons. Technical advances may give birth to new service classes, forms, and brands, which become effective substitutes. Thus, the demand for "family" doctors declined and gave way to demand for internal medicine practitioners and pediatricians. In addition, changes in politics, fashion, or tastes may lead to client erosion. For instance, lawyers specializing in regulatory matters have seen a decline in the demand for their services since President Reagan took office. Developments such as these have the effect of intensifying overcapacity and competition.

As billings of a service decline, firms should give thought to withdrawing or reducing the service in order to invest their resources in more attractive markets. Unless strong retention reasons exist, carrying a weak service is very costly to the organization. The cost of maintaining a weak service is not just the amount of uncovered cost. No financial accounting can adequately convey all the hidden costs. The weak service tends to consume a disproportionate amount of management's time; it often requires frequent fee adjustments; it requires both advertising and selling attention that might better be diverted to making the "healthy" services more profitable; its very unfitness can cause client misgivings and cast a shadow on the organization's image. The biggest cost imposed by carrying weak services may lie in the future. By not being eliminated at the proper time, these services delay the aggressive search for replacement services; they create a lopsided service mix, long on "yesterday's breadwinners" and short on "tomorrow's breadwinners"; they depress current cash and weaken the organization's foothold on the future.

During the period of decline, the firm needs to adopt some temporizing measures while it searches for new pastures. It may have to let go of some professionals, lower its fees, close some offices, and relocate its headquarters. The ultimate task is to discover and exploit new market opportunities. The following story illustrates how a dentist reconceptualized his dental practice in the face of a declining demand for dentistry:

> Dr. Jeffrey Morley, a 29-year-old dentist, operates the Center for Cosmetic Dentistry in San Francisco. "We're artists, and our canvas is the human being. You can't be in the appearance business today without being a psychologist." Dr. Morley and two colleagues, an orthodontist and a jaw surgeon, offer "dental solutions" to solve cosmetic problems. "What it comes down to is this: Buck teeth imply people are dumb. Large canines imply aggressiveness. Weak chins imply passivity, while strong chins imply a macho, studly personality." The dentists probe the patients' desires and recast their mouths using orthodontic wire, caps, bonding materials, or surgery to help them realize the personality they want. "The idea was germinating a long time and just came to fruition last summer. Now, less than a year later, with overhead in excess of $20,000 a month, we're making a profit."[8]

SUMMARY

Most professional service organizations are multiservice firms. They make decisions on the service mix, on each individual service, and on marketing mix strategies for each service at each stage of its life cycle.

Services have to be defined. Services are activities or benefits that one party can offer to another that are essentially intangible and do not result in the ownership of anything. Services are intangible, inseparable, variable, and perishable. Rising costs and increasing competition are forcing professional service firms to search for ways to increase their productivity.

An organization's service mix can be described in terms of its length, width, and depth. Some of the organization's services constitute its core services and others its ancillary services. Organizations like to develop a flagship service or superstar professional to help publicize the organization.

Three levels of the concept of a service can be distinguished. The core service answers the question: What need is the service really meeting? The perceptible service is the form in which the service is seen: it includes the following service attributes: personnel, quality level, service time, waiting time, supporting equipment, and packaging and labeling. The augmented service consists of the perceptible service and the additional services and benefits such as warranties or credit. As competition increases, organizations augment their service offer to compete more effectively.

Services pass through a life cycle consisting of four stages: introduction, growth, maturity, and decline. The S-shaped life cycle is the most common, but other patterns include a scalloped pattern, cyclical pattern, and fad pattern. Each stage of the life cycle presents new marketing challenges and requires adjustments in the target market and marketing mix.

NOTES

1. G. Lynn Shostack, "Breaking Free from Product Marketing," *Journal of Marketing*, April 1977, pp. 73–80.

2. See W. Earl Sasser, "Match Supply and Demand in Service Industries," *Harvard Business Review*, November–December 1976, pp. 133–40.

3. Theodore Levitt, "Product-Line Approach to Service," *Harvard Business Review*, September–October 1972, pp. 41–52; see also his "The Industrialization of Service," *Harvard Business Review*, September–October 1976, pp. 63–74.

4. See Evert Gummesson, "Toward a Theory of Professional Service Marketing," *Industrial Marketing Management*, Vol. 7 (1978), p. 90.

5. Norman Cousins, as quoted in *Time*, June 21, 1982, p. 83, in a report on his graduation address before the Tulane School of Medicine in New Orleans.

6. See Peter W. Bernstein, "Competition Comes to Accounting," *Fortune*, July 17, 1978, p. 92.

7. See Everett M. Rogers, *Diffusion of Innovations* (New York: Free Press, 1962).

8. "Your Suit Is Pressed, Hair Neat, but What Do Your Molars Say?" *Wall Street Journal*, June 16, 1982, p. 1.

9

SETTING FEES

The accountant–client relationship has been likened to that of doctor and patient, priest and penitent, or even husband and wife. Do you haggle with your doctor over his fee, with your wife over the price of her birthday present? Of course not. Nor with your high-toned accountant over his bill. Accounting fees are just not discussed in polite company.

Such niceties are still the rule in corporate–auditor relations, but not in the hotly competitive municipal accounting field. Municipalities *must* make public information about audit contracts. Thanks to a 1976 amendment to the Federal Revenue Sharing Act, which forces local governments to undergo audits, the veil of secrecy surrounding accounting fees has been lifted somewhat. Surprise! Accounting fees aren't quite as haggle-proof as the profession would like you to think.

The soap companies call it "cents-off deals," department stores, "traffic builders." In accounting it's called "practice development." But price-cutting is price-cutting, no matter what you call it.

Among the Big Eight accounting firms, fees range as high as $100 an hour for auditing services. Nonnegotiable? Coopers & Lybrand is auditing the City of Boston for $500,000, about $7 an hour, and the State of Maryland for $587,000, less than $10 an hour. Venerable Ernst & Ernst lost the Boston job with a bid of $45,000 because the city fathers felt the firm did not understand the scope of the job. But E & E won the State of New Hampshire auditing contract for that same amount, beating out bids as high as Deloitte Haskins & Sells' $555,000.

This kind of price-shaving takes its toll. Already it has cut into the average partner's take, causing a decline in partners' income at Coopers & Lybrand and Touche Ross. Peat, Marwick, Mitchell & Co., too, has seen margins sliced.

But why cut prices? Earl C. Keller, professor of accounting at the University of Michigan, explains it this way: "All the CPA firms want to get larger, but the corporate business is not expanding—all they're doing is trading clients." William J. Raftery, director of government services at Main Lafrentz & Co., is frank: "You have to have spare staff on hand for larger clients. We wind up with excess capacity and, just like the Japanese dump steel, you could say there's some dumping of staff." His counterpart at Coopers & Lybrand, James A. Hogan, agrees: "Municipal jobs often come up during accounting's slow season—most fiscal years end June 30—so the people working on a lot of these jobs would be sitting around doing nothing if they didn't have the city audits to occupy their time."

As the municipal market battle continues—and for the first time ever the battle is in the open—some corporate clients are wondering why it's only cities that benefit from price-cutting. They are wondering if they aren't paying some of the cost of municipal audits.

"I suppose there's some social good," says Control Data Corp. comptroller Gary E. Polaczyk, "and from our viewpoint, it's okay as long as it doesn't go too far. If they're undercutting too much, obviously somebody's paying for it."

CDC's auditor, Peat, Marwick, Mitchell audits the City of New York for $1 million a year—around $26 an hour. That is fairly high for a city job, but corporate audit committees across the country would drool at such a cheap contract.

Source: Brian McGlynn, "Excess Capacity?" p. 76. Reprinted by permission of *Forbes* Magazine, June 25, 1979. © Forbes Inc., 1979.

Times have changed with respect to fee setting in most of the professions. Clients are no longer willing to accept silently whatever fee a professional chooses to charge. Government actions (such as the one cited above) and other developments (see Chapter 1) have helped to create a climate where clients are much more informed than ever before about the fees being charged by rival professional service organizations. They are using this increased amount of information to guide them in demanding fees that they see as fair and equitable. Increased price competition—something that was alien to most of the professions—has been the result. And in professions like accounting this competition has heated up far beyond what it was like during the 1979 situation described above.

Increased client sensitivity to fees, and the resulting price or fee competition, has elevated the importance of carefully developing the price or fee component of the marketing mix. Careful attention to fee setting can bring substantial returns to a firm, helping it to attract clients away from competing firms and to obtain clients who previously might have avoided a particular professional service because of a fear that it would cost too much.

The fee-setting process involves multiple considerations. We will address the following issues in this chapter:

1. What should be the objectives of fee setting?
2. What basic strategies are available in fee setting?
3. What tactics are available for implementing fee strategies?
4. How should fees be changed?
5. How can fees be negotiated, billed, collected, and allocated most effectively?

DETERMINING OBJECTIVES
FOR FEE SETTING

The first consideration in setting fees is determining what the firm wants to accomplish with its fee strategy. A firm that seeks to maximize profits will charge different fees than one that seeks to earn merely satisfactory profits. In this section, we will review several alternative fee-setting objectives and discuss their implications for fee-setting strategy.

Current Profit Maximization

Some organizations seek to attain the highest possible current profit levels. Each year, they attempt to set fees and other marketing variables at levels that will maximize profits. They make forecasts about how various marketing mixes will be responded to by clients, competitors, intermediaries, suppliers, regulators, and others, and they choose the mix (and fee) that appears likely to bring the largest profits. Sometimes rather formal, rigorous procedures involving mathematical modeling are used to determine fees and other marketing variables. More frequently, the process is rather informal and intuitive.

In theory, the profit-maximizing firm should set fees or prices using the price-setting approach of economics. This approach involves some mathematical model building that we will not bother to explain in detail here. Essentially, the approach suggests that the firm should attempt to set fees so that the marginal (additional) revenue brought in for the last hour of work billed just equals the marginal cost of doing that last hour of work. In this way, the firm should be in a situation where each hour of work it performs produces more additional revenues than additional costs—since only the last hour billed, which will theoretically be the most expensive to sell and have the highest marginal cost, will have additional costs as high as its additional revenues.

Needless to say, implementing the economics approach to fee setting is very difficult. Generally, using this approach requires a firm to oversimplify the pricing problem to an unreasonable extent. In order to estimate the marginal revenues and costs associated with various fee levels, rigid assumptions must be made about the manner in which competitors, clients, suppliers, regulators, intermediaries, and a firm's own staff will react to different fee levels.

Nevertheless, the emphasis given in the economics approach to examining the reactions of multiple parties and to assessing carefully how much revenues and costs will result from various fee levels is worth close consideration. A firm cannot hope to make any of the fee-setting strategies discussed later in this chapter work in a profit-maximizing way without considering these factors. Even firms that have objectives other than profit maximization will generally find it valuable to consider these factors carefully.

Market Penetration

The importance that clients place on previous experience when choosing among professionals leads many professional service organizations to set objectives involving the *penetration* of certain markets (or the obtaining of high levels of experience in providing certain services). An organization with a market penetration objective will be inclined to want to focus on its competition when setting fees. This will typically lead such a firm to charge fees that are lower than its competition.

Low fees may be particularly advisable if: (1) the market appears to be highly sensitive to fee levels, and therefore a low fee will stimulate more rapid market growth; (2) a low fee would discourage actual and potential competition; (3) a low fee would not be viewed by clients as an indicator of poor quality work; and (4) the more experience the firm obtains, the lower its costs of attracting and servicing clients. If none of these four conditions hold, then a firm may want to avoid fee-cutting as a means of penetrating a market and turn to other marketing tools (or other objectives).

Market Skimming

Some organizations seek to make large amounts of profits from a small number of clients. They therefore charge fees so high that only a limited subset of clients would be attracted. They recognize that they could make more short-run profits by charging lower fees and seeking a larger market, but they prefer—at least for a short time—to "skim" the market of its most profitable sectors and go after those who are not willing to pay higher fees at a later point in time.

This objective will be appealing to firms in situations where: (1) high fees may actually be viewed by targeted clients as an indicator that better quality services are being provided, (2) high fees will not attract new competitors, (3) the costs of attracting and servicing clients do not decline appreciably as more experience is obtained, (4) a shortage of well-qualified professional staff makes it difficult to service more than a few select, high-paying clients, and (5) high fees will not attract the scrutiny of government regulatory officials or the wrath of third-party payers like insurance companies or the government.

Satisficing

Many professional service organizations do not emphasize profitability—either in the short or long run—in the way they conduct their affairs. The world is filled with professionals who just "get by" but continue to practice because of love for their professions. These professionals tend to have objectives of earning a satisfactory level of profits —enough to allow them to cover their expenses, live comfortably (but not extravagantly), and earn reputations for being fair and competent. Fee setting for these people therefore focuses on trying to cover expenses with fees that are viewed as fair and equitable.

STRATEGIC OPTIONS IN FEE SETTING

A professional service organization's fee-setting objectives provide guidance for the development of the two key elements of a fee or pricing strategy: (1) the *average fee level* and (2) the *fee presentation approach.* The organization needs to decide how low or high it wants its fees, on average, to be, and how it wants to present or package fees for clients (e.g., time and expenses, retainer, etc.). We now discuss the strategic options in both of these areas.

Selecting an Average Fee Level

A professional service organization needs to decide where it wants to position itself on a cost or expense dimension. Does the firm want to be seen by targeted clients as cheap, expensive, or somewhere in between? Of course, the selection of a penetration objective will generally dictate the use of a low fee level; while the selection of a skimming objective will generally dictate the use of a high fee level. But for firms interested in profit maximization or satisficing, the choice of an average fee level that will produce desired results is not a simple task. With some target markets, high fees (i.e., a "Cadillac" or premium strategy) may be the best choice for improving profitability, perhaps because these clients equate high fees with high quality, while for other target markets low fees (i.e., a bargain strategy) may be most profitable. The availability of good marketing research data on the perceptions and desires of targeted clients can make it easier to choose a profitable average fee level.

Most organizations use one of three basic calculation methods to help them select a specific average fee level: (1) *cost-oriented methods,* (2) *demand-oriented methods,* and (3) *competition-oriented methods.* Cost-oriented methods will tend to be used by firms with satisficing objectives; while demand-oriented and competition-oriented methods will tend to be used by firms with skimming and penetration objectives, respectively. Profit-maximizing firms will tend to use aspects of all three methods. We will now illustrate how a management consulting firm might use each of these three methods.

Cost-oriented methods.   Setting fees in a cost-oriented way would have a management consulting firm calculating what it costs to provide a given amount of service to a client and then setting a fee to insure that costs are covered and a specified level of profits are earned. Typically, the firm would develop a "multiple" or markup that it could automatically multiply times the hourly/daily salaries of professional staff members to arrive at an hourly/daily fee for their services. Such a multiple would be designed to be large enough to allow the total fees received to cover both overhead expenses and a targeted level of profits. The hourly/daily fees arrived at in this way would be used for determining total charges for clients no matter what specific fee presentation approach was being used(see below).

A management consulting firm might calculate its multiple in the following way.[1] First, it would estimate the total cost per year of maintaining its professional staff (C). It would do this by multiplying the number of hours per year it expects each professional to work (H) times the number of professionals on its staff (N) times the average salary (and benefits) paid to professionals per hour (S). For example, the firm might make the following calculations:

$$C = HNS$$
$$C = 2,000(50) (\$35)$$
$$C = \$3,500,000$$

Next, the firm would determine its total yearly overhead costs (F) by examining its expected expenses for secretarial and clerical staff, marketing staff, office rentals, professional dues, insurance, and so forth. For this example, let us assume that the total comes to $2,000,000.

The firm would then assume that total revenues are equal to total professional costs times the yet unspecified multiple (M) times a "productivity rate" (P) which reflects the proportion of hours worked by the average professional staff member that are billable hours. In other words, for the present example it would be assumed that:

$$R = (C)\,(M)\,(P)$$
$$R = \$3{,}500{,}000(M)\,(.7)$$
$$R = \$2{,}450{,}000M$$

If profits (Z) are equal to

$$Z = R - C - F$$
$$Z = \$2{,}450{,}000M - \$3{,}500{,}000 - \$2{,}000{,}000$$

then the remaining task becomes to figure a value for M that would allow Z to reach a targeted level, say $625,000. This could be done as follows:

$$\$625{,}000 = \$2{,}450{,}000M - \$5{,}500{,}000$$
$$M = 6{,}125{,}000/2{,}450{,}000$$
$$M = 2.5$$

Another way to arrive at this multiple would be to solve the profit formula for M and then plug in the example values (as follows):

$$Z = R - C - F$$
$$Z = HNSMP - HNS - F$$
$$HNSMP = Z + HNS + F$$
$$M = Z/HNSP + HNS/HNSP + F/HNSP$$
$$M = (1/P)\left[\frac{(Z + F)}{C} + 1\right] \qquad (9\text{--}1)$$
$$M = (1/.7)[(625{,}000 + 2{,}000{,}000)/3{,}500{,}000] + (1/.7)$$
$$M = 2.5$$

Equation 9–1 could be used to formulate a multiple to assist many different types of firms in their fee setting. The formula suggests that higher targeted profit levels and larger overhead tend to make multiples higher, while higher productivity rates and higher professional staff costs tend to lower the multiples needed to achieve given profit levels.

Needless to say, there are numerous other variations of cost-oriented fee-setting methods. Formulas exist for deriving many different types of multiples or markups. For example, according to a recent study by

Sogofsky, marketing research firms tend to use six different basic types of formulas for determining fees. These are labeled by him as:

1. Multiple of field costs
2. Multiple of all out-of-pocket costs
3. Multiple of all out-of-pocket costs plus research time
4. Multiple of all out-of-pocket costs plus all labor
5. Different multiples for out-of-pocket costs versus labor
6. Different billing rates for each category of significant costs[2]

And a variety of other cost figures are used in the formulas favored by professionals in other fields.

The major positive feature of cost-oriented methods is their relative simplicity. All one usually needs to do to determine a billing rate for a professional is multiply the person's hourly/daily salary times the calculated multiple. In addition, since these methods have great popularity in the professisons, employing one will often put a firm in a situation where fees are being determined in a very similar way by all competitors—and therefore similar rates are charged by all of them and fee competition tends to be avoided. The popularity of these methods also tends to make clients very familiar and comfortable with the resulting fees, helping to improve communication between clients and professionals.

But these methods have a serious weakness. To calculate a multiple using formula 9–1 or some similar approach amounts to assuming that average productivity rates (or percent billable time) will stay at some fixed level regardless of what multiple is finally selected. In other words, one assumes that the amount of work professionals obtain in a given year is not influenced by what fees are being charged. Of course, this is a very difficult assumption for many professional service organizations to live with. To avoid problems that might occur from making this assumption, an organization may want to resist simply plugging values into a formula to arrive at a multiple. Instead, simultaneous consideration could be given both to possible multiple values and to possible productivity rates. The multiple finally selected should be one that could be confidently predicted to provide a productivity rate that would allow the organization to achieve its targeted profit levels.

Demand-oriented methods.   Instead of focusing first on costs, a management consulting firm could begin its fee-setting process by looking toward its clients and their perceptions of what are appropriate fees for a consultant to charge. The firm would examine its present clients to determine how loyal, how financially sound, and how well informed about competing consultants' fees each client tends to be. The more loyal, financially sound, and uninformed about fees a client seems to be, the more that client would become a candidate for a fee hike (or vice versa). Similarly, potential clients would be examined to see their previous loyalties, their financial strength, and their knowledge of consultants' fees. Lower fees would have to be quoted to those potential clients who have shown loyalty to competing firms and have obtained knowledge (and savvy) about fee structures.

The result of this process might be a situation where the consulting firm would be charging a wide range of different fees to different clients—a very different outcome than one would tend to get with the use of cost-oriented methods. Even more diversity in fees could result if the firm decided to charge more for those services that contain attributes that clients see as desirable. Thus, the firm might charge clients higher fees to provide attributes such as shorter waiting times for completion of projects or greater use of senior people on project teams. However, as clients become more knowledgeable about the fee structures of professionals (as they *are* doing), it will become more difficult for an organization to charge widely varying fees to different clients.

Demand-oriented fee-setting methods can produce considerable profits for an organization while still keeping clients satisfied and feeling like they paid appropriate fees. The major drawback to these methods is their reliance on an ability to estimate how different clients will react to fee changes—something which is extremely difficult to do. We will discuss the problem of estimating price elasticity, or market reactions to fee changes, later in this chapter.

Competition-oriented methods. A management consulting firm could commence its fee-setting task by looking toward competitors' fees before it considers either its costs or the potential reactions of its clients. Depending on its overall fee-setting objective (e.g., penetration, skimming, etc.), competition-oriented fee setting would have the firm selecting fees that are higher, lower, or the same as those of competitors. Competition-oriented fee setting can be successful for an organization if (1) it has accurate information about competitors' fees and (2) clients are aware of fee differentials between competitors and react to those differentials.

A form of competition-oriented fee setting must be employed by professional service organizations confronted with competitive bidding situations. Even if the client is not committed to going with the lowest bid—and it is possible to outbid competitors by showing well on attributes other than fees—it is wise to think in a competition-oriented way about the fee portion of a competitive bid. The problem of competitive bidding has received considerable attention from management scientists and other researchers. Exhibit 9–1 contains a brief summary of what research has revealed on this subject.

EXHIBIT 9-1. An approach to competitive bidding

According to Monroe,[3] the literature on competitive bidding suggests employing the following approach in developing bids:

1. *Estimate costs.* Arbitrary cost estimating should be avoided and careful estimates based on realistic activity levels should be used.

2. *Estimate the probability of winning with various bids.* Estimates must be made of the probabilities of getting competing bids above various bid levels. Three approaches for making these estimates are: (1) The Winning Bid Approach—where only past *winning* bids of competitors are examined to estimate the probabilities of getting competing bids below (or above) various levels; (2) The Average Opponent Approach—where the past winning *and* losing bids of all competitors are examined to estimate the probabilities of an *average* competitor submitting bids below (or above) various levels; and (3) The Specific Opponent Approach—where the past winning and losing bids of all competitors are examined to estimate each competitor's probability of submitting a bid below (or above) various levels. To implement any of these approaches, assumptions must be made about the past and future costs incurred by competitors. In addition, considerable information about past bidding results must be obtained. Such data might be available on competitions for government work, but would be hard to find for private-sector work.

3. *Determine the Best Bid.* The expected profits from making each considered bid should be calculated by multiplying the probability of winning at each considered bid level times the anticipated profits from doing the work at that bid level. The following chart presents an example of such a calculation. Assume that the calculations are being made to bid for something like a consulting project, audit engagement, or building design. The best bid would be $90,000 for a profit-maximizing firm and something lower for a firm with penetration or satisficing objectives.

COMPETITIVE BIDDING EXAMPLE

BID (B)	COST (C)	IMMEDIATE PROFITS (B − C)	PROBABILITY OF WINNING (P)	EXPECTED IMMEDIATE PROFITS [P × (B − C)]
$ 30,000	$50,000	$ −20,000	1.00	$ −20,000
40,000	50,000	−10,000	0.90	− 9,000
50,000	50,000	0	0.80	0
60,000	50,000	10,000	0.70	7,000
70,000	50,000	20,000	0.60	12,000
80,000	50,000	30,000	0.50	15,000
90,000	50,000	40,000	0.40	16,000
100,000	50,000	50,000	0.30	15,000
110,000	50,000	60,000	0.20	12,000
120,000	50,000	70,000	0.10	7,000
130,000	50,000	80,000	0	0

Source: Kent B. Monroe, *Pricing: Making Profitable Decisions* (New York: McGraw-Hill, 1979), p. 224. Reprinted with permission.

174

Selecting a Fee Presentation Approach

In addition to determining the level of fees, an important strategic decision must be made on the presentation approach to use with fees. There are six basic presentation approaches: (1) *time and expenses,* (2) *fixed sum,* (3) *percentage,* (4) *contingency,* (5) *retainer,* and (6) *hybrid.* Of course, several of these approaches could be employed simultaneously by a given firm. Each approach is described and evaluated below.

Time and expenses. With this approach, fees are set by multiplying the number of hours/days of professional service provided by an hourly/daily billing rate and then adding the amount (or some multiple of the amount) of out-of-pocket expenses incurred by the professionals for materials, travel, computer time, and so forth.

The major advantage of the "time and expenses" approach is that it allows the professional service organization to be sure it is covering all its costs. Extra time spent in wrapping up a project can be billed to a client and does not have to reduce the project's profitability. This approach is also often seen as "fair" by clients. In addition, the use of this approach also tends to make staff members more conscious of the need to spend most of their time in billable rather than nonbillable activities—although this approach may sometimes lead people to overemphasize the quest for billable time and underemphasize the need to spend nonbillable time in marketing and professional development activities.

The major disadvantage of the time and expenses approach is the uncertainty and consequent dissatisfaction it creates in clients. Clients like to know what something is going to cost them before they make the decision to buy. But buying professional services by a time and expenses approach usually puts clients in a position where they must make a decision based on only an estimate (provided by the professional) of what the services will cost in total. They worry about projects or litigation taking longer than they should, and this puts a strain on the relationship between professionals and their clients.

Fixed sum. With this approach, fees are set at some fixed amount prior to providing services and are not changed regardless of how much time or expenses are required to provide the services. This approach can alleviate client uncertainty about fees and make them much more comfortable with their relationship with professionals. It can also be used to "hide" high hourly/daily rates that clients may have a difficult time accepting (since they do not earn those amounts). But this approach transfers much of the uncertainty and risk confronted by clients with the time and expenses approach over to the professional service organization. Unforeseen events or lack of cooperation by clients can be disastrous for the accountant, lawyer, consultant, or design professional saddled with major amounts of work billed on a fixed sum basis. The pressures created by having to keep within a fixed sum can even lead firms to compromise their standards and not pursue quality work as vigorously as they would if each hour were being billed.

Percentage. In some professions, the fee is set as a percentage of some "placement" value. Advertising agencies receive a commission of 15 percent on the media space purchased for their clients. Travel agents receive a 10 percent commission on the value of the travel they arrange. Executive recruiting firms receive a percentage of the first-year salary of clients they place in a new job. As an example, Gerald Roche, chairman of Heidrick & Struggles, earned a fee of $333,000 for successfully luring John Sculley, president of Pepsi Cola Company, to take a new job as the president of Apple Computer, Inc.

The percentage approach has the advantage of being straightforward and easy for clients to understand. To the extent that higher placement values yield higher real values for clients, clients should not mind the higher fee. The professional's problem arises when a traditional percentage (such as 10 or 15 percent) is no longer adequate to cover the rising expenses and yield an adequate rate of return. From time to time, advertising agencies try to convince the media to pay higher commissions or these agencies resort to charging clients for certain services in addition to the media commissions they receive.

Contingency. With this approach, fees are determined by taking a percentage of figures such as the amount of a legal judgment or settlement, the cost of constructing a building, the amount of cost savings accomplished by instituting a recommended change, or some other figure that reflects something about how much a professional has accomplished.

The "contingency" approach has the advantage of being relatively simple for clients to understand. It also projects an image of being "fair" to these people. It is hard for people to feel cheated by, for example, a lawyer who takes a reasonable percentage of a personal injury award or an architect who takes a reasonable percentage of the cost of constructing a building. However, this approach can create incentives for professionals to act against their clients' best interests. It can encourage lawyers to do only a little bit of work and accept a small (but sure) settlement instead of doing much litigation to obtain a large (but unsure) award. Or it can encourage an architect to add design features to a building that a client does not really need in order to increase total construction costs.

Retainer. With this approach, fees are set prior to a "covered" time period during which clients will receive up to a predetermined level of services without paying any extra fees. For some prepaid health and legal service firms, the retainer or prepaid fee entitles clients to unlimited services.

This approach has the major advantage of providing some certainty for both professionals and their clients. Both sides are able to predict the financial consequences of their relationship. However, the professional service organization that uses a retainer approach must be skilled at forecasting how frequently its services will be utilized in each time period, just like an insurance company must skillfully estimate how many claims it will receive. If usage is underestimated when determining the fee, then serious losses could result.

Hybrid. For many professional service organizations, the best fee-setting approach will amount to a hybrid or combination approach. A certain law firm may find it best to use a prepaid or retainer approach combined with a time and expenses approach for any hours worked beyond a specified level per year. For example, in 1979, former Illinois Governor Dan Walker offered a service for a prepaid fee of $60 per year that included unlimited telephone consultations, a prepared simple will, and, in most cases, any necessary calls or letters in the client's behalf. If more work were required, the prepaid client would get it at 10 percent to 25 percent off the firm's regular fees.[4]

Actually, the best approach for any given organization will depend on a host of factors, including the organization's objectives, the nature of its target markets, and its competitive situation. For instance, a firm seeking to penetrate a very fee-sensitive market that is being sought by numerous competitors will most likely be forced into using a fixed sum approach and charging very low fees. On the other hand, a firm seeking to skim a fee-insensitive market that has attracted little interest from competitors will most likely turn to a time and expenses approach and charge whatever the market will bear.

TACTICS FOR FEE SETTING

A variety of tactical moves are available to a professional service organization to help make its fee-setting strategy more effective. Fees can be structured and presented to certain clients in ways that will produce added revenues for a firm. Instead of always staying very close to the selected average fee level and always using the same presentation approach, a firm can use fee tactics which introduce variation around a basic fee strategy. Thus, a firm can offer "discounts," demand "premiums," or utilize other fee tactics while still basically pursuing a strategy which, for example, stresses very high fees (on average) and time and expenses presentation approaches.

The offering of discounts is a common fee tactic in the professions.

Firms will often offer to lower a normal hourly/daily rate or other type of fee for clients who:

1. buy a very large volume of services
2. require services in a "slow" time period or season, or
3. need the services to support a socially beneficial venture.

The offering of a discount can make a client feel unique or special. This can mean the difference between obtaining or missing a new client or keeping or losing an old client.

The demanding of "premiums" is another fee tactic that is used by professional service organizations. A request for a higher than normal fee may be a profitable tactic when:

1. clients want work completed in an especially short period of time,
2. particularly unique and specialized services are required, or
3. clients want work done that presents certain risks to the reputation of the professional service firm (e.g., defending a legal client in a highly publicized court case).[5]

A client who does not understand the need to charge premiums in these situations may not be worth going after. Doing time-pressured, difficult, or risky work at normal fee rates can, over the long run, prove to be unprofitable.

Some professional service firms also vary their rates based on the "type of encounter" professionals have with clients. For example, some management consultants charge different rates for having luncheon meetings, doing training or teaching, conducting interviews, writing reports, talking on the phone, and so on. Similarly, doctors often vary their rates for normal office visits, emergency office visits, hospital visits, and so on. If this tactic is used, care must be exercised to establish a fee structure that encourages desired types of encounters and discourages undesirable encounters—without discouraging all types of encounters. A consultant, for instance, does not want to set a high fee for luncheon meetings if that will tend to discourage too many desirable clients from exploring possibilities further.

Another fee-setting tactic commonly used in the professions is the "high estimate." This is where the professional service organization gives a client an overly conservative estimate of how long it will take to provide a service or of how much the service will probably cost. The organization's best guess of what the fees will actually be is significantly lower than what it states in the estimate. Assuming that this high estimate does not lead too many potential clients to use competitors—which is a definite risk of using this tactic—what can be achieved is the delivery of a "pleasant surprise" to many of them when bills are finally delivered. By presenting them with total fees that are less than what they expected, the organization can often obtain more highly satisfied and loyal clients who are willing to pass on good word-of-mouth about the organization.

INITIATING CHANGES IN FEES

No matter what fee strategy a professional service organization chooses to use for a period of time, fees must be changed as cost, demand, and competitive factors evolve. When a change in fees is called for, decisions must be made about the direction and the extent of the change. Should a *general* change in fees be made covering all offerings or should only a *selective* change be implemented? As we discussed earlier, it is useful to consider the reactions of many different people when determining fees, including competitors (Will they undercut your cuts? Will they follow your hikes?), staff members (Will they demand higher salaries if fees are increased?), and regulatory officials. However, the reactions of clients are probably the most important to consider when initiating fee changes.

But trying to predict how clients will react to fee changes can be quite troublesome. The great uncertainty which many people experience when buying professional services tends to make their behavior with respect to fees difficult to understand. This behavior becomes even more troublesome to understand in situations where either buying decisions are made under great time pressure (e.g., selecting emergency medical care, retaining a criminal lawyer) or services are paid for in some significant part by insurance.

Zeithaml recently examined the issue of how *individuals* react to the fees charged by professionals.[6] Drawing from the considerable amount of research that has been done on how consumers react to prices of various *products* when faced with great uncertainty, limited information, time pressure, and so on,[7] she developed several hypotheses about how people react to the fees of professionals. Some of her notions include:

1. People tend to ignore or avoid information about fees prior to purchase, paying most attention to this information after services have been received.
2. People depend upon fees to indicate quality in services high in credence attributes (i.e., those services that they have difficulty evaluating even after they have received them).
3. People may prefer professionals with high fees over those with low fees in situations where high risk is perceived to exist.
4. People will tolerate higher fees for professionals with strongly positive reputations or images.

5. People experienced with a professional service are more likely to use fees as an indicator of quality than people with no experience.

6. Fees may be more important in the decision to return to a professional than they are in the initial decision.

7. When the need for a professional service arises urgently or unpredictably, people do not consider fees in making buying decisions.

8. When insurance covers professional care, fees are not a pivotal factor in the purchase decision.

Although these notions need to be tested by empirical research studies and they may not apply to how *organizations* buy professional services, they still deserve much attentioin. What Zeithaml has suggested, among other things, is that for many professional service organizations the raising of fees may be highly effective. However, for certain market segments which are well informed about fees and have an ability to judge quality work on their own—or for those segments that refrain from using needed professional services because they perceive fees as being unaffordable—the raising of fees would be a reckless move.

What this discussion points to is the need for a professional service organization to conduct research to try to explore the diverse possible client reactions to any contemplated fee change. The techniques available for forecasting client reactions to fee changes—or for studying price elasticity—have essentially been reviewed in Chapter 6. As we discussed there, an organization can seek to forecast demand levels at various fee levels by examining what people say (i.e., intentions surveys, intermediary estimates), what people do (i.e., market tests), or what people have done (i.e., time-series analysis, statistical demand analysis).

FEE COMMUNICATION AND ADMINISTRATION

Fee setting involves dealing with several other problems that deserve some discussion before concluding this chapter. First, in many situations, final fees cannot be determined until after *negotiations* have been conducted between the professional service organization and its clients. Once fees have finally been determined, an approach to *billing* clients must be developed. In addition, an approach to *collecting* delinquent accounts must also be formulated. Finally, some organizations need to reach decisions with regard to whether *fee-splitting* should be done with referral sources. We will briefly discuss how these tasks might be performed in a way that supports and does not detract from an organization's marketing effort.

Negotiations

Some professional service organizations have a policy of never negotiating over fees. Once they determine what they want to charge, they
essentially tell their clients or patients, in a nonthreatening way, to "take
it or leave it." They refuse to haggle over fees. Assuming that the fees
offered have been carefully formulated to take account of cost, demand,
and competitive conditions, such a policy can be highly effective—particularly for the organization with considerable experience and a strong
reputation in a service area. By avoiding negotiations, the organization
does not risk possible damage to its reputation that could arise if it is
perceived as being too nitpicky or too defensive about fees.

But for organizations that find a "take it or leave it" approach
unacceptable—either because certain business is attractive no matter
how it is obtained or because targeted clients seem to *enjoy* negotiating
before buying—negotiations should be approached in a systematic manner. Research should be conducted to obtain as full an understanding as
possible of the financial situation and attitudes of the potential client.
How much can they afford to pay? How much would it cost them *not* to
use the service? What services or expenses do they particularly dislike
paying large amounts for? This information can be obtained by questioning potential clients directly or by talking to others who may be familiar
with their situations.

Once this information has been acquired, the organization should
attempt to formulate an offer that will be perceived by the other party as
a "win." This type of offer would contain concessions that are designed to
give the other party the lower hourly fees, the use of less expensive
supporting equipment, or other changes from previous fee requests that
they desire most. If this offer is not accepted, other concessions should be
considered and offered if deemed appropriate. At all times, discussions
should remain friendly and nonthreatening, with as much a focus as
possible on the benefits of using the service rather than on the costs.

Billing and Collecting

The major idea to keep in mind when designing billing and collecting systems is to *avoid negative surprises.* Clients should be informed
about fees or changes in fees long before they actually receive bills. They
should also receive regular monthly statements (if appropriate). It is also
usually better to send people several small bills rather than a single very
large bill to cover a big project. Whether bills should be itemized or
contain merely a lump sum figure is a matter of some debate. The
disadvantage of itemizing is that it may provide a stimulus for clients to

question a firm's fees and methods, as they may be struck by things like how much they could have saved if less hours had been billed by partners.[8] The advantages of itemizing include what it can contribute to educating clients and building a sense of trust. The approach used should probably be dictated by the preferences of the client.

Getting people to pay bills on time is an important task that should be given priority attention. For one thing, people do not like to call on professionals to whom they owe money, so that if one wants repeat business one must make sure that the old business has paid its way. There is no magic solution to getting people to pay on time. Making the task easier for them by doing things like filling out insurance forms for them, taking credit cards, or (for organizations) helping them find needed credit can sometimes help. So can the sending of appreciation notes to clients who are prompt bill payers. But perhaps the best approach is the use of regular communication to remind them of their obligation. Threatening notes and collection agencies should be used, but only when situations have become unreasonable.

Fee-Splitting

Any marketing program must rely heavily on referral sources for obtaining leads and providing testimonials and recommendations. And one way to insure that referral sources keep working for your organization is to compensate them in some way, perhaps by giving them a percentage of the fees brought in as a result of their referrals. But fee-splitting is a very controversial topic in most of the professions, and it is even banned or considered unethical in some fields and in some locations.

The argument against fee-splitting is that it could lead professionals to refer clients or patients to other professionals because they are being paid to do so and not because they think those professionals will serve people's needs the best. For most professional service organizations, the decision on whether to split fees must be made with extreme caution and with a full understanding of the legal and ethical ramifications of taking this action.

An alternative to fee-splitting is the keeping of a "scorecard" on referrals. The frequency and dollar amounts of referrals could be recorded for all referral sources and receivers. Periodically, meetings could be held with each member of a firm's referral network to review the scorecard and see who is sending more referrals to whom. If referrals are out of balance, then special efforts could be made to rectify the situation in the coming months. If a firm finds that it is giving many more referrals than it receives from another firm for an extended period of time, then an adjustment in referral practices may be in order.

SUMMARY

Fee setting has become a much more challenging task for professional service organizations in recent years. Increased buyer sophistication about fees has created pressures to do fee setting in a cautious, thoughtful manner.

The first consideration in setting fees is the objectives of the organization. Different strategies toward fee setting will be dictated depending on whether an organization seeks to maximize profits, penetrate a market, skim a market, or merely satisfice.

Fee-setting strategy is defined by the average fee level and the fee presentation approach adopted by the organization. Levels can be determined using cost-oriented, demand-oriented, or competition-oriented methods. Possible fee presentation approaches include time and expenses, fixed sum, contingency, retainer, and hybrid. The best strategy for an organization to adopt will depend on its objectives and on the competitive situation it faces. Several fee tactics, such as the use of "high estimates," can make fee strategies more effective.

Fee changes must be initiated with caution. The reactions of other parties to fee changes are difficult to predict. In particular, it is hard to forecast how clients will react to fee changes, as many may even see higher fees as an indicator that better quality services are being provided. Sound research on potential client reactions should precede any fee changes.

Fee setting can also involve negotiations over fees, the development of billing and collection systems, and the determination of a policy with regard to fee-splitting. All of these tasks should be carried out with an eye toward supporting and not hindering the organization's marketing program.

NOTES

1. The discussion of calculating a "multiple," on pp. 170-171, has been adapted from H. Justin Davidson, "Marketing by Consulting Firms," in J.M. Rathmell, *Marketing in the Service Sector* (Cambridge, Mass.: Winthrop, 1974), pp. 205–8.

2. Irwin Sogofsky, "Marketing Research Firms: Stress Your Strong Suit When Pricing Custom Studies," *Marketing News*, May 14, 1982, p. 2-1.

3. Kent B. Monroe, *Pricing: Making Profitable Decisions* (New York: McGraw-Hill, 1979), pp. 223–37.

4. Jack Hafferkamp, "Mass-Merchandising of Legal Services," *Chicago*, July 1979, p. 101.

5. John Robshaw, "Professional Fees—How Much Should You Charge?" *CAmagazine,* September 1978.

6. Valarie A. Zeithaml, "The Acquisition, Meaning, and Use of Price Information by Consumers of Professional Services," working paper, Department of Marketing, Texas A&M University, 1982.

7. For a review see Monroe, *Pricing,* pp. 37–48.

8. Larry E. Greiner and Robert O. Metzger, *Consulting to Management* (Englewood Cliffs, N.J.: Prentice-Hall, 1983), p. 64.

10

MAKING SERVICES ACCESSIBLE:
Channels of Distribution Decisions

The three most important elements for success in business, they say, are location, location, and location. This truism is not wasted on Philadelphia lawyers Peter Levin and Steven Arkans, who run the Legal Service Center clinic there.

After three and one-half years in operation, with more than 20,000 clients, they decided they needed a new branch office.

They leased a big recreational vehicle, spent $4,000 to put in carpets and a desk, and sent their newly created mobile law office into shopping centers.

"We had reservations as to how the public would receive it," Mr. Levin said. "But the reaction has been unbelievably good. When the van is right there when people are shopping, they don't have any hesitancy about knocking on the door."

The overhead on the van is about $1,500 a week, not counting gas. In the first two weeks the mobile office handled 25 clients, who could pay by MasterCharge or Visa.

"There's no mystery about how much the fees will be, because they are clearly posted right on the outside of the van," said Mr. Arkans. An uncontested divorce goes for $245 plus costs, a will runs $45, a real estate settlement costs $245, and a first arrest for drunk driving costs $245.

The mobile office location schedule will vary until client demands set a more permanent one.

Source: National Law Journal, February 16, 1981, p. 39. © Copyright 1983, National Law Journal, reprinted with permission.

Professional service organizations are learning that they can no longer count on clients being willing to come to their offices at any time or in any place. While the days of needing to make "house calls" do not promise to return, most professionals are discovering that they must give increased attention to whether their services are available to target markets in a timely and accessible manner. People simply prefer to use professionals who are nearby, easy to reach, and easy to see when they want to see them. When a person perceives any difficulty in gaining access to a particular professional, they may choose a more accessible professional or even postpone or forego using the service altogether.

The need to be readily accessible to clients has long been recognized by big national CPA and consulting firms. They have typically set up well-staffed offices within a reasonable distance of any large concentration of clients.

But, recently, the need to have accessible branch offices has been recognized by a large number of law,[1] architectural, and engineering firms. They recognize that being physically close to the political "action," to building sites, or to manufacturing plants can give them an advantage in a targeted area over competing nonlocal firms that may be perceived as "outsiders" possessing little commitment to the area. Thus, many Chicago and New York law firms have established offices in Washington, D.C., while many architectural and engineering firms have set up new offices in growing Sun Belt cities. Where they find it impossible to establish branch offices, many firms are increasingly turning to joint-venture and subcontract arrangements with established firms in targeted areas.

In effect, branch offices and collaborating out-of-town firms are becoming the *channels of distribution* for many professional service organizations. They provide a channel or conduit through which a professional service firm can become more accessible to targeted clients. They are serving functions similar to that of wholesalers and retailers of tangible products.

Increased attention to accessibility can also be observed among those professionals seeking to attract more middle-class and lower-class *individuals* as clients. A wave of new types of channels have appeared designed to make it easier and more comfortable for individuals to obtain services. Examples of the use of relatively new channels include:

> The use of mobile offices such as the one described above. Similar ventures have been tried in other cities and by professionals in other fields. For example, PetVacx is a mobile veterinary care operation that parks itself in a different fixed location of the Maryland suburbs of Washington on each day of the week.
>
> The establishment of chain-type tax preparation, legal, dental, and eyecare clinics typified by H & R Block and its affiliated organization, Hyatt

Legal Services. H & R Block's accessible shopping-center locations have helped it grow to where it now prepares one out of every ten federal returns.[2] On a somewhat smaller but still significant scale are the Jacoby & Myers Legal Clinics, which now have over one hundred affiliated offices in California and New York. Other clinics like Sterling Dental Centers, Retail Dental Centers, and Pearle Vision Centers have become major factors in the markets in which they operate. Many of these chains have used franchising to expand and several have located themselves within major department stores like Sears, Montgomery Ward's, K-Mart, and Zayre's.

The establishment of legal, dental, and other types of cooperatives, where a group of professionals band together to offer groups of individuals special services and special fees. For example, people who pay a small fee to join the Consumer Services Cooperative in Maryland are given the privilege of using a panel of affiliated lawyers at significantly discounted rates. Another example is provided by the National Marketing Cooperative for Dentistry, which refers patients to its member dentists after receiving calls on a toll-free number (800-DENTIST).[3]

The use of videotape-based matching services. This has been used by a group of psychotherapists in the Washington, D.C., area. In the comfort of the matchmaker's living room, people in search of psychotherapy can watch *Therapist Preview*, where different therapists appear on tapes presenting their philosophies and backgrounds.[4]

And other new channel arrangements can be expected to appear in the near future.

Clearly, no single channel of distribution is right for all professional service organizations. Moreover, experience with many channels is still too new for someone to form a complete judgment about most of them. But no matter what channel arrangement an organization uses, the channel should provide:

1. Locations for delivering services that are convenient and attractive to large numbers of targeted clients.
2. Offices that all work cooperatively to provide a coordinated marketing program.

In this chapter, we will focus on how both of these desired channel features can be obtained by a professional service organization.

SELECTING LOCATIONS

Decisions concerning the locations of offices can be divided into two basic tasks. First, an organization must decide whether each targeted geographic segment deserves being served by its own office. Second, an organization must decide upon the best physical site to locate each office it decides it needs. We will discuss each of these tasks separately—although in reality they should be addressed in an interrelated fashion.

Does an Area Need an Office?

As a professional service firm grows from a small local practice to a regional, national, or international firm, management must make decisions on how many branch offices to open and where they should be located. Here is an example:

> Management Analysis Center (MAC) is a medium-sized (100+ professionals) management consulting firm headquartered in Cambridge, Massachusetts. It has branch offices in Chicago, Palo Alto, Los Angeles, Washington, D.C., and London. MAC's management must decide on a number of location issues. Should the firm serve the New York City area, where many clients are located, from its Boston office, or should it open an office in Manhattan? Should the firm open an office in Houston where management consulting services are growing very rapidly, or should Houston be prospected and serviced from Los Angeles? Should the firm open an office in the Far East, either in Japan or Australia, where some of its clients do business and many new accounts might be cultivated?

When a professional service organization decides to target a portion of its marketing effort toward a given geographic area—whether it is a region, state, county, city, or neighborhood—it should do so based on a careful analysis of the market potential of the area. Techniques such as those reviewed in Chapter 6 (e.g., chain ratio method) should be employed to forecast how much in billings can be expected from an area if a strong marketing program is targeted toward it. Consideration should be given to the difference in billings that could occur as a result of establishing an office in the area as compared to either providing service from out-of-town or collaborating with existing area firms. Will the new office add billings the firm would not obtain otherwise, or will it merely lead to the spreading around of the existing level of billings?

In addition to considering how revenues might be affected by the establishment of an office in a targeted area, the impact of such a move on costs must also be examined. Both the new costs and the *cost savings* of establishing a branch office must be considered.

Table 10–1 contains a listing of possible ways that setting up a branch office might affect the financial situation of a professional service organization. Forecasts of the market potential of the targeted area should be combined with assessments of the financial consequences and probability of occurrence of the effects listed in the table. Eventually, an overall judgment can be made of the benefits and costs of opening a branch. For some professionals, the best solution may involve the establishment of a *temporary* branch office designed to serve a particular client for the duration of a project or contract. The use of temporary offices is reasonably common in the architectural and engineering professions.

TABLE 10-1
POSSIBLE EFFECTS OF OPENING A BRANCH OFFICE

COULD INCREASE REVENUES BY:	COULD REDUCE COSTS BY:
1. Allowing prospective clients to phone or visit with less expense and difficulty.	1. Cutting the time and expenses needed for travel and phone calls to have discussions with clients.
2. Allowing the firm to respond faster to inquiries and requests from prospective and existing clients with phone calls, meetings, or visits.	2. Allowing more efficient office management systems (e.g., word processing) to be used without having to replace old systems.
3. Increasing the visibility of a firm, making it more likely to be considered by prospects.	
4. Suggesting to clients that a firm is more "personal" and has a strong commitment to serving their local geographic area.	
5. Motivating staff members to work harder at marketing the services of "their" office.	

COULD REDUCE REVENUES BY:	COULD INCREASE COSTS BY:
1. Creating an uncoordinated marketing effort.	1. Creating an uncoordinated marketing effort containing wasted time and expenses.
2. Making it more difficult to maintain quality control.	2. Requiring much travel time and expenses for having high-level people work at attaining coordination and control.
3. Taking talented personnel away from the "home" office where they might be able to attract more work through already established contacts and networks.	3. Requiring the firm to move existing staff or hire new staff.
4. Inviting competing firms to increase their efforts in the area.	4. Adding real estate, leasing, utility, security, and other expenses for running the office.
	5. Stimulating competitive reactions that make it necessary to use more expensive forms of promotion.

Different firms in the same profession are likely to come up with very different judgments about how to deal with branching. For example, Mahon reports that in the CPA field "Ernst and Ernst for years apparently pursued a policy of having small offices in many locations, while Price Waterhouse concentrated on a few number of very large offices."[5] The former strategy may have been seen as a way to increase the firm's visibility, while the latter strategy may have been viewed as a way to control costs (perhaps because visibility was not seen as a problem). What any organization decides to do about branching will be determined to a degree by how well it feels it can coordinate and control the activities of its branch offices or channels. We will address the subject of channel coordination and control after reviewing some issues about site location.

Selecting an Office Site

When an organization decides it needs to establish an office in a geographic area—or when it decides it needs a new office in an area where it already has one—numerous factors must be considered. Foremost among these factors are the *attitudes and behavior* patterns of targeted clients. If the targeted clients prefer the ambiance and are more likely to enter shopping-mall offices rather than offices in high-rise buildings, then various shopping malls should be evaluated as possible sites.

On the other hand, if targeted clients prefer to go to high-rent districts to obtain services—because they also like to visit the nearby shops and restaurants—then sites in these districts should be considered. In addition, the mode of transportation typically used by targeted clients when they come to visit should be examined. If people typically come by automobile, then a site with good access roads and easy, inexpensive parking is essential. Consideration should also be given to whether available sites can have interior decorating that clients find appealing. We will discuss how internal "atmospherics" can be used to project certain images and help an organization promote its services in Chapter 11.

Other factors to consider in selecting a site include:

1. *Where competitors are located.* In some professions, having sites closer to targeted clients than competitors can make a difference. Even the Big Eight CPA firms are apparently trying to "out-locate" each other, as two of them recently moved their Washington, D.C., area offices out to suburban locations near eagerly sought high-technology companies in the area.[6]

2. *Proximity to frequently used facilities.* Locating near hospitals, courthouses, universities, and libraries can be very helpful, as long as the site is still attractive to clients.

3. *Proximity to "facilitating intermediaries."* Locating near bankers, consultants, lawyers, accountants, laboratories, insurance companies, or others who supply supplemental services to clients (e.g., financing, consulting, tests) can be convenient for everyone, and it can also increase the frequency of referrals provided by these intermediaries, who may be prone to say: "Why don't you go see the ———— next door?"

4. *Proximity to restaurants and clubs.* Having convenient places to entertain clients can be helpful, particularly because it may help to overcome the

resistance of staff members to spend time entertaining and "selling" prospective or previous clients.

5. *The costs of mortgages, leases, utilities, security, parking, maintenance, and so forth.* Cost is a major factor in choosing a location. Firms typically face a choice between a high-cost location in the central business district near clients and referral sources and a low-cost location that will involve more travel time. A recent development that is making lower costs possible in central business districts involves fully equipped offices available under time-sharing plans. Thus in downtown Chicago, physicians can lease a one-room fully equipped office for $20 an hour, and this rate includes a well-staffed reception area, answering service, a medical technician, and maintenance.

6. *Anticipated trends in population, real estate prices, shopping patterns, and other features of an area.* An office needs to be well situated in future years as well as in the present.

7. *The flexibility of the arrangement for the site.* Can office space be rearranged or expanded if it becomes necessary? Can the site be abandoned without overwhelming costs if it is later deemed inappropriate?

There is no magic formula for combining all these factors into a decision about a site. However, some organizations formulate point systems where each site is given a total score determined by calculating a weighted sum of scores given to each factor. Weights are assigned to each factor based on how important that factor is to an organization. Exhibit 10–1 presents an example of how a point system might be applied by a particular law firm choosing between two sites. In this case, the greater expense of site 1 is compensated for by its greater client favorability and

EXHIBIT 10–1. Example of a site selection point system

Selection Factor	Importance Weight for Factor (5 = very imp., 1 = not imp.)	Scoring for Site 1*	Scoring for Site 2*
Client favorability	5	5	3
Absence of competitors	1	1	2
Proximity to facilities	2	5	4
Proximity to intermediaries	3	4	3
Proximity to entertainment	2	4	3
Low costs	4	2	4
Favorability of future trends	4	3	3
Flexibility	3	3	4
Total weighted score		85	80

*5 = Has very much of factor.
1 = Has very little of factor.

closer proximity to everything, making it a preferable site. Such a point system can definitely help an organization choose better sites, as can the use of certain elaborate mathematical models that have been employed extensively by big retail chains. But, ultimately, no matter what approach is used, research on each prospective site must form the basis for decision making.

COORDINATING AND CONTROLLING
CHANNEL MEMBERS

The professional service firm has three basic organizational structures it can employ to achieve coordination and control with a set of branch offices (and/or collaborating firms): a *macropyramid* structure, an *umbrella* structure, and a *conglomerate* structure.[7] The macropyramid structure has *all* planning and strategic decision making being done at a home or central office, with branch offices being left to implement strategies and carry out operations under a strict set of guidelines or procedures. The umbrella structure gives more autonomy to each branch and allows them to develop their own plans and strategies, as long as they remain consistent with the overall mission and strategic direction of the firm. The conglomerate structure gives even more autonomy to the branches, even allowing them to develop their own missions and strategic directions. What ties the branches together under this structure is only a dependence on a common financial resource base, such as a group of founding partners or investors. Figure 10–1 depicts the basic differences among these three structures.

The macropyramid structure obviously provides the most coordination and control, but the other two structures, by allowing offices to adapt to local conditions, can occasionally be profitable. Even if an umbrella or conglomerate structure is pursued, an emphasis on coordinating and controlling branch-office activities should still be present. Among other things, coordination and control are needed to make a marketing program function smoothly, with no offices working at cross-purposes to one another. Moreover, coordination and control are needed to keep work quality high so as not to damage the national (or regional) reputation of the firm.

An example of what can go wrong when adequate coordination and control are not achieved is provided by a recent experience of Kirkland and Ellis, a 240-lawyer firm based in Chicago. According to an article in *Forbes*, the firm ran into the following problem in 1978:

> After its Chicago headquarters represented Westinghouse in an antitrust suit against 29 uranium producers, the court discovered that the firm's

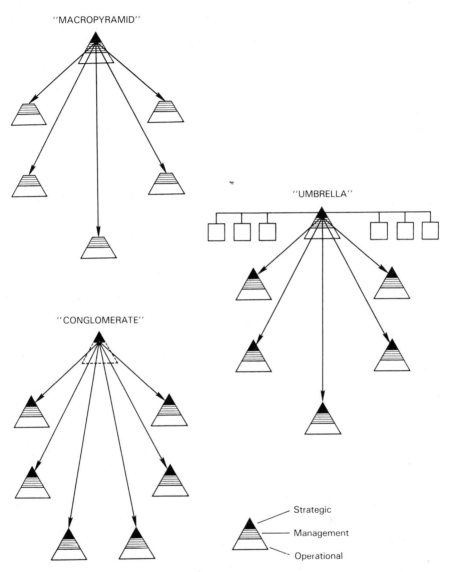

Source: Adapted from Simon Majaro, *International Marketing* (London: Allen and Unwin, 1977). Reprinted with permission.

FIGURE 10–1.   Three alternative organizational structures for attaining coordination and control of channel members

Washington office had done some work for the American Petroleum Institute, among whose members were three of the companies being sued by Westinghouse. Not only was Kirkland and Ellis dropped from the case, but it is now also being sued by a Westinghouse shareholder for the fees that it collected—perhaps as much as $2.5 million.[8]

Regardless of what organizational structure is employed, three basic approaches are available for improving coordination and control with branch offices or collaborating firms. First, the home office can offer *information and expertise* that channel members become dependent upon, making them more willing to go along with home-office programs and procedures. Second, the home office can offer *financial incentives* that encourage cooperation and support. Finally, the home office can create *legal agreements* that essentially force channel members to give cooperation and support.

The "information and expertise" approach can be highly effective and is unlikely to cause some of the conflicts that the other approaches can produce. This approach can be used when channel members have a need for data, guidance, specialized personnel, or other resources in order to serve their constituencies most effectively. The home office can essentially offer needed information and expertise it holds in exchange for cooperative actions by the channel members. When Big Eight CPA firms provide branch offices with elaborate manuals, training sessions, and easy-to-complete planning forms to guide their marketing effort—as several of the firms do—they do so with the hope that the branch offices will find it so easy and effective to simply use the supplied materials that all recommended policies and procedures will be automatically followed. In a similar vein, home offices that make certain highly skilled professionals or support personnel (e.g., proposal writers, marketing researchers) readily available to branch offices do so partly in the hope that these people will be used automatically by the branches and will help shape some consistency in the overall marketing program.

The offering of financial incentives, which can be done in conjunction with the offering of information and expertise, is a somewhat riskier but potentially more effective way of gaining coordination and control with channel members. Commissions, bonuses, and other incentives can be offered to top management and individual professionals of channel organizations if they contribute to the achievement of marketing goals established by the home office. Thus, these people might receive financial rewards if they identify a certain number of "live" leads in targeted segments during a year or if they win a given percentage of the competitive bidding situations they enter during the year. Such incentives can serve as a potent motivator of desired behaviors. However, the risk of using incentives is that it may lead channel personnel to focus too much on obtaining the rewards instead of managing with a broader perspective designed to help the entire organization carry out its basic mission. Conflicts and jealousies can also erupt over the way rewards are allocated.

The approach of setting up legal agreements—essentially to force coordination and control—may be necessary when the channels of distribution are made up of other organizations or legal entities. Having a carefully drawn joint-venture or subcontracting agreement can help to insure that certain marketing functions are performed by all parties. The danger with legal agreements is that conflicts can arise during the process of drawing them up, and even more serious and bitter conflicts (and lawsuits) can develop if an agreement is broken.

One form of legal agreement that can be used to achieve coordination and control with channel members is the *franchise* agreement. We will conclude this chapter with a short discussion about franchising.

Franchising

Historically, franchising has been an extremely popular way to distribute all types of commercial products and services. Cars, gasoline, fast food, hotel accommodations, and countless other things have been distributed effectively in this way. Recently, franchising has received considerable trial as a means of distributing professional services such as legal, dental, tax preparation, and eyecare services.

A *franchise system* has been defined by Stern and El-Ansary to denote:

> The licensing of an *entire* business format where one firm (the franchisor) licenses a number of outlets (franchisees) to market a product or service and engage in a business developed by the franchisor using the franchisor's trade names, trademarks, service marks, know-how, and methods of doing business.[9]

Thus, a professional service organization serving as a franchisor might provide the other organizations that are its franchisees a name (e.g., Jacoby and Myers Legal Clinic), know-how about how to run an automated office, national advertising support, advice on fee setting, and so forth. In exchange for this, the franchisees (which would be under separate ownership) might provide the franchisor with some opening franchise fee, additional fees based on a percentage of billings per year, the performance of certain marketing functions, the maintenance of certain required appearance and quality standards, and so forth.

Franchising can provide numerous benefits to both the franchisor and the franchisee. The franchisor can obtain a less costly way of expanding to reach new markets, since the franchisees bear much of the expense of expansion. In addition, the franchise agreement provides the franchisor with a means of coordinating and controlling the activities of its distribution channels (the franchisees).

The franchisee can obtain the following benefits from the arrangement, according to an article on franchising dental care by McIntyre and Weinrauch:[10]

1. Easier entry to markets
2. Financial aid for getting started
3. Less risk
4. Marketing expertise
5. Managerial expertise
6. Financial expertise
7. Name recognition
8. Centralized purchasing
9. Site selection expertise

Franchisees in other professions could probably obtain similar benefits.

Nevertheless, franchising has several drawbacks for both franchisors and franchisees. Franchisors can find themselves in situations where they have less control and are earning less money than they would if they owned and staffed all facilities and offices themselves. On the other hand, franchisees can readily find themselves in situations where they are mistreated by franchisors and have no recourse but to mount expensive lawsuits to obtain fair treatment. Most importantly, both franchisors and franchisees can find themselves extremely limited in terms of the market segments they can attract. Just like many people prefer to avoid fast-food franchises, many clients simply prefer to obtain professional services from more individualistic organizations.

SUMMARY

Professional service organizations are paying more attention to how accessible their services are to clients. New types of service distribution channels are emerging to provide clients with services they can obtain in a timely and convenient fashion.

One common decision that must be made about distribution is where to establish branch offices. Should a targeted geographic area have an office? If so, what site should be selected? A host of factors must be considered in making these judgments. The most important factors to consider have to do with how clients will react to having an office in various locations.

Coordination and control of the activities of channel members is essential for a smoothly functioning marketing program, regardless of whether a macropyramid, umbrella, or conglomerate organizational structure is employed. Coordination and control can be achieved by providing needed information and expertise, by offering financial incentives, and by setting up legal agreements. The franchise agreement is a type of legal agreement that is being used with increasing frequency in the professions.

NOTES

1. See Anthony Spaeth, "Long Arm of the Lawyers," *Forbes,* August 6, 1979, p. 55.

2. See Carol E. Curtis, "Life After April 15," *Forbes,* April 13, 1981, p. 130.

3. See "Coop to Market Traditional Dentistry," *Marketing News,* May 29, 1981, pp. 5–6.

4. See Stephanie Mansfield, "And Today's Feature: Screening the Shrinks on Tape," *Washington Post,* October 22, 1982, p. C1.

5. James J. Mahon, *The Marketing of Professional Accounting Services* (New York: Wiley, 1978), p. 129.

6. See Leslie Zupan, "Big 8 Mount New Campaigns," *Washington Business Journal,* August 23, 1982, p. 1.

7. These structures have been adapted from those suggested in Simon Majaro, *International Marketing* (London: Allen and Unwin, 1977).

8. Spaeth, "Long Arm," p. 55.

9. Louis W. Stern and Adel I. El-Ansary, *Marketing Channels* (Englewood Cliffs, N.J.: Prentice-Hall, 1977), pp. 407–8.

10. See Bonnie J. McIntyre and J. Donald Weinrauch, "Opportunities and Challenges in Franchising Professional Dental Care," in J.H. Donnelly and W.R. George, eds., *Marketing of Services* (Chicago: American Marketing Association, 1981), pp. 99–103.

11

COMMUNICATIONS:
Personal Contact and Selling

"We can now aim a rifle instead of a shotgun at the architectural business," King Graf, executive business development vice president of the giant practice, Hellmuth, Obata and Kassabaum, told a seminar on architectural marketing. HOK now employs 850 people. "To compete for major work we had to be a major size. We decided to develop a business plan that would allow us to grow," said Graf. "To do that, we decided to prepare and implement a business market strategy which would feed the firm."

HOK spends at least 6 percent of its fee income on marketing. As Graf put it, "Make a friend before you need a friend . . . we want potential clients who, when they have a building program, will put us on their list." HOK goes about marketing with ruthless efficiency. Its marketing directors and coordinators meet twice a year to discuss "what types of projects we consider will be active in the next six months." They draw up a priority list of perhaps three possible industries and, from that, a list of companies or institutions within those industries. The list is circulated. If anyone in HOK knows the vice president of construction or of "facilities" in any of the firms on the list, they will phone them and ask for a preliminary interview. According to Graf, over 90 percent accept.

HOK has extensive libraries containing publications in which the names of those responsible for buildings in the remaining firms (or institutions, or universities—or whatever) can be looked up. Brochures are sent to them with a covering letter and, according to Graf, "30–40 percent respond to that letter—we phone again a month later and ask for a preliminary interview." Again, he says, over 90 percent accept. The interview itself is carefully planned. "It is very important to find out who you are going to be talking to and make sure to show and talk about material relevant to him—and to talk accurately and confidently about the design of a quality facility for him," said Graf.

HOK never assumes that potential clients will know how large and diverse the practice is or the buildings it has designed. (HOK has not only designed a wide range of building types, including hospitals, offices, prisons, schools, and airports but offers a wide range of skills, from engineering to graphics, and from land-use planning to interior design.) First, they are shown a slide of HOK's logo and then a map showing how its various offices are distributed throughout the United States. Then some slides of a few projects which are likely to be familiar to the potential client—the National Air and Space Museum in Washington ("the most visited museum in the world—the potential client has probably been there"); the Winter Olympic stadium at Lake Placid ("the U.S. ice hockey team beat the Russians there in 1980, so that building takes on a new dimension"); the Dallas/Fort Worth regional airport ("the country's largest airport"); and so on. Initially the slides are what Graf describes as "soft pictures, people using the building." The potential client will then think, "So HOK designed that." Then, after explaining briefly the diversity of the practice, projects of specific interest to the particular potential client are shown. "Be as specific as possible as quickly as possible."

After the interview, "invite the vice president to your office and walk him through the drafting office where he can see the title blocks on the drawings . . . keep in touch, call routinely, invite him again, put him on your mailing list." The idea, of course, is that when the potential client comes to build, HOK will be among the practices he will consider as architects. "Once you are on that list," said Graf, "go into a reactive posture—and you all know how to do that."

The quality of staff, not only as architects, but in the way they project themselves, is vital in obtaining contracts, according to Jerry Sincoff, HOK's executive vice president for project operations. "When we all went to school we didn't learn about personality development," he said, "but it is important to have people in the office who can speak about themselves—and the firm—in a fine clear way." It is talking to and being with the client that is important, he said. As soon as HOK gets wind of a potential contract, a project manager and other members of the team who will work with the client are selected. "We always try to select people who are available, persuasive and credible for that specific project," said Sincoff. "Together they plot a strategy for winning this one."

Enthusiasm in the "wrapping up" process is essential, he said. "Tell the client you really want to work on his job." Clients are kept happy, he said, by "quality design, quality management and quality service," so HOK aims, he said, for a "quality product, approximately on time and approximately within budget." And for the next project, said Graf, it helps to have a list of known, tested, satisfied clients to use as references, but "call and check them out before you put them on that list."

Source: Excerpted from "HOK: Soft Pictures, Hard Sell," *Architectural Journal,* April 1982, pp. 39–40. Reprinted with permission.

The manner in which in-person communications are conducted with members of target markets is a crucial element of any marketing program. For most professional service organizations, *personal contact* is probably the most important of all the tools available within the communications element of the "marketing mix." Personal contact—or personal selling—typically plays a larger role in persuading clients to buy a professional service than various forms of public relations and advertising that can also be used for promotional purposes. The risk that most perceive in selecting a professional makes it necessary to be able to reassure and persuade them through direct, personal messages rather than just impersonal media.

Because of its predominant importance in communications, we will discuss personal contact first in this chapter and treat the other communications tools of public relations (including brochure and newsletter development) and advertising in the next two chapters. However, by separating our discussion of the different communications tools into three chapters, we do not mean to suggest that personal contact, public relations, and advertising should be distinctly independent activities. To the contrary, all of these activities should be performed with a recognition that they are interdependent and require joint planning. For example, the personal contact program should support any advertising program, and vice versa. Figure 11–1 shows all the communications tools available to the professional service organization, pointing out how they are interdependent.

As our opening story about HOK suggests, the personal contact or selling program of a professional service organization cannot be organized in a haphazard fashion. A systematic program is needed, and several factors must be considered in developing the program. First, the organization should consider how much emphasis and resources it wants to devote toward personal contact versus other promotional tools. The legal and ethical rules governing "solicitation" in the given profession must be consulted, and if certain forms of selling seem to be prohibited, then less emphasis may have to be given to personal contact—although certain more subtle forms of selling are certain to be permissible. In

FIGURE 11-1. Communications tools for professional service organizations

addition, the feelings of prospective clients and of staff members (who have to sell) about various promotional tools must be weighed.

Once the level of emphasis and resources for personal contact has been determined, other issues to address in the personal contact planning process include:

1. How should the personal contact effort be organized? Who should do the selling and how should they be assigned to sales targets?

2. How can enough time be allocated to personal contact by the professionals who have been selected to do it? How can selling be made more convenient and more financially rewarding for staff members?

3. How can the major steps of the personal selling process—lead-finding and qualifying, courting, proposal preparation, presentation, and negotiating and closing—be carried out more effectively?

The remainder of this chapter contains an in-depth examination of each of these questions.

ORGANIZING FOR SELLING

The marketing-oriented, responsive, professional service organization will have its entire staff doing selling in one form or another. From the way people answer the telephone to the way they conduct themselves in public places, the staff of such an organization will project various explicit and implicit sales messages that present the organization as friendly, conscientious, professional, and competent. But the bulk of the personal selling in an organization will typically be done by a limited number of people. We will now discuss who those people should be and how they should be organized.

Who Should Sell?

Most professional service organizations will find that it is preferable to have the professionals who perform professional services also be the primary sellers of those services. Such an approach is consistent with being client oriented, since clients generally prefer dealing with and buying from the professionals who will be doing the work for them rather than "front-persons" or full-time salespersons. In a situation which they approach with great uncertainty anyway, clients do not want to feel uncertain about the professionals they will be working with. They would rather get to know professionals before using them, and feel reassured that the professionals understand their problems and are highly competent and experienced practitioners.

The notion that professional services should be sold primarily by practicing professionals has been advanced by several authors. In one of the most important early discussions of this subject, Wittreich stated: "The service firms represented by true professionals (i.e., those who can do the work) are far more valuable to their clients than those represented by professional salesmen."[1] A similar conclusion was reached more recently by Gummesson, who stated: "The person who is a marketer of the service usually must also be prepared to take part in the operation of assignments."[2]

In discussing this issue with respect to architects and engineers, Coxe concluded: "Clients have demonstrated a clear preference for marketing organizations composed of closer-doers, where the professional making the sale can assure the client that he or she will be personally involved, to a credible degree, during the execution of the project."[3] And Denney stated the following about selling by accountants:

> One of the fundamental misconceptions many accountants have about marketing is that all of this activity should generate new business without any personal effort on their part. They think that someone else can bring in the new clients and then they can take over and do the work. Unfortunately, they're wrong.
>
> A well-conceived marketing plan merely identifies growth opportunities and presents an organized approach to maximize these opportunities. While some aspects of a marketing plan (such as advertising, a firm brochure, or contributions to a worthwhile cause) do not require much person-

al contact, the successful marketing of accounting services really becomes, basically, a personal marketing activity.

It takes an accountant to sell accounting services. The public relations firm, the ad agency, the graphics artist, and the consultant can't do the final selling. *You* have to make the plan work. You have to do the personal marketing.[4]

The need to have professionals who can both provide services and sell them can put a strain on a firm. An emphasis on selling can turn off highly competent professionals, who may choose to seek employment where they merely have to practice their profession. Attracting and maintaining a high-quality professional staff—and keeping quality control high—can therefore be difficult when selling is emphasized. Nevertheless, most firms find it worthwhile to encourage professionals to develop selling skills. Fortunately, there are training programs and seminars available for teaching people how to sell more effectively. For example, Exhibit 11–1 presents an outline of a seminar on developing selling skills offered for professional service organizations by a consulting firm that specializes in the marketing problems of lawyers and accountants. And numerous less specialized selling seminars are available on a regular basis around the country.

However, regardless of how much training certain people receive, they may simply not be cut out for selling. Good salespeople must therefore be sought during the recruiting process. But trying to predict the professionals who will be successful salespeople is not easy. No published research has been done on the traits to look for in hiring professionals to sell professional services. And, for that matter, the considerable amount of research that has been done on the traits of successful salespersons of other goods and services has not produced definitive conclusions.[5]

Nevertheless, numerous lists of the traits of good salespersons have been offered. Mayer and Greenberg, for example, offered one of the shortest lists.[6] Their seven years of fieldwork led them to conclude that the effective salesperson has at least two basic qualities: (1) *empathy*, the ability to feel as the buyer does, and (2) *ego drive*, a strong personal need to make the sale. Using these two traits, they were able to make fairly good predictions of the subsequent performance of applicants for sales positions in three different industries.

To arrive at a policy concerning the traits to look for to find professionals who can sell, the organization should examine the traits of its own successful "salespersons." There may be unique aspects of the organization's situation that allow only certain kinds of people to excel at bringing in new business. Successful salespersons should be compared to less successful ones to see if any distinguishing characteristics stand out. The knowledge acquired from such a comparison should be incorporated into the recruiting process.

EXHIBIT 11-1.   Advanced marketing–selling program

This program would be complementary to and build on the Basic Marketing–Selling Orientation. We believe that this new program should have the following objectives:

- Introduce professionals to the concept of professional selling.
- Understand the principles that form the foundation of the selling process.
- Become acquainted with the communications skills needed for effective selling.
- Provide opportunities for professionals to practice integrating selling principles with selling skills.
- Apply the newly learned selling principles and skills to actual selling situations.
- Provide opportunities for professionals to position themselves to sell prospective clients.
- Introduce the process for targeting and planning approaches to sell prospective clients.

To achieve these objectives, we recommend a two-day training program that uses lecture–discussion, guide design exercise, additional case studies, and independent role plays as the basic program approach. The proposed topics that would be included are as follows:

DAY 1

8:30–9:00 A.M. (.5 hours) Lecture–Discussion	1. Introduction to the Concept of Prospecting and Qualifying Prospects
9:30–12:00 A.M. (3 hours) Case Study & Group Discussion	2. Reviewing Actual Case Data on a Small Closely Held Prospective Company and Developing an Approach to Qualify and Sell the Prospect
1:00–1:30 P.M. (.5 hours) Lecture–Discussion	3. Introducing the Concept for Selling Professional Services
1:30–2:30 P.M. (1 hour) Lecture & Group Exercise	4. Understanding the Principles Underlying the Professional Selling Process
2:30–3:30 P.M. (1 hour) Lecture & Group Exercise	5. Understanding the Communications Skills for Selling Effectively Professional Services
3:30–5:00 P.M. (1.5 hours) Group Exercise	6. Integrating the Selling Principles and the Communications Skills

DAY 2

8:00–12:00 A.M. (4 hours) Role Plays & Group Discussion	7. Making the Professional Selling Process Work in Actual One-to-One Selling Situations
1:00–5:00 P.M. (4 hours) Role Plays & Group Discussion	8. Continuation of the Selling Process in Actual Selling Situations
5:00–5:30 P.M. (.5 hours) Lecture–Discussion	9. Wrapping up the Professional Selling Process

Source: Marketing Institute International Corporation, Washington, D.C. (MII-CORP), 1982. Reprinted with permission.

Sales Assignments

Once an organization determines who should do its selling, it must decide on how to assign these people to various selling responsibilities. Two interrelated issues must be addressed: (1) who should perform various selling functions? and (2) who should be assigned responsibility for different target markets? We will address both of these questions below.

Assignment of Selling Functions. Weld Coxe, a well-known management consultant for architects and engineers, sees a need for firms in those fields to have the following people performing various selling functions:

1. *Closer*: One who ultimately delivers the professional proposal to the client and wins the contract.
2. *Courter*: One who, during the get-acquainted stage, wins the confidence of the client in the firm's ability to do the job.
3. *Lead finder*: One who knocks on doors or otherwise finds the leads to be courted and closed.
4. *Coordinator*: One who maintains the firm's selling resources and pulls together the statements of qualification, proposals, interviews, presentations, and so on, whenever they are needed in the selling process.
5. *Marketing manager/director*: One who is ultimately responsible for seeing that it all happens.[7]

Similar labels would apply for other types of professional service organizations. These labels could be used to describe functions that must be performed in selling to either new or existing clients. An existing client can still be probed for leads, courted, and so on.

Several options exist for assigning personnel to the various selling functions. First, an organization could rely on "pure" marketing and selling personnel—or staff members who are not "doers" or providers of the actual professional services—to do everything but "closing," which would be done primarily by doers. This approach has the advantage of taking much of the demands of doing selling off of overly busy doer/ professionals, helping to make sure that all the selling functions get completed properly. The disadvantage of this approach is that clients may not like being contacted initially or courted by sales or marketing personnel, preferring to have all their dealings from the very beginning with the professionals who might be serving them.

A second approach to assigning personnel to selling functions would be to use junior professionals for most of the lead-finding and courting and senior people only for closing. Pure marketing personnel would be used more in a research support and prodding (i.e., reminding doers to perform their selling functions) capacity rather than in a selling one. This approach has the advantage of giving junior people exposure and experience in selling. It also gives clients the opportunity to deal with doers from the very beginning. It will not, however, satisfy those clients who prefer to deal with the "boss" or the "big hitters" all along.

A final approach would be to allow high-level doers who like to sell and who are good at selling to do most of the lead-finding, courting, and closing. Again, pure marketing personnel would be used more in a research support and prodding capacity. This approach will work well when clients prefer to deal with top people. The approach also helps to insure that the best sellers do most of the selling. The problems with this approach are that it makes it harder to give junior people experience in selling, it can lead to less quality-control activity, and it is expensive. Having senior people working at lead-finding instead of building up billable hours can be costly.

The best approach for any given professional service organization to use in assigning selling functions will depend on several factors. Consideration must be given to the desires and preferences of clients, the capabilities and interests of staff members, the selling activities of competitors, and so forth. The organization may find that one assignment approach works best for all target markets or that different approaches should be used for different markets.

Assignment to Target Markets. Someone in the organization must be assigned the responsibility of coordinating the selling effort toward each target market and, perhaps, toward each targeted client. Market managers, client officers, client managers, account executives, or individuals with similar titles must be assigned the task of making sure that all necessary information is gathered about targeted clients and that all necessary selling functions are performed for those clients. In addition, some individuals must be made responsible for selling to or cultivating referral sources. The top marketing official of the organization will have to work hard to make sure that all these individuals are performing their selling tasks properly.

Numerous options exist for assigning people to target markets. Different people—who could be "pure" marketing, junior, or senior people depending on what has been decided about who should perform the bulk of the selling functions (see above)—could be assigned to coordinate selling for different geographic markets, for different types of services, for different types of clients, or for different types of referral sources. No assignment scheme is best for all professional service organizations. The best scheme will be the one that allows all targeted clients to be researched fully, called on frequently and appropriately, and serviced properly. Such a scheme should minimize duplicated effort and also minimize chances for conflict or disagreement over "turf" between staff members.

ALLOCATING TIME AND EFFORT TO SELLING

The need to have busy professionals—who may prefer doing other things with their time than selling—devote much time and effort to selling creates problems for many organizations. And some organizations have an opposite problem. They find that certain key people spend too much time and effort in selling. These organizations would be better off if these high-fee people had more billable hours and spent more time and effort trying to improve quality control.

Striking a balance in terms of the time and effort devoted by professionals to selling requires careful analysis, planning, and control. The organization must consider how it wants to assign the various selling functions, as discussed previously, and then devise methods to make it convenient and rewarding for each professional to devote approximately the amount of time and effort toward selling that the assignment approach calls for. Several methods for making selling more convenient and more rewarding for professionals are discussed in the following two sections.

Making Selling More Convenient

The top marketing official, or a member of this person's staff, should have the responsibility of continually prodding and reminding professionals to perform their selling functions. "Tickler" lists should be sent to all selling professionals on a regular basis, providing a specific breakdown on which prospective clients need to be called, which old clients need to be entertained, which referral sources need to be interviewed, and so on during a stated time period. In addition to these lists, the marketing staff could provide professionals with recommended scripts or statements that could be used in discussions with clients. For example, one large East-coast engineering firm provides all its engineers with a stack of preprint-ed small cards containing a list of statements and questions that can be used when telephoning either prospective clients or old clients. This firm also determines how frequently each client should be called based on an estimate of the potential of each client. This is calculated by multiplying (1) the expected size of a client's contracts times (2) the estimated probability of obtaining those contracts with a good sales effort.

Other ways to make selling more convenient, and therefore more likely to be done in appropriate amounts by professionals, involve the combining of selling with other activities. Mixing selling and other activi-ties is particularly important for smaller organizations that cannot afford marketing staff support to make the performance of selling functions more convenient. In the following paragraphs, we shall elaborate on how selling can be mixed with "doing," marketing research, and pleasure-seeking.

Mixing Doing and Selling.　　Many opportunities for selling one's services emerge while services are actually being provided. Clients can be urged to continue using the organization's services, to try other services offered by the organization, or to recommend the organization to others. This selling can be done in a subtle, indirect way or in more overt, direct ways.

One clearly effective way to sell one's services is simply by doing good work in a friendly, industrious, honest, and patient manner. The clients who receive this type of service feel they have been treated in a valued and respected manner. The following quote from a recent article on marketing for physicians states this viewpoint in another way:

> While the huge majority of patients can't judge their doctor's techni-cal ability, they can and do judge whether they have been treated with respect and concern by a fellow human being who wants what is best for them. They know if they have been made welcome and comfortable during their frequently reluctant and apprehensive visits to the doctor's office. They know if their sometimes poorly articulated questions have been heard and answered.
>
> "The most successful doctor," says Millard Mills, management consul-tant from Waterloo, Iowa, now retired, "answers five questions with every medical problem except the minor ones: (1) What is wrong? (2) What caused it? (3) What should be done about it? (4) What will it cost? (5) How long will it take?"[8]

The professional who sells in this manner will do little things like keep records of names, stories, or background details that clients enjoy talking about. This type of professional will also do things like put clients on hold when they phone so that files can be quickly checked for purposes of starting conversations with comments that show great familiarity with the situation of the phone callers. The phone will also be used by these professionals to call clients to follow-up on services or to offer new suggestions or ideas at unexpected times (to show that the client is on their minds).

Other slightly more overt ways of mixing doing and selling involve the discussion and endorsement of other new or different services provided by the organization. Discussion of such services can sometimes be stimulated by having staff members who specialize in these other services work for a period of time on the "team" providing the original services. Thus, accounting firms will sometimes put management services or tax experts on audit teams in the hope that they will have the opportunity to discuss their more specialized services with clients. *Cross selling* of services can also be done to a degree through the recommendations made by professionals in final reports or closing presentations.

Of course, it is possible to be quite direct and overt with clients about one's desire to keep them loyal and ready to supply good word-of-mouth recommendations. Many clients will actually think more highly of a professional who regularly tells them that their business is deeply appreciated and that referrals would be most welcome. They might see such a professional as being more forthright and honest. However, overt selling to existing clients must have limits, since too much selling can lead people to view professionals as possessing too much "hype" and not enough substance.

Mixing Research and Selling. Since finding time for doing marketing research can be just as difficult for many professional service organizations as finding time for selling, one way to make it more likely that significant amounts of both are done is by combining them. It is possible to conduct marketing research studies in such a way that *subtle* selling is being done while collecting information. Professionals can be asked to conduct telephone or personal interviews with existing or prospective clients about their anticipated service needs, their decision-making procedures, and the attributes they seek in professionals. The subtle selling can be done by impressing respondents with polite, intelligent questions and astute side comments. The idea is to leave respondents with a positive impression of the professionalism and competence of the interviewer, making it more likely that they will call on the interviewing organization when services are required. Needless to say, the information obtained during these interviews can also be valuable in its own right for making various targeting, positioning, fee-setting, distribution, and promotion decisions (see Chapter 7).

However, we must offer one important warning about mixing marketing research and selling: *Do not allow overt selling to be done during a research interview.* In conducting research interviews, respondents should feel that the interview is being done to gather information and not to sell anything. If respondents perceive an interview as actually being a sales call—either because questions or comments are not subtle enough or because sales "pitches" are really being made—they may refuse to cooperate and may also form a negative impression of the interviewing organization. For this reason, all questionnaires should be pretested and reviewed carefully before being used with targeted clients.

Mixing Pleasure and Selling.   Making selling a form of entertainment for professionals is another way to get more selling done. Thus, professionals can be encouraged—and perhaps given funds—to interact with existing and prospective clients or referral sources at favored restaurants, country clubs, political groups, civic organizations, alumni gatherings, trade association meetings, or other places where they enjoy themselves. This *classic* approach to developing a professional practice still has much value in today's more sophisticated marketing environment.

The professional service organization that intends to make significant use of this approach must carefully target the organizations and places it chooses to frequent. Professionals should spread themselves around to different places and not concentrate at one particular club. Where possible, research should be done on the club memberships and leisure-time preferences of key individuals in targeted markets. For example, several Big Eight CPA firms have been known to keep extensive files on the club memberships and association activities of chief financial and executive officers of targeted companies.

Opportunities to interact with valuable referral sources in entertaining settings should also not be overlooked. Several Big Eight CPA firms, for example, have lavish "Alumni Banquets" for their former employees, providing an entertaining way to see old friends and make contacts with people who may now be serving in capacities where they select CPAs for their organizations. Besides former employees, other people who can often serve as valuable referral sources (depending on the profession) include:

1. Former employees of clients.
2. Trade association officers and staff members.
3. Faculty members at nearby universities.
4. Professionals in the same field who are not competitors (because their organizations are much larger, much smaller, or nonlocal).

5. Facilitating intermediaries who provide complimentary or supporting services (e.g., lawyers, bankers, consultants, specialist physicians, etc.).
6. Former classmates.

These and other carefully selected people should be regularly invited to lunch, golf, tennis, parties, conferences, or other enjoyable pursuits.

There are, of course, limits to how much entertaining/selling a professional service organization can do. These activities can be extremely time-consuming and expensive and can often yield inferior results to less-expensive, public-relations forms of promotion (see Chapter 12). Professionals often have difficulty distinguishing their organizations from competitors and describing their organization's distinctive competencies between drinks, golf strokes, or poker hands. Printed and visual materials, and someone's full attention, may be necessary to convey the appropriate messages. A decision on how much entertaining/selling should be done has to be based on careful examination of the preferences and decision-making processes of targeted clients.

Making Selling Rewarding

Professionals can be encouraged to spend more time selling by offering monetary and status incentives. Bonuses, higher salaries, commissions, attributions, prizes, or other monetary rewards can be offered to professionals for achieving any of a variety of different goals in their selling pursuits. Rewards can be based on the number or the billings of new clients a person brings in, the number of "live" or "qualified" leads from targeted markets the person identifies, or some other performance indicator. The indicator and rewards must be selected carefully, as it is possible to misdirect or over-incentivize selling activity through the types of monetary rewards being used. As we discussed earlier, an organization can have too much effort directed toward selling and too little toward quality control. Bonuses and salary increases are probably less likely to produce these types of problems than commissions, attributions, or prizes.

Care must also be exercised in using *status* rewards to encourage selling. People should be promoted and given other status privileges (e.g., better offices, more secretarial and staff support) if they are productive at selling. But promotions should not occur if people are *only* productive at selling and not at performing other necessary professional duties. It is important to have top-level people who can do competent work as well as sell. These kinds of people allow an organization to retain existing clients—something which is easier and less costly to do than attracting new ones.

CARRYING OUT THE MAJOR STEPS IN
PERSONAL SELLING

The literature on selling is filled with tips and suggestions on tactics for selling more effectively. In this section, we will discuss the major steps and tactics that people have found helpful in selling professional services. The discussion will focus on selling to *new* clients. The steps are shown in Figure 11–2 and discussed below.

Lead-Finding and Qualifying

Some professional service organizations are able to generate enough promising leads based on word-of-mouth recommendations from satisfied former clients. Moreover, other organizations are able to generate enough leads through the effective use of public relations and/or advertising. (We cover public relations and advertising in Chapters 12 and 13.) But professional service organizations typically must supplement public relations and/or advertising with the work of people engaged in lead-finding, since it is often more cost-effective to identify certain promising leads in this way.

Identifying clients who are likely to require certain professional services within a short period of time is a task that requires considerable planning and discipline. Whether this task is assigned to full-time sales personnel or to professionals serving as doer/sellers, it must be performed in a focused, systematic manner. As our opening example to this chapter stressed, it helps to aim rifles at business prospects instead of shotguns.

Persons assigned to lead-finding should therefore be instructed to limit their search to only given target markets. Probably the best place for them to obtain leads within their assigned target markets is from existing clients in those markets. These people can be casually but directly questioned (during work sessions, social gatherings, or phone conversations) about their knowledge of impending work elsewhere in their own organizations or in organizations just like their own. They may know about what is going on in other organizations through trade association activities, former colleagues who have moved on, business contacts, and so on.

Other valuable sources of leads include:

1. *Surveys of targeted clients.* Questions can be asked in telephone and personal interview surveys about anticipated service needs. Of course, overt sales calls should not be made immediately on leads identified in this way, unless an unsolicited request for such a call is made by the surveyed party. An immediate follow-up sales call can lead clients to question the

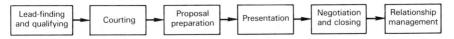

FIGURE 11–2. The major steps in personal selling

integrity of the survey and of the surveying organization. Instead, attempts should be made to "bump into" these leads at professional meetings or social gatherings, or to have some intermediary set up an introductory meeting or provide a referral.

2. *Surveys of referral sources.* In addition to checking with current and prospective clients, people who regularly provide referrals should be contacted periodically to check if they are aware of any potential work. Trade association staff members, facilitating intermediaries who provide complementary and support services, and others should all be questioned regularly.

3. *News reports and articles.* Stories written or broadcast about targeted clients sometimes indicate that services will be needed. The sighting of such stories can provide an opportunity to send congratulatory letters or make introductory phone calls. Clipping services can be hired to allow better monitoring of these stories.

4. *Annual reports and other organizational publications.* Future service needs can sometimes be revealed in publications put out by corporations or other organizations. And future service needs might be inferred by examining organizational trends revealed in data displayed in these publications.

5. *Government files.* If services are being sold that would be useful to people who have just filed for building permits, patents, copyrights, stock offerings, automobile licenses, and so forth, then the relevant government files should be checked on a regular basis.

6. *Reporting services.* Professionals in fields like architecture, engineering, and management consulting regularly consult the *Commerce Business Daily, Engineering News Record, Dodge Reports,* and other reporting services that provide listings of leads. Unfortunately, many of the leads provided by these sources are rather old and hotly pursued by numerous competitors.

7. *"Cold" calls.* Targeted clients can simply be called on by phone or in person, asked if they expect to need services, and then be given some type of initial sales presentation.

Once a potential lead has been identified, a method must be devised (unless "cold" calls have been used) for making initial contact with the lead and establishing that professional services are indeed going to be required (i.e., "qualifying" the lead). In most cases, it is preferable if this initial contact can be made in the way discussed above in reference to leads identified through surveys. That is, the lead should be "bumped into" or an introduction or a referral should be provided by an intermediary. However, if a subtle initial contact cannot be arranged, then a more overt, direct sales call can often be equally effective (unless it is prohibited by codes of ethics). In fact, many types of clients will respond well to direct sales calls, particularly if the caller can impress the potential client as being someone who is "on top of things" by knowing that services are being sought. Moreover, many organizational buyers have become used to having sales calls (including cold calls) from certain professional service organizations (e.g., engineering firms) and are quite willing to be approached by CPAs, lawyers, consultants, and other professionals.

Regardless of what type of initial contact is made with a potential lead, the meeting or conversation must be well planned. Any research that has been done to identify the potential lead should be drawn upon to develop fact-finding questions that will allow the salesperson to obtain a clear picture of the needs that must be served. Questions must also be prepared to obtain information about buying procedures, buying criteria, possible competitors, deadlines, and so forth. Enough information can hopefully be obtained from this initial contact to allow the professional service organization to decide whether it wants to pursue the lead in a vigorous manner.

Pursuing a lead will involve an investment of time and money. The cost of cultivating a prospect includes travel, food, and entertainment costs, proposal preparation costs, and time "write-offs." The professional therefore must feel strongly that he or she will receive value for this investment. An estimate of the *value of cultivating a specific prospect* should be made. Prospect value is given by:

Prospect value = Present value of the earnings stream if the prospect
   is converted into a client
   $\times$ the probability of converting the prospect into a client
   $-$ the cost of trying to convert the prospect into a client

By preparing these estimates for a pool of prospects, the professional can determine which prospects to cultivate, given a limited time budget for new client development.[9]

Courting

Those leads that an organization decides to pursue, including those it obtains through its public relations or advertising, must typically be courted for a period of time before they make their buying decisions. According to Wittreich, there are two basic approaches that can be used in courting clients:

1. *The extrinsic.* This approach is used when the service organization has only minimal understanding of the client's problem, and its primary emphasis is on extolling its own problem-solving abilities via such devices as: describing a generalized approach to most problems ("persuasion by meth-

od"); describing the abilities, experience, etc., of key personnel of the firm ("persuasion by personnel"); or describing specific problems solved for other clients ("persuasion by success story").

2. *The intrinsic.* This approach is applicable when the primary emphasis of the service organization is on coming to grips with a problem of interest and importance to the client, which it shows, for example, by indicating a grasp of the problem in sufficient magnitude to generate both confidence and interest in further discussion, then taking a tentative "pass" at the problem with further discussions and/or memoranda, which reinforces the initial confidence. Presumably, this promise would later be fulfilled by actually conducting a project (in terms of specific information, recommendations, action programs, etc.) in such a manner as to fully justify the initial confidence.[10]

Wittreich argues that the intrinsic is the preferable approach. It is an approach that exhibits more sensitivity to client needs and to the uncertainty clients experience in buying professional services. It does not attempt to bowl clients over, as the extrinsic approach often does, with imposing descriptions of methods, personnel, or success stories—which they may have difficulty understanding or appreciating. The intrinsic approach may make use of descriptions of methods, personnel, or success stories, but they do not form the basis for keeping courtships going. The intrinsic courtship is built around a focus on the problems of clients.

Implementing an "intrinsic" approach requires a willingness to be patient and to commit considerable resources to courting. Talented staff professionals must devote large amounts of time toward *listening* and gathering information on the needs and preferences of clients. However, focusing the courtship on what clients need or want instead of on what the professional service firm has to offer improves the likelihood of being able to "close" the selling process with the acquisition of a new, valued client.

Proposal Preparation

From being something that was only expected of professionals if they were seeking government grants or contracts, proposals are now being requested routinely by corporations and institutions before selecting auditors, attorneys, management consultants, architects, engineers, and other professionals. Proposal writing has become a major expense for many professional service organizations, eating up huge amounts of staff time and involving large outlays for artwork, printing, research, editing, and other activities.

Here are a few of our suggestions for writing successful proposals:

1. Base most of the content of the proposal on what marketing research and courting activities have suggested about client needs and preferences.

Focus on how the needs of this client can be satisfied, not on how other clients have been served in the past.

2. Go easy on the "boilerplate." Clients prefer it when it appears that the entire proposal has been tailored specifically for them. Any sections with general statements about organizational capabilities and credentials should not be allowed to overshadow more client-specific material.

3. Have some type of unifying theme in the proposal that will make it easier for the client to distinguish how your organization will deal with his or her problems compared to strategies of competing organizations. The theme selected should be consistent with your organization's overall positioning strategy.

4. Avoid the creation of unrealistic expectations about what your organization can accomplish. If clients have it in writing that they can expect incredible achievements, it leaves room for great dissatisfaction (and perhaps lawsuits) if only modest achievements occur.

5. Try to have early drafts of the proposal reviewed by noninvolved staff members, outside experts, and, if possible, people in the prospective client's organization. Timely criticism and feedback, particularly from the client, can keep a proposal on the right track.

Experts on proposal writing have developed numerous other personal tactics for writing winning proposals. The hiring of an expert proposal writer with a good track record may be a wise investment for certain organizations, especially given the increased number of clients who want proposals.

Presentations

The type of presentation we are talking about here is the presentation made before a prospective client during the final stages of the buying process. Frequently, several different organizations are asked to make competing presentations at this point. We are not referring to "canned" presentations that can be used during initial sales calls on prospective clients, although some of our suggestions may prove helpful for designing these types of presentations.

Our earlier recommendations concerning how to court sales and how to write proposals would all apply to the design of presentations. Research on client needs and preferences, acquired during the lead-finding and courting stages, should form the basis for forming the content of the presentation. Moreover, the presentation team must come prepared to handle objections, state a unified theme, spend only a limited time on credentials, and create realistic expectations. Other suggestions we can offer are:

1. Be clear about the groundrules and procedures for the presentations. How much time is available for questions? Who will be attending? Is a point system being used to judge presenters?

2. Watch out for "little" interpersonal-relations aspects that can make communications less persuasive. Presenters should dress appropriately, be equally courteous to men and women, make eye contact when speaking, and avoid any other actions (e.g., smoking, joke-telling) that the attendees are known to dislike.

3. Have the doers participate in or make the presentation. Clients like to see how the people they will be working with perform under pressure.

4. Avoid being overly "slick" in the use of audio-visual materials. Good slides, pictures, charts, transparencies, videotapes, or films can all be useful supplements. But they should not be allowed to "run on their own," limiting the opportunity to let prospective clients evaluate how the *people* they might employ can think and interact on their feet.

5. Listen to the audience and show eagerness to do the work they describe. Demonstrate that two-way communication will take place throughout the relationship. Also, show prospective clients that their work is definitely wanted and will remain wanted.

The importance of developing effective presentation skills cannot be underestimated, as the following illustration shows:

> A regional office of a large management consulting firm was experiencing a low closing rate in its bids for various corporate assignments. The branch manager decided to hire a speech professor from Northwestern University to observe his staff's presentations and help improve their presentation skills. The professor videotaped their presentations, pointed out a large number of communications mistakes, helped edit their "scripts," and substantially raised the staff's communications skills. The firm's closing rate increased dramatically following this training.

Negotiating and Closing

At this point, we would like to comment on how to "close" sales. A key factor in being able to close sales is being well prepared for the selling session with information about what the client sees as his or her major objections to buying the service and major benefits of buying the service. The salesperson has to come to a session prepared to counter objections and reinforce perceived benefits. Use of the intrinsic approach to courting (described above), with its emphasis on understanding client problems, can help obtain much of the needed information. Additionally, information should be sought from facilitating intermediaries and anyone else who may have useful insights into the thought processes of the client.

Some techniques available for trying to overcome objections include trying to have the client clarify and define the objections, questioning the client in such a way that the client has to answer his or her own objections, denying the validity of the objections, and turning objections into reasons for buying. Training of salespersons and preparations for selling sessions must focus on the development of these techniques.

If objections are handled well, then it may be time for the salesperson to make a final push to close the sale. Good salespersons can often spot a signal that a client is ready to close from a comment, question, or physical action by the client. The final push can be made by recapitulating the points of agreement, offering to help write up an agreement, asking whether the client wants A or B, getting the client to make minor choices among possible variations, or indicating that a decision must be made now or something will be lost (e.g., the chance to use a given professional, the chance to thwart an external threat). The salesperson can also offer the client specific inducements to finally close the sale, such as concessions in fees or an offer of supplementary free services.

Closing the sale may hinge on the firm commanding effective negotiation skills. Issues often have to be resolved regarding who and how many professionals will work on the project, how soon the project needs to be started and completed, the fee level and basis, the sharing of risks, and so on. Part of a professional's training should include exposure to negotiation concepts and skills. The professional should be able to close the sale without making concessions that will hurt the firm's long-run profitability.

A sale can be closed as long as a *zone of agreement* exists.[11] A zone of agreement can be considered as the range of acceptable outcomes that simultaneously exists for the negotiating parties. This concept is illustrated in Figure 11–3. If the two parties are negotiating the fee, each privately establishes the threshold value that he needs. The seller has a reservation price, s, which is the *minimum* he will accept. Any final-contract value, x, that is below s represents a price that is worse than not reaching an agreement at all. For any $x > s$, the seller receives a surplus.

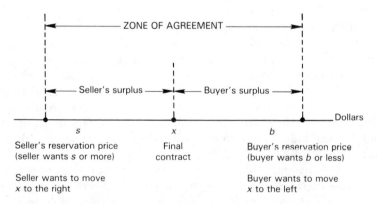

Source: Howard Raiffa, *The Art and Science of Negotiation* (Cambridge, Mass.: Harvard University Press, 1982), p. 46. Reprinted by permission.

FIGURE 11–3. The zone of agreement

Obviously, the seller desires as large a surplus as possible while maintaining good relations with the buyer. Likewise, the buyer also has a reservation price, b, that is the *maximum* he will pay; any x that is above b represents a price that is worse than no agreement. For any $x < b$, the buyer receives a surplus. If the seller's reservation price is below the buyer's, that is, $s < b$, then a zone of agreement exists, and negotiation will determine where x will fall within the zone.

There is an obvious advantage in knowing or probabilistically assessing the other party's reservation price and in making one's own reservation price seem higher (for a seller), or lower (for a buyer) than it really is. However, the openness with which buyers and sellers reveal and use their reservation prices or otherwise practice strategic misrepresentation is often dictated by the personalities of the negotiators, the circumstances of the negotiation, and the expectation of future relations.

Negotiation involves strategic decisions before negotiation begins and tactical decisions during the negotiation sessions.

A negotiation strategy can be defined as a commitment to an overall approach that has a good chance of achieving the negotiator's objectives. Some negotiators pursue a "hard" strategy with opponents, while others pursue a "soft" strategy. Fisher and Ury propose an intermediate strategy that they call "principled negotiation."[12] They claim that this strategy will result in outcomes favorable to its adopter regardless of the strategy selected by the other party. The strategy of principled negotiation is:

> to decide issues on their merits rather than through a haggling process focused on what each side says it will and won't do. It suggests that you look for mutual gains wherever possible, and that where your interests conflict, you should insist that the results be based on some fair standards independent of the will of either side. The method of principled negotiations is hard on the merits, soft on the people.[13]

Similarly stated strategies have been referred to as "win/war" strategies, integrative bargaining, or using a strategy of flexible rigidity (flexible with respect to bargaining means, rigid with respect to goals). Exhibit 11–2 describes the four basic points of the principled negotiation strategy.

Negotiation tactics can be defined as maneuvers to be made at specific points in the negotiating process. Bluffs, last-chance offers, hard initial offers, and other tactics are discussed in both scholarly and "how-to" books. Many sources offer checklists of tactical dos and don'ts such as "Don't tip your hand too early" and "Do negotiate on home ground whenever possible." These lists of possible tactics are usually a shotgun blast of widely varied actions and rarely are consistent with a specific overriding bargaining strategy.

EXHIBIT 11-2.   The principled negotiation approach to bargaining

---

In research known as the Harvard Negotiation Project, Roger Fisher and William Ury arrived at four points for conducting "principled negotiation" that have a high chance of concluding successfully for both parties. They are described below.

1. *Separate the people from the problem.* Because people, not machines, are conducting the face-to-face bargaining, it is easy for emotions to become entangled with the objective merits of the issue being negotiated. Framing negotiation issues in terms of the personalities involved rather than the interests of the parties can lead to ineffective bargaining. Negotiation deteriorates when it becomes a test of wills instead of a joint problem-solving activity. Separating the people from the problem first involves making accurate perceptions. Each party must understand emphatically the power of the opponent's viewpoint and try to feel the level of emotion with which they hold it. Second, emotions brought into or evolving out of negotiations should be made explicit and acknowledged as legitimate. Openly discussing emotions of both parties while not reacting to an emotional outburst helps keep negotiations from degenerating into unproductive name-calling sessions. Thirdly, clear communications must exist between parties. Listening actively and acknowledging what is being said, communicating about problems rather than the opponent's shortcomings, and directly addressing interests rather than speaking first to be heard are methods of improving the chances of jointly beneficial solutions by better communication techniques. In general, separating the people from the problem means looking at the issues side by side rather than face to face.

2. *Focus on interests, not positions.* The difference between positions and interests is that one's position is something the person decided upon, while one's interests are what caused the person to adopt the position. Thus a bargaining *position* may be that a contract must include a stiff penalty for late shipment; but the party's *interest* is to maintain an unbroken flow of raw materials. Reconciling interests works better because for every interest there usually exist several possible positions that could satisfy that interest. Also, opposing positions may hide shared and compatible interests (e.g., we want the predictability of a steady flow of orders, you want the security of an unbroken flow of raw materials). Making certain that interests are understood by all parties and then being flexible as to the means of achieving these interests, while negotiating firmly for the interests themselves, is an effective strategy. As Fisher and Ury state it:

Fighting hard on the substantive issues increases the pressure for an effective solution; giving support to the human beings on the other side tends to improve your relationship and to increase the likelihood of reaching agreement. It is the combination of support and attack which works; either alone is likely to be insufficient.

3. *Invent options for mutual gain.* Inventing options for mutual gain involves the search for a larger pie rather than arguing over the size of each slice. Developing options requires innovative thinking such as brainstorming sessions where judgment of options is undertaken only

after many options have been invented. Looking for options which offer mutual gain facilitates the desirable condition of side-by-side bargaining and helps identify shared interests.

4. *Insist on objective criteria.* When an opposing negotiator is intransigent and argues his position rather than his interests, a good strategy is to insist that the agreement must reflect some fair objective criteria independent of the position of either side. This will help reach solutions on principle, not pressure. By discussing objective criteria instead of stubbornly held positions, neither party is yielding to the other; both are yielding to a fair solution. Such objective criteria may be market value, depreciated book value, competitive prices, replacement costs, wholesale price index, etc. This approach works best when each issue is seen as requiring a joint search for objective criteria, and each party is open to reason as to the standards best reflecting objectivity. Deviation from a fair, objective standard should be made only when a better one is offered, not because the opposing party is applying pressure, threats, or other means of imposing his will.

Relationship Management

Once the contract is signed, the professional has to exercise good follow-up skills and make sure that the project runs smoothly. The professional needs to inform the client of the progress being made, and any unusual developments. The professional should manage the client relationship in a way that is open, friendly, and satisfying.

Some firms have installed a system called relationship management to manage the most important accounts. For many firms, the top five or ten clients account for a disproportionate share of sales. The idea is that each major account should be the responsibility of a relationship manager. Relationship managers call or visit these accounts on a regular basis, make useful suggestions, and serve them in a number of ways. Here are two examples:

> An architect in Atlanta designs store units for a national restaurant chain headquartered in New York City. When he travels to New York, he always contacts the marketing vice president of the restaurant chain to take him out to dinner and a show. He also invites this manager to skiing trips and golf outings. Some people call this LGD marketing, that is, "lunch, golf, and dinner marketing."

> A management consulting firm noticed that certain clients gave it repeat business and others did not. It discovered that some of its consultants were good at managing client relationships and others were only good at managing projects. The consulting firm identified its key clients and made sure that consultants skilled in relationship building were assigned to them.

Relationship management will undoubtedly play a larger role in the future. Here are the main steps in establishing a relationship management program in a professional service firm:

- *Identify the key clients meriting relationship management.* The firm can choose the five or ten largest clients and designate them for relationship management. Additional clients can be added who are growing exceptionally rapidly, or who are a key to understanding new developments in the industry.
- *Assign a skilled relationship manager to each key client.* The current professional can be assigned, or someone who is more skilled at relationship management. The relationship manager should have characteristics which match or appeal to the client.
- *Develop a clear job description for relationship managers.* It should describe their reporting relationships, objectives, responsibilities, and evaluation criteria. The relationship manager will be the primary party responsible for the client, the focal point for all information about the client, and the mobilizer of the firm's services for the client. Each relationship manager will have only one or a few relationships to manage.
- *Appoint an overall manager to supervise the relationship managers.* This person will develop job descriptions, evaluation criteria, and resource support to increase the effectiveness of this function.
- *Each relationship manager must develop long-range and annual client relationship plans.* The annual relationship plan will state client and profit objectives, strategies, specific actions, and required resources.

The main point about relationship management is that firms need skills in managing their relationship with clients, especially key clients. Under the marketing concept, an organization primarily manages its clients more than its products.

SUMMARY

Personal contact—or personal selling—typically plays a larger role in persuading clients to buy a professional service than various forms of public relations and advertising that can also be used for promotional purposes. However, all promotional activities are interdependent and should therefore be the subject of joint planning.

Organizing for personal selling involves determination of who should do selling and how these people should be assigned to selling functions and targeted clients. Most organizations find it desirable to have significant portions of their selling done by professionals who provide services. Clients generally prefer to buy professional services from the people who will be performing work for them rather than from sales or marketing personnel who never provide services. Using "doer/sellers" for closing sales is particularly important, and it may be wise to use this type of salesperson for lead-finding or courting.

Getting professionals to spend an appropriate amount of time at selling (i.e., not too little or too much) can be difficult. Support and prodding from marketing personnel can help to make sure that the right amount of selling gets done by each individual. Adequate amounts of time for selling can sometimes be attained by having professionals mix selling with either doing, marketing research, or pleasure-seeking.

Carrying out the personal selling function involves six steps: lead-finding and qualifying, courting, proposal preparation, presentation, negotiating and closing, and relationship management.

Lead-finding should be done in a focused and systematic manner. Existing clients should be looked to first for leads, but surveys, news articles, annual reports, reporting services, and cold calls can all be used for lead-finding. Whenever possible, courting should be done in an intrinsic manner, meaning that the primary emphasis of the courting process should be on the problems of the client, not on the credentials of the professional service organization. Proposals should be carefully researched and effectively presented. Negotiation and closing can be accomplished in a number of different ways, with good research on buyer decision making being helpful for developing appropriate comments and questions. Finally, the professional must deliver good work and manage the client relationship well as a basis for future business.

NOTES

1. Warren J. Wittreich, "How to Buy/Sell Professional Services," *Harvard Business Review*, March–April 1966, p. 129.

2. Evert Gummesson, "The Marketing of Professional Services—An Organisational Dilemma," *European Journal of Marketing*, Vol. 13, No. 5 (1979), p. 309.

3. Weld Coxe, *Managing Architectural and Engineering Practice*, (New York: Van Nostrand Reinhold, 1983), p. 59.

4. Robert W. Denney, "How to Develop—and Implement—a Marketing Plan for Your Firm," *Practical Accountant*, July 1981, p. 28.

5. See Adrian B. Ryans and Charles B. Weinberg, "Sales Force Management: Integrating Research Advances," *California Management Review*, Fall 1981, pp. 75–89.

6. David Mayer and Herbert M. Greenberg, "What Makes a Good Salesman?", *Harvard Business Review*, July–August 1964, pp. 119–125.

7. Coxe, *Managing*, p. 58.

8. "Keeping Your Practice Healthy," *American Medical News,* January 30, 1981, p. 2.

9. For a mathematical formula for estimating prospect value, see Philip Kotler, *Marketing Management: Analysis, Planning and Control,* 4th ed. (Englewood Cliffs, N.J.: Prentice-Hall, 1980), pp. 568–69.

10. Reprinted by permission of the Harvard Business Review. Excerpt from "How to Buy/Sell Professional Services" by Warren J. Wittreich (March–April 1966). Copyright © 1966 by the President and Fellows of Harvard College; all rights reserved.

11. See Howard Raiffa, *The Art and Science of Negotiation* (Cambridge, Mass.: Harvard University Press, 1982). Reprinted by permission.

12. Roger Fisher and William Ury, *Getting to Yes: Negotiating Agreement Without Giving In* (Boston: Houghton Mifflin, 1981).

13. *Ibid,* p. 57.

12

COMMUNICATIONS:
Public Relations Tools

You might call Myles Schneider the running footman.

You also might call him up on Tuesday nights for some free foot (and related leg, knee, hip, and back) advice.

Any other time you might call him up and hear one or another of eight taped footnotes—he calls it his "Foot Facts" program.

Myles Schneider, podiatrist, is into public service with almost as much passion as he devotes to his running, and his practice.

Besides the foot line he conducts Tuesdays with his partner, Paul Ross, at their Bethesda office and the tapes—he's currently preparing eight more—he also:

- Offers free examinations of children's feet. "We now know a lot of problems—even back problems—sports injuries, a lot of these things are predictable and if you can catch it early enough, you can prevent it."

- Lectures (for free) to PTA groups or running groups on how to avoid sports injuries and what to do about them when they do happen.

- Talks (for free) to grade-school classes (complete with slides) with good footsie techniques, even for the youngest athletes.

- Conducts free courses for trainers and coaches on how to evaluate injuries and help teams as well.

- Conducts a program in which high school track teams may come in (with their coach) for individual evaluations—for about $10 a head (or pair of feet). Each youngster gets a full half-hour diagnostic session, complete with treadmill and "whatever else needs to be done" to discover what problems there may be, or are likely to be.

Backed up by his doctor of podiatry degree from the Ohio College of Podiatric Medicine, Schneider's sophistication in the field led to his first book (with colleague, Dr. Mark Sussman), *How to Doctor Your Feet Without the Doctor,* a valuable self-help syllabus with photographs, diagrams, and a lot of common sense (Running Times, Inc.).

It has now led to a section on sports medicine in a forthcoming book on biking and a second book of his own which will provide do-it-yourself formulas for any amateur sportspeople, be they swimmers, runners, skiers, tennis players, to determine how much, how fast, how long each individual can push him or herself without getting hurt.

Source: Excerpted from Sandy Rovner, "Health Talk: The Footman Runneth," *Washington Post*, February 27, 1981, p. C5. Reprinted with permission.

Myles Schneider makes use of a wide range of promotional tools. He recognizes that much can be done to develop a professional practice by employing a variety of relatively low-cost, public relations approaches. Speaking, writing, telephone messages, and the like all help to improve his image and reputation with his target markets. His personal selling task is made easier because of the support provided by his public relations program.

In this chapter, we review a variety of communications techniques that fall in between the two headings of "personal selling" and "advertising." These techniques do not involve one-on-one or face-to-face communication (as personal selling does), nor do they involve the payment of money for time or space in the media (as advertising does). The techniques are basically public relations or credibility enhancement techniques that have obtained widespread acceptance in the professions. In fact, many of the techniques received widespread use long before overt solicitation and advertising became common in the professions.

Since the role of public relations vis-à-vis marketing is often a matter of considerable debate in many organizations, we feel compelled to address first the question of how public relations should fit with (or within) a professional service organization's overall marketing program. After this has been clarified, we devote the remainder of the chapter to exploring the potential of the following public relations tools:

1. Written materials—including brochures and newsletters
2. Firm identity media
3. Public service activities
4. Publishing

5. Speeches
6. Events—including seminars
7. News
8. Atmospheres

We review the scope of each of these categories and offer several suggestions on how to make the various tools work most effectively.

THE ROLE OF PUBLIC RELATIONS

In carrying out its activities, a professional service firm needs to consider not only the interests of its clients but also the interests of other publics who may be affected by its activities. We define a public as follows:

> A **public** is any group that has an actual or potential interest
> or impact on an organization's ability to achieve its objectives.

Figure 12-1 shows the key publics that a professional service firm needs to consider in serving its current and potential clients. Employees represent an internal public and the other groups represent external publics.

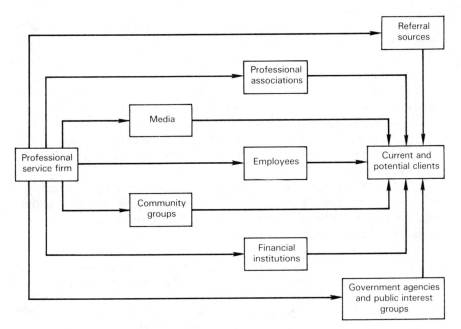

FIGURE 12-1. A professional service firm's publics

Although organizations must put their primary energy toward managing their clientele effectively, their success will be affected by how various publics view their activity. Organizations are wise to spend some time monitoring key publics, anticipating their moves, and dealing with them in constructive ways.

Most organizations use public relations professionals to plan programs for their various publics. Public relations people monitor the attitudes of the firm's publics and disseminate information and communications to build goodwill. When negative publicity breaks out, they act as trouble shooters. They also counsel management to eliminate questionable practices so that negative publicity does not arise in the first place.

Public relations is often confused with one of its subfunctions, such as press agentry, company publications, lobbying, fire fighting, and so forth. Yet it is a more inclusive concept. The most frequently quoted definition of PR is the following:

> **Public relations** is the management function which evaluates public attitudes, identifies the policies and procedures of an individual or an organization with the public interest, and executes a program of action to earn public understanding and acceptance.[1]

Sometimes the following short definition is given, which says that PR stands for *performance* (P) plus *recognition* (R).

When marketing has been proposed as a useful function to install in organizations that already are receiving PR help, the existing public relations people have reacted in different ways. Some PR people feel that they are doing the organization's marketing work and that there is no need to hire a marketing person. Other PR people feel that they could learn quickly whatever is involved in marketing and that there is no need to add a marketer. Still other PR people see marketing and PR as separate but equal functions and do not feel threatened. Finally, other PR people see marketing as the dominant function to which they will one day have to report.

For our purpose, we shall view public relations as primarily a communications tool to advance marketing objectives of the organization. We see the following three important differences between public relations and marketing:

1. Public relations is primarily a communications tool, whereas marketing also includes need assessment, service development, fee setting, and distribution.
2. Public relations seeks to influence attitudes, whereas marketing tries to elicit specific behaviors, such as buying and providing referrals.

3. Public relations does not define the goals of the organization, whereas marketing is intimately involved in defining the organization's mission, target markets, and services.

Thus, public relations should essentially be used to maintain and enhance an organization's image. While many PR activities will stimulate inquiries or even buying by clients, the main purpose of these activities should not be to change people's behavior. Instead, PR should be oriented toward the task of forming, maintaining, or changing attitudes, with behavior change as a secondary objective.

Figure 12–2 presents a five-stage process that should be carried out to implement a successful PR program. First, the organization's relevant publics must be identified. An active program to communicate with and relate to everyone is impossible to mount, so those publics that are of greatest interest to the organization must be identified. These relevant publics will consist of more than just targeted clients, as PR must also be directed at referral sources, competitors, regulatory officials, potential employees, and others.

Once the organization has identified its various publics, it needs to find out how each public thinks and feels about the organization. Personal or small-group interviews might be conducted with members of each public, or a small survey might even be done. Data obtained on public knowledge and attitudes about the organization can then be used to take the next step of establishing image and attitude goals for key publics. The organization should set up specific, realistic, and measurable goals reflecting how it wants to be seen and thought about by its relevant publics within a given period of time.

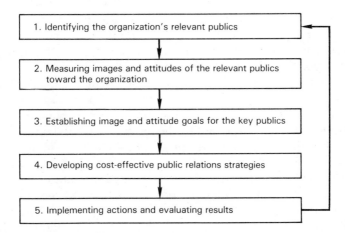

FIGURE 12–2. The public relations process

The next step involves the development of cost-effective PR strategies to attain the stated goals. The various PR tools discussed later in this chapter must be evaluated to see whether they can be used at a reasonable cost to reach targeted publics and achieve desired perceptual and attitude changes. Those tools which seem like they would be nice to use, but which also are expensive and have questionable value for reaching and influencing targeted publics, may have to be dropped in favor of more functional tools. For example, a fancy new brochure may have to be dropped in favor of a speakers' program or a newsletter.

Finally, the strategies selected must be implemented and evaluated. The persons and organizations responsible for performing various tasks must be monitored carefully and the results they achieve must be assessed. Again, data should be obtained on public knowledge and attitudes to see whether goals are being achieved. Where results are disappointing, new goals and/or strategies should be considered.

We now review the various PR tools available to a professional service organization. (See Exhibit 12–1.)

WRITTEN AUDIO AND VISUAL MATERIALS

Professional service organizations rely extensively on written materials to communicate to their target publics. A large consulting firm, for example, might make use of materials such as a brochure, annual report, in-house magazine, newsletters, pamphlets, and nonproprietary research reports. It might also make use of audio-visual materials such as slide shows, photographs, videotapes, film, and audio cassettes.

In preparing each publication, the public relations personnel must consider *function*, *aesthetics*, and *cost*. For example, the function of an annual report is to inform interested publics about the organization's accomplishments during the year as well as about its financial status, with the ultimate purpose of generating confidence in the organization and its leaders. Aesthetics enter in that the annual report should be readable, interesting, and professional. If the annual report consists of only a typewritten document with no pictures or graphics, some publics may form a negative impression of the organization. Cost acts as a constraint in that the organization will allocate a limited amount of money to each publication. The public relations personnel have to reconcile considerations of function, aesthetics, and cost in developing each publication.

Two forms of written materials that are used widely in the professions are brochures and newsletters. We discuss each of these tools more fully in the following sections.

EXHIBIT 12–1.   The blue-chip lawyers discover marketing

They hire public relations agents to trumpet their accomplishments and professional marketers to analyze their "client bases." They publish glossy brochures to promote their strong points. They hungrily eye their competitors' business. Their sales pitches are designed to lure new clients and impress old ones. Who are they? Meet America's corporate lawyers.

A tough competitive environment is forcing the most conservative members of a conservative profession out of the library. Once anxious to avoid publicity, and required by law to seek assignments only through social contacts and professional reputation, lawyers are now embracing promotion to sell their services. And all their messages say the same thing: Hire us. "In its own way," says Robert B. Krueger, a Los Angeles attorney, "every firm of any size in the country is out there marketing like hell." After making an unsolicited presentation, Krueger himself recently won the business of a corporation that controls vast natural-resource reserves.

GETTING ON TV

Corporate law is a new game with new rules. In New York, a public relations woman suggests that reporters interview partners at top-ranked Weil, Gotshal & Manges. Houston's respected 125-lawyer Bracewell & Patterson hires a hard-talking marketing consultant who refers to potential clients as "prospects." McGuire, Woods & Battle, an old-line Richmond (Va.) practice, publishes an eight-page hardbound book to tell its story. Three partners of McDermott, Will & Emery, one of the country's largest firms, fly from Chicago to New York to lunch with the editor of a legal newspaper. In Minnesota's Twin Cities, the public TV station every evening ends *The Nightly Business Report* with an acknowledgment that it was sponsored by Robins, Zelle, Larson & Kaplan, one of the state's big firms.

Although none of the top firms has yet bought display space in the *Yellow Pages* or run commercials on *60 Minutes*, many other selling tools are gaining acceptance. The most common is the use of public relations firms. Both of Cleveland's legal giants—Squire, Sanders & Dempsey and Jones, Day, Reavis & Pogue, which are among the 10 largest firms in the country—get public relations advice. This month the large New York firm Rosenman Colin Freund Lewis & Cohen hired an agency. Hill & Knowlton Inc., an international PR company, currently claims a roster of about 20 legal clients, and publicists all over the United States have been signing up lawyers. For retainers that start at about $1,500 a month and hourly rates that climb to $150, the publicists set about the business of building their clients' images. That includes ghostwriting bylined articles for trade journals and editorial pages and promoting court victories and other professional accomplishments.

POWER OF THE PRESS

But the gold mine is the business pages of major newspapers and magazines. "They are beamed right at customers," says one lawyer. The PR people cajole and chatter. They pass on good news and sit on bad, always working to promote their clients as quotable experts—or, if they hit the jackpot, as subjects of glowing features.

And there are success stories. Some lawyers have long used the press and other marketing tools to their advantage, even without professional advice. Takeover celebrity Joseph H. Flom—of Skadden, Arps, Slate, Meagher & Flom—is the most frequently cited example. "If you could point to one firm that caused all this," says New York public relations man Alfred H. Horowitz, "it's Skadden Arps. They came from nowhere." The firm denies use of any image-building consultant, but it grew quickly in the 1970s, just when Flom's dramatic work was getting frequent and admiring attention in the media. The managing partner of another of the country's largest firms says he and his partners are becoming so irked by the media popularity of certain competitors that they may hire a press agent themselves. He complains: "We won a major case in the Supreme Court in the securities field, a landmark case. My partner argued it. We briefed it. We won it. The case was written up in *The New York Times*. And who did they quote as to the significance? Somebody at Skadden Arps. They never called us."

Source: Condensed from article by the same title, *Business Week*, April 25, 1983, p. 89ff.

Brochures

Professional service firms are increasingly using brochures as a marketing tool. (See Exhibit 12–2.)

Many professional service organizations have made huge investments in firm brochures, only to see the printed product wind up gathering dust on storeroom shelves. The process of developing brochures can be extremely time-consuming and conflict-provoking, as professionals can become hung up in arguments over the brochure's content and appearance. The end product often ends up being a bunch of compromises that nobody feels comfortable about using. Moreover, brochures can often become out of date very rapidly, since personnel changes and changes in client preferences occur all the time.

Consequently, the professional service organization must think long and hard about whether it wants to go through the expense and effort of developing a brochure. The money required to print a first-class brochure can often be put to better use with other public relations tools such as small pamphlets, newsletters, or reprints of articles about the organization. These other materials can be sent or given to prospective clients instead of a brochure.

Perhaps the most important thing to consider in deciding whether to develop a brochure is what the competition is doing. If directly competing organizations use 20-page, 4-color brochures to appeal to desired clients, then it may be necessary to do the same. However, the

EXHIBIT 12–2.   Law firms catch brochure fever

Some are pinstriped and dignified, some red, white and shiny. They're from the stodgiest of firms and the flashiest. They're the latest in law firm marketing techniques—brochures.

The legal profession is joining a trend with bankers, brokers and other professionals. Law firms are deciding that they, too, must develop their images to keep and attract clients. Some are projecting that image through brochures alone, while others are opting for a full-fledged corporate makeover, including a fancy logo and stationery.

The legal profession is "one of the last holdouts," according to Michael Kaiser of Los Angeles, head of a design group that recently completed a brochure for the 60-year-old law firm of Hill, Farrer & Burrill. "Law firms never had to put down on a piece of paper what they really are as a company," Kaiser said.

Some firms still have a hard time doing that, in part because marketing by brochure seems only a stone's throw from advertising, still considered by some firms to be unlawyerlike. "The big firms are a little worried about hyping themselves," said Kaiser. "They were brought up with a certain ideal."

The Minneapolis firm of Larkin, Hoffman, Daly & Lindgren, Ltd., decided to take the plunge last year. It produced a slick, pinstriped brochure that has met generally favorable reviews.

The firm decided to go ahead with the brochure, according to marketing director Jan Tiffany, to raise its profile and to make current and prospective clients more aware of its capabilities. It mailed its brochure directly to clients and also printed excerpts in *Corporate Report*, a regional business news publication.

"It's time to reexamine the traditional way law is practiced, the conventional wisdom," the brochure begins. In an obvious bid for new business the brochure continues: "The more you know about the law firm you are considering, the more likely you are to make the choice that is right for you."

Austin Anderson, director of the Institute of Continuing Legal Education in Ann Arbor, Michigan, thinks law firms are rightly concerned with keeping and increasing their business. "They will suffer in the long run if they don't have some form of client-retention program," said Anderson, who is writing a book on marketing for firms with 25 or fewer lawyers.

But he isn't convinced that lawyers know how to use brochures effectively. He emphasized that firms must think through the purpose of brochures. "Are they for attracting clients or recruiting lawyers? Does the firm want to give a general description or explain its specialties?" Different answers mean getting out different kinds of information to the public.

Anderson said firms might do better communicating with their clients regularly through newsletters or updates. "Keep the client informed and involved," he said. "It doesn't have to be extensive."

Still, brochures and other types of information are flowing more regularly from lawyers' offices these days. Their effectiveness might be summed up in a letter a Concord, New Hampshire, lawyer sent the Larkin firm: "Many thanks for sending along a copy of your firm's very handsome and impressive brochure. As they say at the ballpark, 'You can't tell the players without a scorecard.' "

—Martha Middleton

Source: "Brochure Fever: Law Firms Dive into Marketing," *American Bar Association Journal,* July 1983, pp. 881–82. Reprinted with permission.

resulting brochure should not be a copy of competing documents—it must make the organization look *different* from its competitors. It is better to differentiate a firm by using no brochure at all (and other materials) than to use a brochure that copies that of a competitor.

If an organization chooses to produce a "different" brochure, the following suggestions should be considered:

1. *Give the brochure a definite role to play in the marketing program.*[2] Determine when, where, how, by whom, and to whom the brochure should be distributed. Should it be sent to anyone who makes an inquiry or only be handed out when personal selling is being done? The appropriate role will depend on the organization and the characteristics of its external environment.

2. *Make the appearance and content of the brochure consistent with the "positioning" strategy of the organization.* Pictures, graphics, typefaces, colors, paper quality, and other characteristics should all project the image that the organization wants targeted publics to perceive it as having.

3. *"Copy test" the brochure before having it printed.* People from the targeted audiences for the brochure should be shown unfinished or rough mockups of the text and pictures of the brochure to test how readable they find it, how well they remember main copy points, what image they feel is projected, and so forth. Glaring weaknesses or oversights can often be identified at this stage, saving the organization embarrassment and money.

Newsletters

It is becoming more common for organizations in all the professions to use newsletters as a vehicle for communicating regularly with clients, referral sources, colleagues, or other targeted publics. Newsletters can provide people with timely and useful information, making them feel more appreciative and favorable toward the publishing organization. The most important consideration in developing a newsletter is having its contents be of great interest to the targeted publics. As Stover puts it:

Keep in mind that the newsletter should be largely "you"-oriented—i.e., toward the reader—rather than "we"-oriented—i.e., toward the firm—since readers are primarily interested in items that may benefit *them*, not in news about your firm.[3]

Thus, CPA firms will want to include articles with tax tips, architectural firms will want to include articles with new design ideas, and management consulting firms will want to include articles summarizing management theories and research. Material describing personnel changes and organizational accomplishments should be kept to a minimum.

Newsletters can be prepared in basically three different ways. First, an organization can prepare a newsletter in-house, using original writing, graphics, and photography. This approach has a personal touch, and it gives the organization complete control over the content of the newsletter. However, in-house development of a newsletter can be very time-consuming and expensive. Ideas for articles are often hard to generate and good writing requires the use of highly skilled (and sometimes expensive) individuals. Using a clipping service to find reprintable articles from other sources can make the task easier, but this can cost a significant sum.

A second way to prepare a newsletter is to use a preprinted or commercially prepared newsletter, adding the organization's name at the masthead. Several of these newsletters are available for accounting firms and other professional service organizations.[4] Although high-quality writing, professional appearance, and ease of publication can be obtained by using these materials, the newsletter will probably lack a personal touch, with carefully targeted stories, that could make it particularly attractive to targeted publics.

A final way to prepare a newsletter is to combine some original writing with materials provided by a client communications service.[5] These services provide a group of original stories and news items on a regular basis to affiliated firms. Although a finished product is not obtained from these services, flexibility in putting together one's own newsletter is enhanced. The resulting document can have a more tailored or personal look without the need to develop all new stories. According to Schwersenz, this approach has been gaining favor among regional and local CPA firms.[6]

FIRM IDENTITY MEDIA

Frequently, each of the organization's separate materials takes on its own look, which not only creates confusion but also misses an opportunity to create and reinforce an *organizational identity*. In an overcommunicated society, organizations have to compete for attention. They should at least try to create a visual identity which the public immediately recognizes. The visual identity is carried through the organization's permanent media such as logos, stationery, brochures, signs, business forms, call cards, and atmospherics.

The firm identity media become a marketing tool when they are attractive, memorable, and distinctive. The task of creating a coordinated visual identity is not easy. The organization should select a good graphic design consultant. A good consultant will try to get management to identify the essence of the organization, and then will try to turn it into a big idea backed by strong visual symbols. The symbols are adapted to the various organizational media so that they create immediate organization recognition in the minds of various publics. Arthur Andersen, the public accounting firm, has made good use of its symbol of two handsome mahogany doors, on its various media.

PUBLIC SERVICE ACTIVITIES

Performing various public service activities can accomplish a number of objectives for a professional service organization. Public service activities can help improve the public image of an organization, leading people to see the organization as a "good citizen." These activities also frequently provide a way to meet and impress potential clients or referral sources. In addition, public service activities that involve the provision of free or discounted services to needy clients can often be used as a means of providing new personnel with training and experience.

Public service activities can take many forms. Donations can be made to outside parties in the form of:

1. Unrestricted monetary gifts
2. Grants to support research studies, special educational programs, building funds, conferences, publications, scholarships, endowed professorships, etc.
3. *Pro bono* work (or free provision of services)
4. Allowing free use of facilities or equipment (e.g., meeting rooms, copying machines, computers)

Many professional service organizations also encourage their personnel to contribute to and participate in political activities.

There is a wide range of organizations that members of the firm can join or support, and thereby gain exposure for the firm. They include chambers of commerce, religious groups, civic groups, government commissions, political parties, and business and professional associations.

The selection of public service activities for a given organization should depend on several factors, including the political and charitable preferences of staff members. Perhaps the most important factor to consider is how each activity might benefit the professional service organization. In other words, those activities that allow the organization to exhibit "enlightened self-interest" most effectively probably deserve the most careful consideration. Thus, if a CPA or consulting firm sees great benefits for itself from giving financial support to business schools—because the goodwill created will enhance its ability to recruit staff from the schools—then the provision of this support should be a high priority public service activity. Several large professional service firms have established scholarships and endowed chairs at select colleges to help the schools and bring recognition to their firms.

To make sure that public service activities are given adequate attention, many professional service organizations set up guidelines or rules for staff members to follow. People are urged or required to give certain amounts per year to certain causes or devote certain percentages of their time to *pro bono* work or politics. For example, several of the Big Eight CPA firms require their partners to contribute 4 percent of their cash earnings to nonreligious charitable organizations.[7]

PUBLISHING

Writing articles and books that display the expertise of an organization's professionals is an excellent way to enhance an organization's credibility and image. Several principals at McKinsey & Company—such as David Hertz and Charles Ames—would regularly publish articles in the *Harvard Business Review* to call attention to new business ideas and tools. Published articles and books often generate inquiries on their own, and any publicity they receive can generate many more inquiries. They cal also serve to make referral sources more inclined to make positive recommendations. Additionally, copies or reprints of publications can be used to supplement (or even replace) materials like brochures and pamphlets.

For most organizations, balance should be sought in the types of publications obtained. Having everything published in a few very academic journals is probably not as useful as having a mix of publications in academic *and* trade or practitioner journals that are read by targeted publics. A few "letters to the editor" should also be part of this publications mix. In addition, in some professions, the writing of a column for a newspaper, magazine, or newsletter can be helpful.

SPEECHES

Public speaking can allow an organization to communicate with and impress targeted publics. If the organization has people who perform well in speaking engagements, efforts should be made to find these people opportunities to speak before targeted publics. But speaking engagements must be selected carefully so that only those that reach a large number of targeted publics and/or those that provide great prestige are pursued. It is easy for a good public speaker—who will tend to get many invitations to speak—to get overbooked and overworked making speeches before groups containing people who are of marginal interest to the organization.

A related public relations tool is *teaching*. Many organizations have staff persons who teach courses at colleges and universities during their spare time. Having people teach allows the organization to obtain some of the prestige that comes from having a university affiliation. Teaching also helps to keep the teachers current about professional developments. Moreover, considerable exposure to future potential clients or referral sources can be obtained in the classroom. However, teaching can often be very time-consuming and difficult, and it frequently takes years before one hears from former students about their interest in acquiring professional services.

EVENTS

The professional service organization can increase its newsworthiness by creating or participating in events that attract the attention of target publics. Thus an organization might conduct a seminar or conference; organize a major exhibit at a conference or trade show; sponsor tours, demonstrations, benefits, awards, or celebrations; or throw a big office party. Each well-run event not only impresses the immediate participants, but also serves as an opportunity to develop a multitude of stories directed to relevant media vehicles and audiences.

Seminars have recently become very popular as a public relations tool for professional service organizations. Law and accounting firms are frequently conducting seminars on changes in various laws, management consulting firms are conducting seminars on new planning and research techniques, design firms are conducting seminars on new construction techniques, and so on. Seminars provide a good way of impressing participants with the expertise of the organization's personnel in a carefully controlled setting. However, seminars can be very expensive, and they require considerable planning and attention to details if they are to run smoothly. Exhibit 12–3 contains a checklist for running a seminar that has been offered by Robert Denney, a marketing consultant to CPA firms.

NEWS

One of the major tasks of the public relations personnel is to find or create favorable news about the organization and market it to the appropriate media. Media coverage of public service activities, publications,

EXHIBIT 12–3. A seminar checklist

Here are 20 points to keep in mind in giving a seminar:

1 Select a seminar coordinator.

2. Determine the purpose of the seminar (public relations, to develop leads, to sell new services, or to provide additional information to clients).

3. Choose an appropriate subject.

4. Prepare an invitation list (clients only or others as well).

5. Decide on a sponsor.

6. Decide where to hold the seminar (your offices, the sponsor's offices, or outside).

7. Select the speakers (from your firm only or outsiders as well).

8. Choose an agenda.

9. Decide on a date, time of day, and length of seminar (avoid holidays and attendees' busy periods).

10. Decide whether to charge for attendance and, if so, how much.

11. Decide whether to include lunch, cocktails, or dinner.

12. Prepare announcements (they should be received at least three weeks before the seminar).

13. Decide how to promote the seminar (direct mail, written invitation, or other).

14. Determine how attendees will register (mail, phone, or both).

15. Send confirmations of registration.

16. Notify attendees of any materials to be read in advance.

17. Decide on materials to be used at seminar (charts, illustrations, workbooks, worksheets, and/or other).

18. Decide on whether to use visual aids and, if so, the form and content.

19. Prepare name tags and tent cards for attendees.

20. Prepare a participant evaluation sheet for the seminar.

Source: Robert W. Denney, "How to Develop—and Implement—a Marketing Plan for Your Firm," *Practical Accountant*, July 1981, p. 22. Reprinted with permission.

speeches, and events can be sought, as well as coverage of personnel changes and the acquiring of new clients. The appeal of obtaining publicity or news coverage is that it is "free advertising"—that is, it represents exposures at no cost. As someone said: "Publicity is sent to a medium and prayed for while advertising is sent to a medium and paid for." However, publicity is far from free because special skills are required to write good publicity and to "reach" the press. Good publicists cost money.

Getting media organizations to accept press releases and press conferences calls for marketing skill. A good public relations person understands the needs of the press for stories that are interesting and timely. News releases should be well written and eye-catching. Press kits should be available in case the media wants more information about the organization. The PR person will make a point of knowing as many news editors and reporters as possible and helping them interview the organization's leaders when news breaks out. The more the press is welcomed by the organization, the more likely it is to give it more coverage and good coverage.

Atmospherics

The office buildings, office furnishings, and office layouts of a professional service organization can be useful aids in selling. They can also send silent but persuasive messages of their own to prospective clients. Many professional service organizations use the *office tour* as a vehicle for describing the capabilities of the organization. Different departments and personnel are pointed out and examples of previous work by the organization are shown (i.e., architects show models or drawings of buildings, CPAs show annual reports, etc.). The interior design of the office may also send silent messages of prosperity, modernism, uniqueness, tradition, or other characteristics to visitors.

Office tours should not be left to the whims of individual staff members. And interior design should not be left completely in the hands of hired interior designers. Both should be planned with careful attention to how they might impact the selling and marketing of the organization's services.

Tours should be designed so that all important people are available and introduced and so that relevant materials are displayed in easily sighted locations. Furthermore, interiors should be designed to be pleasing to target markets and to project an image consistent with the organization's overall positioning strategy. Thus, a drugstore law firm that targets lower-class and lower-middle-class clients will probably want to decorate its offices somewhat like the firm described below:

> Blue fans whirr on the floor. There are a couple of potted plants, inexpensive paneling, a kind of everyman's furniture. This look is all in the master plan: Don't put the client off. This could be his first trip to a lawyer. Make the guy feel at home, or at least somewhere between a haircut and a root canal.[8]

On the other hand, a dentist seeking upper-class patients might be inclined to decorate in this way:

> Instead of a sterile white color scheme she has chosen soft sand-colored tones—suede cloth for the walls, wool for the carpeting, and laminated leather for the reception area.

"I like soft neutral colors and I wanted the office to be a reflection of me. But more than that, I feel that there shouldn't be anything jarring in a dental office, like bright colors," says Boston periodontist Dr. Marilyn Canis.

Instead of waiting in an enclosed reception room there's an open feeling created by the rounded lines of dividers, the curve of a built-in desk, the sculptured look of a banquette seating.

Once in the dentist's chair, the patients are treated to such pleasing distractions as a custom-designed stained glass window, luxuriant plants and contemporary art on the walls.[9]

Well-trained and experienced interior designers should be able to work with professional service organizations to obtain the desired atmosphere.

SUMMARY

A wide range of communications techniques falls in between the two headings of "personal selling" and "advertising." The techniques in this category have typically been labeled as public relations techniques. This book assumes that public relations is a tool used to advance the marketing purposes of the organization.

Seven different classes of public relations tools are available to the professional service organization. Written and audio-visual materials can be developed in the form of brochures, newsletters, annual reports, pamphlets, film, cassettes, and so on. They all can be useful in persuading clients of the value of an organization's services. Firm identity media, such as logos, stationery, signs, and calling cards, can help to project a desired image for the organization. Public service activities help an organization look like a good citizen and frequently provide a way to meet and impress potential clients. Publishing allows an organization's personnel to display their knowledge and expertise, enhancing the organization's credibility. Speeches add to the prestige of an organization and provide a means of obtaining personal contact with prospective clients. Events, such as seminars, provide another forum for impressing prospective clients in a personal way, and events can often be used to generate free publicity. News about the organization can be offered to the media in the hope of getting free exposure to targeted markets and publics. Finally, atmospheres can be designed to send silent messages about the firm's prosperity, modernity, uniqueness, or other characteristics to visitors.

NOTES

1. *Public Relations News,* October 27, 1947.

2. Mary Gallagher, "After Bates: A Checklist for Firm Marketing," *Bar Report,* August–September 1981, p. 6.

3. Beryl C. Argall Stover, "Firm Brochures and Client Newsletters—Two Vital Marketing Tools," *Practical Accountant,* July 1981, p.34.

4. See Stover, "Firm Brochures," and Jack Schwersenz, "Marketing Your Services," *CPA Journal,* October 1979, pp. 11–18.

5. Schwersenz, "Marketing."

6. Ibid.

7. See Peter W. Bernstein, "Competition Comes to Accounting," *Fortune,* July 17, 1978, pp. 88–96.

8. Paul Hendrickson, "Counsel over the Counter," *Washington Post,* September 9, 1982, p. E13.

9. Virginia Bohlin, "Resting, Relaxing at Dentist's," *Boston Globe,* March 6, 1981, p. 42.

13

COMMUNICATIONS:
Media Advertising

Law firms are not immune from going the bankruptcy route. In the case of one Boston firm, advertising was blamed for "doing the firm in."

At first, it sounded like an idea that couldn't miss—28 lawyers forming a professional corporation, Springer and Langson, to offer quality legal services at fees less than those charged by traditional law firms. How would it get its clients? Through advertising. Did it work? No.

Boston lawyer and firm founder Robert Springer's "mind started spinning," he said, as he was reading the Supreme Court's *Bates* decision. He envisioned an "upside-down law firm," in which fees could be kept down because inexperienced lawyers would see clients first, while experienced ones stood ready to help at a home office. "So many things don't take the most experienced" to accomplish, Springer explained.

The firm pumped $300,000 into what he called "first class" advertising that was also "terribly unsuccessful." "We just did not get a sufficient response. We got 10 responses to a 30-second television ad. We needed 30 or 40," he explained.

What went wrong? Springer said that he and members of his firm wanted to attract a middle-class-and-above clientele because "you can't go below that level and survive." But he believes that those who can afford to pay reasonable fees generally aren't looking for lawyers. "They already have one," he said, "or bump into them at a cocktail party."

The public isn't ready for lawyers to advertise, he thinks. "Maybe in 10, 15, or 20 years people will be able to accept this as a way of life," he said, "and not look down on firms that do advertise. It costs a lot of money.... It's an expensive procedure with high overhead."

The ads began running in May 1979. In October of that year, the firm closed and went into bankruptcy.

"And that's all I can tell you about this very exciting, very interesting, and totally disastrous experiment," he concluded.

Source: Martha Middleton, "Ad Campaign Fails, Law Firm Goes Bankrupt," ABA Journal, January 1981, p. 25. Reprinted with permission.

Advertising is not a panacea for a professional service organization facing a shortage of clients. As the firm described above found out, advertising can be expensive, risky, and ineffective. But advertising in the professions has also produced highly publicized success stories like the following:

> The San Francisco CPA firm of Siegel, Sugarman, and Seput began its practice in July 1977 with just the three partners and annual billings of $8,000. By 1981 their annual billings had grown to $1.75 million and the number of employees to 27. This growth has been attributed more to advertising ($100,000 in 1981) than to referrals. Says Arnold Siegel: "We rely on advertising and the referrals it generates for new business development. We do nothing else to attract clients other than advertising."[1]
>
> Jacoby and Myers started using television advertising almost immediately after the June 1977 Supreme Court *Bates* decision. They had seven legal clinics when the TV ads began running. Within one year after it started using television, the firm had expanded to 22 offices.[2]
>
> The Michael Baker Corporation is a civil engineering firm that was faced with the completion of its two biggest jobs—the Trans-Alaska Oil Pipeline and Haul Road and the Interstate Highway—in 1976. After considerable research, the firm targeted the coal industry as a high-potential market and began running full-page advertisements in *Coal Age* and other industry publications. By 1981, the firm had gone from near-zero billings in the coal industry to over $5 million.[3]

Clearly, advertising has gained considerable acceptance in the professions in the relatively short time since the famous *Bates* decision of the Supreme Court.[4] Advertising—or the use of *nonpersonal forms of communication conducted through paid media under clear sponsorship*—is being done by professional service organizations in a wide variety of media. Advertisements for professionals have appeared in newspapers, magazines, radio, television, outdoor, novelties (e.g., calendars, pens), directories, references, programs, circulars, and direct mail media.

SHOULD PROFESSIONALS
ADVERTISE?

Should a professional service organization use advertising? We cannot provide a definitive answer to this question. Unless state laws or codes of ethics prohibit advertising, we can see no strong reason for most professional service organizations *not* to use advertising. We do not feel, for example, that advertising can ruin an organization's reputation—*provided* its advertisements are tasteful and honest. On the other hand, we do not believe that all professional service organizations should use advertising.

The decision on whether or not to advertise should be made after considering a variety of factors, including the effectiveness of personal contact and public relations efforts. If an extensive personal contact and PR program is not attracting a sufficient number of targeted clients, then advertising may be needed to increase the number of clients. Advertising can reach more people cheaper (per exposure) and faster than personal contact efforts, and it can help make those efforts more effective. Clients may be more receptive to personal selling initiatives after exposure to an advertisement. Or salespersons may find it useful to refer to advertisements during presentations. A good advertising campaign can also serve to motivate individuals to put forth a more intense selling effort.

Other factors to consider in reaching a decision about whether to advertise include the types of services being offered, the types of markets being targeted, and the advertising policies of competitors. Naturally, an organization that offers highly specialized services—that cannot be described appropriately in a short advertisement—would be less inclined to advertise. But for organizations selling relatively uncomplicated services to markets accustomed to seeing the advertising of competitors, advertising may be a necessity.

If a professional service organization chooses to advertise, we recommend using the services of an advertising agency to develop an advertising program of any reasonable size. An agency's valuable help in writing copy, creating artistic effects, or selecting media can often be acquired at a nominal charge. Agencies typically charge a client a fee for developing and placing advertisements that approximates what it would cost the client if it chose merely to place the advertisement in the media on its own. Agencies normally receive a 15 percent discount from the media when they place advertisements, and they use this 15 percent to cover their expenses (for developing copy, selecting media, etc.) and their profit.

In this chapter, we review the five major decisions that a profession-

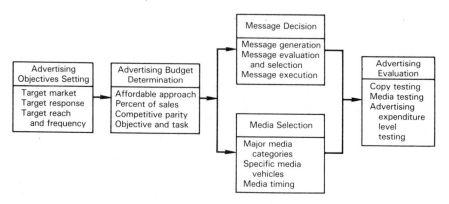

FIGURE 13–1. Major decisions in advertising management

al service organization (and its advertising agency) must make to mount an advertising program. These decisions are summarized in Figure 13–1 and discussed in separate sections below.

SETTING ADVERTISING OBJECTIVES

Before an advertising program and budget can be developed, advertising objectives must be set. These objectives must flow from prior decision making on the target market, market positioning, and marketing mix.

Developing advertising objectives calls for defining the target market, target response, and target reach and frequency.

Target market. A marketing communicator must start with a clear target audience in mind. The audience may be potential buyers of the organization's services, current users, deciders, or influencers. The audience may consist of individuals, groups, particular publics, or the general public. The target audience will critically influence the communicator's decisions on *what* is to be said, *how* it is to be said, *when* it is to be said, *where* it is to be said, and *who* is to say it.

Consider this in terms of a small architectural firm in an eastern city seeking to obtain design work on office buildings and laboratories for high-technology businesses. The architectural firm must decide whether to aim its communications at only the top management of the high-tech companies or at all the employees of those companies. Beyond this, the firm may want to develop communications to reach consultants, construction companies, and other potential influentials in the architect choice process. Each target market would warrant a different advertising campaign.

Target response.   Once the target audience is identified, the marketing communicator must define the target response that is sought. The ultimate response, of course, is purchase behavior. But purchase behavior is the end result of a long process of client decision making. The marketing communicator needs to know in which state the target audience stands at the present time and to which state it should be moved.

Any member of the target audience may be in one of six *buyer readiness states* with respect to the service or organization. These states are *awareness, knowledge, liking, preference, conviction*, and *action*.[5] The communicator normally assumes that clients pass through these stages in succession on the way to purchase. In this case, the communicator's task is to identify the stage that most of the target audience is in and develop a communications message or campaign that will move them to the next stage. To move people from, for example, an awareness to a knowledge stage, an architectural firm might develop advertisements that emphasize the design services the firm is most experienced at delivering; or to move people to an action stage this firm might develop advertisements that stress the urgency of obtaining services before some undesirable event occurs (e.g., competitors will build first, services will become more expensive). It would be nice if one message could move the audience through all the stages, but this rarely happens. Most communicators try to find a cost-effective communication approach to moving the target audience one stage at a time. The critical thing is to know where the audience is and what the next feasible stage is.

Clearly, this analysis can lead to many specific communications objectives for advertising. Colley has distinguished 52 possible advertising objectives in his Defining Advertising Goals for Measured Advertising Results (DAGMAR).[6] The various possible advertising objectives can be sorted into whether their aim is to inform, persuade, or remind. The *inform* category includes such advertising objectives as telling the market about a new service, suggesting new uses for services, informing the market of fee changes, explaining how the service works, describing various available services, correcting false impressions, reducing clients' fears, and building an organizational image. The *persuade* category includes such advertising objectives as building firm preference, encouraging switching to the advertiser's firm, trying to change the client's perception of the importance of different service attributes, persuading the client to purchase now, and persuading the client to receive a sales call. The *remind* category includes such advertising objectives as reminding clients that the service might be needed in the future, reminding them where to obtain it, and keeping it in their minds during off-seasons.

Target reach and frequency.   The third decision is to determine the optimal *target reach and frequency* of the advertising. Funds for advertising are rarely so abundant that everyone in the target audience can be reached, and reached with sufficient frequency. Marketing management must decide what percentage of the audience to reach with what exposure frequency per period. For example, the architectural firm discussed above could decide that it would use direct mail advertising and would buy 1,000 advertising exposures. This leaves many choices as between target reach and frequency. It could send one letter to 1,000 different executives in high-tech companies. Or it could send two different letters a month apart to 500 executives, and so on. The issue is how many exposures are needed to create the desired response, given the market's state of readiness. One exposure could be enough to convert executives from being unaware to being aware. It would not be enough to convert executives from awareness all the way to preference.

DETERMINING ADVERTISING BUDGETS

Advertising budgets can be determined in several ways. Four possible methods include:

1. *The affordable method.*   Advertising budgets are set at the highest level that can be afforded.
2. *The percentage-of-revenues method.*   A given percentage of current or anticipated revenues is budgeted for advertising.
3. *The competitive-based method.*   A given proportion of what a competitor or group of competitors spends on advertising is budgeted for advertising.
4. *The objective-and-task method.*   The amount budgeted for advertising equals what it is expected to cost to perform the tasks that will allow the achievement of specific advertising objectives.

We prefer the last method. It is important to consider the potential effects of different levels of advertising when determining the budget, and the first three methods do not do this particularly well. The affordable and percentage-of-revenues methods, for example, fail to account for the possibility that certain high levels of advertising might generate enough new business to allow a firm either to afford *more* or spend a *lower* percentage of revenues. These two methods tend to treat advertising as a residual or a "throwaway" instead of something that should be allocated according to what it can do for an organization. In addition, the competitive-based approach takes a rather simplistic view of what different advertising levels will accomplish, essentially assuming that the effectiveness of different levels will depend only on how those levels compare to the spending levels of competitors (and not on a host of factors).

The objective-and-task method forces one to think in a more sophisticated way about the effects of different levels of advertising. A total advertising budget is arrived at after adding together separate advertising allocations, each designed to perform a certain task to help accomplish a specific objective. For example, a management consulting firm interested in attracting more business from hospitals and health care facilities would have to think about how much advertising would be needed to make 500 hospital administrators in the Midwest have some level of knowledge about the firm's capabilities. Would $5,000 in advertising in trade journals accomplish this task? If not, how about $7,500? And what would be necessary to make 1,000 midwestern hospital board members at least aware of the consulting firm? After figuring the estimated cost of achieving these and other objectives, the firm would add up all the costs to arrive at a total advertising budget. If the advertising objectives of the firm are sound and attainable, the total budget should turn out to be both affordable and a reasonable percentage of revenues at the end of the year.

We should emphasize that the appropriate amount to budget for advertising will vary across professions, organizations, and target markets. There are no minimum amounts or recommended ranges that we can suggest for advertising budgets for particular types of firms. Experience with advertising in the professions is still too new to be able to make any blanket statements about needed advertising budgets. Positive results have been reported from both small and big advertising campaigns. For example, the Kansas City CPA firm of Donnelly, Meiners, and Jordan (24 people) reported excellent results from a campaign that cost $23,000 over a six-month period.[7] On the other hand, attorney James Sokolove, whose chain of 17 law offices (with 70 lawyers) has become highly visible in the New England region, claims: "One lawyer spending $5,000 a year on advertising is not going to make it." Sokolove's chain—which is actually a cooperative formulated to do mass advertising and marketing—budgeted $800,000 for media advertising during 1983.[8]

In addition to estimating the total size of the required advertising budget, decision makers must determine how the budget should be allocated over different market segments (and subsegments), geographic areas, and time periods. In practice, advertising budgets are allocated to segments of demand according to their respective populations, usage levels, or some other indicator of market potential. It is common to spend twice as much advertising money in segment B over segment A if segment B has twice as much of some indicator of market potential. In fact, however, the budget should be allocated to different segments according to their expected marginal response to advertising. A budget is well allocated when it is not possible to shift dollars from one segment to another and increase total market response.

FORMULATING THE MESSAGE

Given the advertising objectives and budget, management has to develop a creative message. An ideal message is one that would manage to get *attention*, hold *interest*, arouse *desire*, and obtain *action* (known as the AIDA model). In practice, few messages will take the client all the way from awareness through purchase, but nevertheless the AIDA framework suggests some desirable qualities.

The professional service organization and its advertising agency must go through three steps to formulate effective messages: message generation, message evaluation and selection, and message execution.

Message generation. Message generation involves the developing of alternative messages (appeals, themes, motifs, ideas) that will hopefully elicit the desired response in the target market.

Messages can be generated in a number of ways. One approach is to talk with members of the target market and other influentials to determine the way they see the service, talk about it, and express their desires about it. A second approach is to hold a brainstorming meeting with key personnel in the organization to generate advertising ideas. A third method is to use some formal deductive framework for teasing out possible advertising messages.

One framework calls for generating three types of messages: rational, emotional, and moral.

1. *Rational messages* aim at passing on information and/or serving the audience's self-interest. They attempt to show that the professional service will yield the expected functional benefits. Examples would be messages discussing the quality, value, and timeliness of an organization's work. When Booz-Allen and Hamilton, Inc., the giant management consulting firm, used the following headline in one of their recent advertisements, they were employing a rational message:

237 of the Fortune 500 companies have used Booz-Allen in the last 3 years. What about your company?

2. *Emotional messages* are designed to stir up some negative or positive emotion that will motivate purchase. Emotions such as fear, guilt, humor, pride, and joy can be stimulated by creative messages. When the Law Offices of James Sokolove run a television advertisement that starts out with a serious car crash, an emotional response from the audience to "get even" is sought that will lead them to seek legal assistance from a firm that claims it can help them collect for losses incurred in such accidents.[9] And when Wisconsin lawyer Ken Hur advertises his "No Frill Will—$15.00" on the side of an old hearse,[10] he is hoping for humor to work as a persuasion device. But caution must be exercised in using certain types of emotional appeals. For example, advertisers have found that fear appeals work up to a point, but if there is too much fear the audience will ignore the message.[11]

Additionally, researchers have found that humorous messages are not necessarily more effective than straight versions of the same messages.[12]

3. *Moral messages* are directed to the audience's sense of what is right and proper. Advertisements by professionals urging people to take actions like completing their tax forms properly, getting physical or dental checkups, or seeking a malpractice award can be seen as taking on a moral or righteous tone.

Another deductive framework is to examine the organization's actual and desired position in the perceptual maps of targeted clients with the intent of locating themes that would shift the market's view of the organization in the desired direction. Advertisements can be designed to (1) change the beliefs that clients have about the attributes of the organization and/or its services, (2) change the perceived importance of different attributes to clients, or (3) introduce new attributes not generally considered by the market. For example, when a physician advertises being board certified in a particular specialty, it may be done with a desire to introduce the attribute of board certification into the patient's decision making.

Message evaluation and selection.   The task of selecting the best message out of a large number of possibilities calls for evaluation criteria. Twedt has suggested that contending messages be rated on three scales: *desirability, exclusiveness,* and *believability.*[13] He believes that the communications potency of a message is the product of the three factors because if any of the three has a low rating, the message's communications potency will be greatly reduced.

The message must first say something desirable or interesting about the professional services being offered. This is not enough, however, since many rival professional service organizations will be making similar claims about their offerings. Therefore, the message must say something exclusive or distinctive that does not apply to every rival organization or competing offering. Finally, the message must be believable or provable. By asking clients to rate different messages on desirability, exclusiveness, and believability, managers can make sure these messages will be evaluated for their communications potency.

An example of a group of messages that seemed to possess Twedt's three features is provided by the well-publicized advertising campaign run recently by the Big Eight CPA firm of Deloitte Haskins & Sells. All of the messages in this campaign contained a desirable or interesting headline such as the following:

- "What kind of accounting firm doesn't stop at the bottom line?"
- "You're probably going to pay too much in personal income taxes this year."
- "Did your accountants tell you what happened in Washington last week?"

These headlines were followed up by text that described something exclusive about Deloitte Haskins & Sells, such as its unique decision tables for evaluating internal controls or its client newsletter that covers Washington developments. Finally, the messages projected believability by containing claims about the firm's experience and expertise.

Message execution.   The impact of a message depends not only upon *what* is said but also upon *how* it is said. In fact, message execution can be decisive for those professional services that are hard to differentiate in other ways (e.g., financial audits, land surveys, real estate closings). The message has to be given a *style, words*, an *order*, and *format* that will win the target audience's attention and interest.

Any message can be put across in different *execution styles*. The use of pictures, spokespersons, music, and art can be varied to create many different looks and sounds for an advertisement. Advertisements can have a "want-ad" style, an "announcement" style, a "testimonial" style, a "slice-of-life" style, a "technical report" style, and so forth. For example, an ad announcing the opening of a new office would have an announcement style, while an ad containing an endorsement of a professional service organization by a celebrity or satisfied former client or patient would have a testimonial style. A slice-of-life style ad might show people in real-life situations where a professional service could be helpful, while a technical report style ad might contain a description of the results of a new study completed by the advertiser.

Words that are memorable and attention-getting must be found. This is nowhere more apparent than in the development of headlines and slogans to lead the reader into the ad. There are six basic types of headlines: *news* ("Bankruptcies on the Rise. . .Our Consultants Can Help Protect You"); *question* ("How Much Money Did Your Accountant Save You Last Year?"); *narrative* ("Tears Came to Her Eyes When I Told Her How Much Money She Would Get in the Settlement"); *command* ("Protect Your Loved Ones—Write a Will"); *1-2-3 ways* ("12 Ways to Save Money on Your Income Tax"); and *how-what-why* ("Why People Keep Coming Back for Our Designs").

The *ordering* of ideas in an ad can be important. Three issues arise.

1. The first is the question of *conclusion drawing*, the extent to which the ad should draw a definite conclusion for the audience or leave it to them. Experimental research in the field of communications seems to indicate that explicit conclusion drawing is more persuasive than leaving it to the audience to draw their own conclusions. There are exceptions, however, such as when the communicator is seen as untrustworthy or the audience is highly intelligent and annoyed at the attempt to influence them. This last situation might occur frequently in the professions, suggesting that conclusion-drawing should be used with great caution in advertising professional services.

2. The second is the question of one- versus two-sided arguments—that is, whether the message will be more effective if one or both sides of the argument are presented. Intuitively, it would appear that the best effect is gained by a one-sided presentation—that is the predominant approach in sales presentations, political contests, and child rearing. Yet the answer is not so clear cut. The major conclusions from research in the communications field are that (a) one-sided messages tend to work best with audiences who are favorably disposed to the communicator's position, whereas two-sided arguments tend to work best with audiences who are opposed; (b) two-sided messages tend to be more effective with better-educated audiences; and (c) two-sided messages tend to be more effective with audiences who are likely to be exposed to counterpropaganda.

3. The third is the question of *order of presentation*—whether communicators should present their strongest arguments first or last. Presenting the strongest arguments first has the advantage of establishing attention and interest. This may be especially important in newspapers and other media where the audience does not attend to all the message. In a two-sided message, the issue is whether to present the positive argument first (primacy effect) or last (recency effect). If the audience is initially opposed, it would appear that the communicator would be smarter to start with the other side's argument. This will tend to disarm the audience and allow the speaker to conclude with the strongest argument.[14]

Format elements can make a difference in an ad's impact, as well as in its cost. If the message is to be carried in a print ad, the communicator has to develop the elements of headline, copy, illustration, and color. Advertisers are adept at using such attention-getting devices as *novelty and contrast, arresting pictures and headlines, distinctive formats, message size and position,* and *color, shape,* and *movement.* For example, large ads gain more attention, and so do four-color ads, and this must be weighed against the higher costs. If the message is to be carried over the radio, the communicator has to carefully choose words, voice qualities (speech rate, rhythm, pitch, articulation), and vocalizations (pauses, sighs, yawns). If the message is to be carried on television or given in person, then all of these elements plus body language (nonverbal cues) have to be planned. Presenters have to pay attention to their facial expressions, gestures, dress, posture, and hair style.

MEDIA SELECTION

Media selection is another major step in advertising planning. Some media thinking should take place before the message development stage and even before the advertising budget stage. For it is essential to determine which media are used by the target audience and which are most efficient costwise in reaching them. This information affects the advertising budget size and even the type of appeal to use.

There are four basic steps in the media selection process: choosing among (1) major media channels, (2) specific media vehicles, (3) specific advertising vehicles, and (4) timing.

Choosing among major media channels. The first step is to determine how the advertising budget will be allocated among the major *media channels*. The person assigned to media planning has to examine the major media channels for their capacity to deliver reach, frequency, and impact. Table 13–1 lists the major media channels: namely, electronic, print, signs, direct, and special media. Within each channel are media categories: thus electronic includes the categories of television, radio, and cinema. The firm has to decide which media channels and categories would be most cost-effective in carrying its messages. Table 13–2 presents specific profiles of the more important media categories. Media planners must consider the following variables:

1. *Target audience media habits.* For example, radio and television are the most effective media for reaching teenagers.

2. *Type of offering.* Media types have different potentialities for demonstration, visualization, explanation, believability, and color. For example, television is the most effective medium for demonstrating how a complex personal service is administered.

3. *Message.* A message announcing a special seminar or lecture will require radio or newspapers. A message containing a great deal of technical data might require specialized magazines or mailings.

4. *Cost.* Television is very expensive, and newspaper advertising is inexpensive. What counts, of course, is the cost-per-thousand exposures rather than the total cost.

On the basis of these characteristics, the media planner has to decide on how to allocate the given budget to the media categories. For example, the Kansas City CPA firm, Donnelly, Meiners, and Jordan (discussed earlier) divided its first $23,000 (for six months) advertising budget in the following way: $4,500 for magazine advertising, $2,500 for radio, and $5,500 for newspapers (with $2,900 for printing, $1,200 for production, $400 for photography, and $6,000 for the advertising agency's fee).[15]

Each media category has its own advantages and limitations. They are listed after each media category in Table 13–1.

Selecting specific media vehicles. The next step is to choose the specific media vehicles within each media category. For example, the accounting firm of Deloitte Haskins & Sells has placed its full-page ads in the *Wall Street Journal* and *Inc.*, a magazine for small business. Peat, Marwick, Mitchell & Company has advertised specific services in *Business Week* and *Forbes*. The media planner turns to several volumes put out by Standard Rate and Data that provide circulation and cost data for differ-

TABLE 13–1
MEDIA CHANNELS AND AD VEHICLES

Vehicles → / Channels and Categories ↓	Commercials	Display Ads	Classified Ads — Listings	Flyers	Posters	Letters and Memos	Brochures	Newsletters and Bulletins	Business and Greeting Cards	Specialty Items	Business Reply Cards
Electronic											
TV	✔										
Radio	✔										
Cinema	✔										
Print											
Newspapers		✔	✔	✔							✔
Newsletters		✔	✔	✔		✔					✔
Magazines		✔	✔								✔
Journals		✔	✔								✔
Directories		✔	✔								✔
Mail				✔		✔	✔	✔	✔	✔	✔
Signs											
Transit					✔						✔
Billboard					✔						
Outside bldg.					✔						✔
Interior				✔	✔	✔	✔	✔	✔		✔
Direct											
Hand distribution				✔	✔	✔	✔	✔	✔	✔	✔
Pickups				✔	✔	✔	✔	✔	✔	✔	✔
Special Media											
Score sheets		✔									
Programs		✔	✔								
Sky writing											
T-shirts		✔									

Source: Arthur Sterngold, unpublished paper, 1980.

TABLE 13–2
PROFILES OF MAJOR MEDIA CATEGORIES

Medium	Volume in Billions (1982)	Example of Cost (1983)	Advantages	Limitations
Newspapers	$18.3	$10,049 one page, weekday *Chicago Tribune*	Flexibility; timeliness; good local market coverage; broad acceptance; high believability	Short life; poor reproduction quality; small "pass-along" audience
Television	10.6	$2,500 for 30 seconds of prime time in Baltimore	Combines sight, sound, and motion; appealing to the senses; high attention; high reach	High absolute cost; high clutter; fleeting exposure; less audience selectivity
Direct mail	10.3	$1,110 for the names and addresses of 20,000 architects and engineers	Audience selectivity; flexibility; no ad competition within the same medium; personalization	Relatively high cost; "junk mail" image
Radio	1.2	$190 for one minute of prime time in Baltimore	Mass use; high geographic and demographic selectivity; low cost	Audio presentation only; lower attention than television; nonstandardized rate structures; fleeting exposure
Magazines	3.7	$45,665 one page, four color in *Newsweek* $4,160 one page, black and white, in *Architectural Record*	High geographic and demographic selectivity; credibility and prestige; high-quality reproduction; long life; good pass-along readership	Long ad purchase lead time; some waste circulation; no guarantee of position

Note: The volume in billions in column 2 is from *Advertising Age*, December 13, 1982, p. 3, and March 22, 1982, p. 10. Miscellaneous media add another $9.7 billion.

ent magazines regarding ad sizes, color options, ad positions, and quantities of insertions. Beyond this, the media planner should evaluate the different magazines on qualitative characteristics such as credibility, prestige, geographic editioning, occupational editioning, reproduction quality, editorial climate, lead time, and psychological impact. The media planner should make a final judgment on the magazines which provide the best reach, frequency, and impact for the money using calculations of the *cost per thousand persons* reached by each vehicle. Thus, if one magazine charges $5,000 for a full-page advertisement and reaches 500,000 people, it would have a cost per thousand of $10 and would probably be favored over a magazine with a one-page ad cost of $2,000, a reach of 167,000 people, and a higher cost per thousand of approximately $12.

The result of the assessment of vehicles will be a plan like one recently developed for Ballinger Co., an architectural and engineering firm in Philadelphia that was seeking more commissions designing large-scale laboratories and high-technology facilities. In their first year of using advertising (1982), Ballinger ran half-page ads in publications such as *National Real Estate Investor, Hospitals, Trustee, Architectural Record,* and *Buildings Journal.* Page ads were run in *Chemical Week, Drug and Cosmetic Specialty,* and *Corporate Design.* The media planner from Ballinger's advertising agency explained the plan this way:

> With *National Real Estate Investor,* we can reach builders/developers, real estate investors, financial managers, and corporate readers. With *Hospitals* and *Trustee,* we can have the best coverage of the governing boards and trustees of hospitals and health care institutions. A publication like *Chemical Week* or *Drug and Cosmetic Specialty* allows us to reach readers in chemical/pharmaceutical companies who administer the $44 billion spent annually on new plant design and construction.[16]

Selecting specific ad vehicles. The next step calls for selecting the specific ad vehicles to use in connection with the specific media vehicles. For example, a firm can advertise in a magazine in three ways: display ad, classified ad, and business reply card. Table 13–1, which we looked at earlier, shows the ad vehicles that are appropriate to each media category. Thus commercials only apply to electronic media, whereas business reply cards can be used in a number of different media channels.

Deciding on media timing. The third step in media selection is *timing.* It breaks down into a macroproblem and a microproblem. The macroproblem is that of *seasonal timing.* For most professional services, there is a natural variation in the intensity of interest at different times of the year. Interest in tax advice, for example, grows larger as April 15 comes closer. Most marketers do not attempt to time their advertising when there is little or no natural interest. This would take much more money and its effects would be dubious. Most marketers prefer to spend the bulk of the advertising budget just as natural interest is beginning to ripen for the offering and during the height of interest. Counterseasonal advertising is still rare in practice in all types of industries.

The other problem is more of a microproblem, that of *short-run timing* of advertising. How should advertising be spaced during a short period, say a month? Consider three possible patterns. The first is called *burst advertising*, and consists of concentrating all the exposures in a very short space of time, say all in one week. Presumably, this will attract maximum attention and interest and, if recall is good, the effect will last for a while. The second pattern is *continuous advertising*, in which the exposures appear evenly throughout the period. This may be most effective when the audience buys or uses the service frequently and needs to be continuously reminded. The third pattern is *intermittent advertising*, in which intermittent small bursts of advertising appear in succession with no advertising in between. This pattern presumably is able to create a little more attention than continuous advertising, and yet has some of the reminder advantages of continuous advertising.

EVALUATING ADVERTISING

The final step in the effective use of advertising is that of *evaluating advertising*. The most important components are copy testing, media testing, and expenditure-level testing.

Copy testing can occur both before an ad is put into actual media (copy pretesting) and after it has been printed or broadcast (copy post-testing). The purpose of *ad pretesting* is to make improvements in the advertising copy to the fullest extent prior to its release. There are three major methods of ad pretesting:

1. *Direct ratings.* Here a panel of target clients or of advertising experts examine alternative ads and fill out rating questionnaires. Sometimes a single question is raised, such as "Which of these ads do you think would influence you most to buy the service?" Or a more elaborate form consisting of several rating scales may be used, such as the one shown in Figure 13-2. Here the person evaluates the ad's attention strength, read-through strength, cognitive strength, effective strength, and behavioral strength, assigning a number of points (up to a maximum) in each case. The underlying theory is that an effective ad must score high on all these properties if it is ultimately to stimulate buying action. Too often ads are evaluated only on their attention- or comprehension-creating abilities. At the same time, it must be appreciated that direct rating methods are judgmental and less reliable than harder evidence of an ad's actual impact on a target client. Direct rating scales help primarily to screen out poor ads rather than identify great ads.

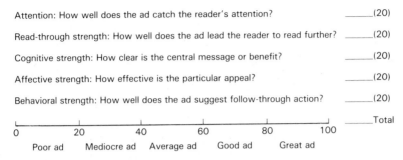

Attention: How well does the ad catch the reader's attention? _____(20)

Read-through strength: How well does the ad lead the reader to read further? _____(20)

Cognitive strength: How clear is the central message or benefit? _____(20)

Affective strength: How effective is the particular appeal? _____(20)

Behavioral strength: How well does the ad suggest follow-through action? _____(20)

_____Total

| | | | | | |
0   20   40   60   80   100
Poor ad   Mediocre ad   Average ad   Good ad   Great ad

FIGURE 13–2. Rating sheet for ads

2. *Portfolio tests.* Here respondents are given a dummy portfolio of ads and asked to take as much time as they want to read them. After putting them down, the respondents are asked to recall the ads they saw—unaided or aided by the interviewer—and to play back as much as they can about each ad. The results are taken to indicate an ad's ability to stand out and have its intended message understood.

3. *Laboratory tests.* Some researchers assess the potential effect of an ad by measuring physiological reactions—heartbeat, blood pressure, pupil dilation, perspiration—using such equipment as galvanometers, tachistoscopes, size-distance tunnels, and pupil dilation measuring equipment. These physiological tests at best measure the attention-getting and arousing power of an ad rather than any higher state of consciousness that the ad might produce.

There are two popular *ad posttesting methods*, the purpose of which are to assess whether the desired impact is being achieved or what the possible ad weaknesses are.

1. *Recall tests.* These involve finding persons who are regular users of the media vehicle and asking them to recall advertisers and products contained in the issue under study. They are asked to recall or play back everything they can remember. The administrator may or may not aid them in their recall. Recall scores are prepared on the basis of their responses and used to indicate the power of the ad to be noticed and retained.

2. *Recognition tests.* Recognition tests call for sampling the readers of a given issue of the vehicle, say a magazine, asking them to point out what they recognize as having seen and/or read. For each ad, three different Starch readership scores (named after Daniel Starch, who provides the leading service) are prepared from the recognition data:

• *Noted.* The percent of readers of the magazine who say they had previously seen the advertisement in the particular magazine.

• *Seen/associated.* The percent of readers who say they have seen or read any part of the ad that clearly indicates the names of the service of the advertiser.

- *Read most.* The percent of readers who not only looked at the advertisement, but who say that they read more than half of the total written material in the ad.

- The Starch organization also furnishes Adnorms—that is, average scores for each product class for the year, and separately for men and women for each magazine, to enable advertisers to evaluate their ads in relation to competitors' ads.

It must be stressed that all these efforts rate the communications effectiveness of the ad and not necessarily its impact on attitude and behavior. The latter are much harder to measure. Most advertisers appear satisfied in knowing that their ad has been seen and comprehended, and appear unwilling to spend additional funds to determine the ad's sales effectiveness.

Another advertising element that is normally tested is media. *Media testing* seeks to determine whether a given media vehicle is cost-effective in reaching and influencing the target audience. A common way to test a media vehicle is to place a coupon ad and see how many coupons are returned. Another media testing device is to compare the ad readership scores in different media vehicles as a sign of media effectiveness.

Finally, the advertising expenditure level itself can be tested. *Expenditure-level testing* involves arranging experiments in which advertising expenditure levels are varied over similar markets to see the variation in response. A "high spending" test would consist of spending twice as much money in a similar territory as another to see how much more sales response (orders, inquiries, etc.) this produces. If the sales response is only slightly greater in the high-spending territory, it may be concluded, other things being equal, that the lower budget is adequate.

SUMMARY

Advertising has produced some notable success stories in the professions since it first began to be used after the Supreme Court's *Bates* decision in 1977. Advertising has also had its failures. Whether a professional service organization should use advertising is something that requires careful analysis and consideration. Advertising should be looked at in terms of what it can contribute to the overall communications program, along with personal contact and public relations.

Five major decisions must be made if an advertising program is to be employed. First, advertising objectives must be set which indicate a target market, target response, and target reach and frequency. Second, an advertising budget must be appropriated, preferably using the objective-and-task method. Next, the message must be formulated, with the wording and format of appeals being evaluated and tested. Next, the media channels, categories, and vehicles must be selected. Finally, the advertising program must be evaluated for its effectiveness.

NOTES

1. Ellen Terry Kesster, "Advertising Accounting Services: How Effective Has It Been?" *Practical Accountant*, July 1981, p. 40.

2. *Target Selling*, a brochure distributed by the Television Bureau of Advertising.

3. Bergen F. Newell, "Advertising Strikes a New Vein," *Magazine Age*, December 1982, pp. 60–63.

4. For a discussion of the early legal developments see Paul N. Bloom, "Advertising in the Professions: The Critical Issues," *Journal of Marketing*, July 1977, pp. 103–10.

5. There are several models of buyer readiness states. See, for example, Robert J. Lavidge and Gary A. Steiner, "A Model for Predictive Measurements of Advertising Effectiveness," *Journal of Marketing*, October 1961, pp. 59–62.

6. See Russell H. Colley, *Defining Advertising Goals for Measured Advertising Results* (New York: Association of National Advertisers, 1961).

7. Gerard J. Meiners, "A Local CPA Firm's Experiences with Advertising," *Practical Accountant*, July 1981, pp. 45–48.

8. Alan Radding, "Boston Attorney Calls on Telemarketing," *Advertising Age*, October 25, 1982, p. 67E.

9. Bernie Whalen, "Legal Services Marketing Enters New Era with Ad Co-op's 'Slick,' Professional TV Commercial," *Marketing News*, March 5, 1982, p. 1.

10. "For Lawyers, the Adman Cometh," *Time*, August 24, 1981, p. 40.

11. See Michael L. Ray and William L. Wilkie, "Fear: The Potential of an Appeal Neglected by Marketing," *Journal of Marketing*, January 1970, pp. 55–56; and Brian Sternthal and C. Samuel Craig, "Fear Appeals: Revisited and Revised," *Journal of Consumer Research*, December 1974, pp. 22–34.

12. See Brian Sternthal and C. Samuel Craig, "Humor in Advertising," *Journal of Marketing*, October 1973, pp. 12–18.

13. Dik Warren Twedt, "How to Plan New Products, Improve Old Ones, and Create Better Advertising," *Journal of Marketing*, January 1969, pp. 53–57.

14. See C.I. Hovland, A.A. Lumsdaine, and F.D. Sheffield, *Experiments in Mass Communication*, Vol. 3 (Princeton, N.J.: Princeton University Press, 1948).

15. Meiners, "Local CPA."

16. Herb Drill, "Architect Draws on Ads," *Advertising Age*, May 17, 1982, p. 48E.

14

MARKETING PLANNING AND CONTROL

Mark Ronner, Ph.D., is an economist who set up a consulting firm in Washington, D.C., in 1982, right after completing four years as a high-level official in the federal government. Mark went into this venture with the hope of providing economics advice, analysis, and testimony for law firms and corporations involved with government regulatory proceedings. A few months after opening his firm, Mark decided he needed to take marketing more seriously. His somewhat random approach to contacting and courting prospective clients had not allowed him to obtain the volume and mix of clients he had hoped to have by that time. He therefore retained a marketing consultant who had been recommended by a friend to give him some direction for his marketing efforts.

The consultant and Mark immediately agreed that a marketing plan should be developed—Mark needed a carefully designed marketing program to help him build his practice. But both agreed that before such a plan could be written, a more careful examination of Mark's external environment and his past marketing actions should be made. Hence, it was agreed that the consultant would first perform a marketing audit of Mark's firm.

The marketing audit mainly involved a lengthy interview in which Mark was probed by the consultant for information about potential markets, competitors, legal trends, distinctive competencies, fees, promotional efforts, and so on. Documents and data that Mark had available in his office were also reviewed. The consultant offered much advice during the course of the interview and also wrote a follow-up audit report containing additional comments and suggestions.

The consultant's report acknowledged that Mark did indeed have valuable services to offer to law firms and other prospective clients. His government background, his eight years as an economics professor at a major university, and his academic credentials clearly differentiated him as someone uniquely qualified to provide economics advice, analysis, and testimony in government regulatory matters. But the report pointed out that prospective clients might not immediately recognize what someone with Mark's unique skills could do for them. The report therefore emphasized how important it was for Mark to try to educate prospective clients about how he could help them win cases.

The consultant recommended that Mark should aim his educational effort at only a limited number of narrowly defined target markets. The report urged Mark to do some exploratory research immediately in order to identify some initial target markets. Additionally, more formal research on the potential of various markets was recommended for the near future. Mark was advised to consider a variety of approaches for carrying out the educational effort, including the use of seminars, a newsletter, the direct mailing of an article he wrote, and cold-calling, followed up (where mutually agreed to) by a written proposal.

Mark found the audit report to be very provocative and set out to implement some of its suggestions. He immediately began talking to various experts he knew about the potential of working on different types of cases. He also began to gather statistics on how frequently different types of cases were arising. After several weeks of implementing audit recommendations, he felt ready to write his marketing plan for 1983. In the plan he established marketing goals for different target markets, strategies for educating and appealing to those markets, time schedules for conducting seminars and implementing mailings, and a marketing budget.

Marketing cannot help a professional service organization very much if it is used in a random and haphazard fashion. As Mark Ronner discovered, it is important to treat marketing systematically, with regular use of control mechanisms like a marketing audit and regular development of a marketing plan.

This chapter will argue that formal planning and control systems are beneficial on the whole and needed for the improvement of organizational performance. The fact that many business firms use modern planning/control systems and that an increasing number of professional service organizations are introducing these systems indicates some apparent satisfaction with the results of these systems. Melville C. Branch has perceptively summarized the main benefits of a formal planning system:

1. Encourages systematic thinking-ahead by management.
2. Leads to a better coordination of company efforts.
3. Leads to the development of performance standards for control.

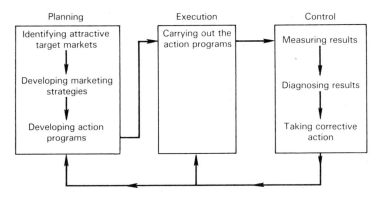

FIGURE 14–1. The marketing planning and control system

4. Causes the company to sharpen its guiding objectives and policies.
5. Results in better preparedness for sudden developments.
6. Brings about a more vivid sense in the participating executives of their interacting responsibilities.[1]

The relationship between marketing planning and control is shown in Figure 14–1 and constitutes a three-step process. The first step calls upon the organization to plan its marketing effort, specifically to identify attractive target markets, develop effective marketing strategies, and develop detailed action programs. The second step involves executing the action programs in the marketing plan, both geographically and over time. The third step calls for marketing control activity to make sure that the objectives are being achieved. Marketing control requires measuring results, analyzing the causes of poor results, and taking corrective actions. The corrective actions consist of adjustments in the plan, its execution, or both.

With some organizations that are relatively new to marketing—such as Mark Ronner's—it may be necessary to commence the planning/control process by first carrying out an aspect of the third step in Figure 14–1; that is, it may be best to have a marketing audit done *before* the development of a marketing plan. The analysis done during an initial audit can often provide valuable input to a marketing plan.

In the following pages, we will first deal with marketing planning and then with marketing control.

MARKETING PLANNING

When a professional service organization *establishes* a marketing planning system it faces three questions: (1)How sophisticated should the planning system be? (2) What procedures should be used to carry on the planning process? (3) What should the contents of a marketing plan be? We now address these issues.

Degrees of Sophistication in Marketing Planning

Most organizations start with little or no formal planning and over the years upgrade their planning systems. In fact, planning systems tend to evolve through the following stages.

Unplanned stage. When organizations are first established, their founders are so busy obtaining financing, attracting clients, and seeking facilities that they have little time for formal planning. Management is totally engrossed in making the day-to-day decisions required for survival. There is no planning staff and hardly any time to plan.

Budgeting system stage. Management eventually recognizes the desirability of installing a budgeting system to improve the management of the organization's cash flow. Management estimates the expected revenues and costs for the coming year. Each department or group manager prepares a budget for that unit. These budgets are financially oriented, not strategically oriented. Budgets are not the same as plans.

Project planning stage. Many organizations find that they need to develop plans for specific projects. Thus, a plan may be developed for opening a branch office or for developing a brochure. But this does not constitute strategic planning.

Annual planning stage. Management eventually recognizes the need to develop an annual planning system based on *management by objectives.*[2] It has three options.

The first is *top-down planning,* so called because top management sets *goals* and *plans* for all the lower levels of management. This model is taken from military organizations where the generals prepare the plans and the troops carry them out. This goes along with a Theory X view of employees, that they dislike work and responsibility and prefer to be directed.[3]

The second system is *bottom-up planning,* so called because the various units of the organization prepare their own goals and plans based on the best they think they can do, and they send them to upper management for approval. This style is based on Theory Y thinking about human nature, that employees like work and responsibility and are more creative and committed if they participate in the planning and running of the organization. Bottom-up planning is most often found in collegial organizations, like professional service organizations, and in smaller organizations.

Most organizations use a third system known as *goals down–plans up planning.* Here top management takes a broad look at the organization's opportunities and requirements and sets organizational goals for the year. The various units of the organization are responsible for developing plans designed to help the organization reach these goals. These plans, when approved by top management, become the official annual plan.

Long-range planning stage. In this stage, the organization refines the planning system in a number of directions to improve its overall effectiveness. The major change is the addition of *long-range planning.* Management realizes that annual plans make sense only in the context of a long-range plan. In fact, the long-range plan should come first and the annual plan should be a detailed version of the first year of the long-range plan. The long-range plan, however, is reworked each year (called *rolling planning*) because the environment changes rapidly and requires an annual review of the long-run planning assumptions.

A further development is that the various plans begin to take on a more *strategic character.* When an organization first turns to long-range planning, it usually assumes that the future will largely be an extension of the present and that past strategies, planning forms, and planning procedures will remain appropriate. Eventually, management begins to recognize that the environment is full of probabilities, not certainties, and that broader strategic thinking is required. The planning format is redesigned to stimulate managers to contemplate and evaluate alternative strategies that will leave the organization as well off as possible.

As the organization gains experience with planning, an effort is made to *standardize the plan formats* so that higher management can make more meaningful comparisons among similar units. It is important that the plans written for comparable units follow the same or a similar format to permit intelligent comparison by higher management.

As the planning culture takes hold in the organization, further improvements are introduced. Managers receive more training in the use of *financial analysis* and are required to justify their recommendations in terms of financial benefits and costs. The managers might also be asked to develop *contingency plans* showing how they would respond to specific major threats and opportunities that might arise. These and other developments mark the emergence of a true strategic planning culture in the organization.

Designing the Marketing Planning
Process

A planning system doesn't just happen. An appropriate system must be designed that will be acceptable to the managers and compatible with the level of information and skill at their disposal. Often the initial system will be designed simplistically so that managers get accustomed to writing plans. As experience is gained, changes and improvements will be made in the planning system to increase its effectiveness. Eventually, managers will accept planning not as a chore to meet their bosses' needs but as a tool to increase their own effectiveness.

Someone has to be responsible for developing the initial planning system. This planning director may find it useful to hire an outside consultant to help planning get started. A consultant may be able to provide valuable perspectives on planning as well as specific procedures and forms. The value of having easy-to-complete planning forms should not be underestimated, as they can make the difference between planning that gets done and planning that never gets beyond someone's good intentions.

Many professional service organizations will need multiple marketing plans—one for each major category of services provided. The planning director should not necessarily write all or even some of these plans. If the planning director will have little to do with plan execution, he or she should work to educate and assist others in writing plans. *A maxim of planning is that planning should be done by those who must carry out the plans.* By involving account supervisors, client managers, and similar people in planning their operations, they are (1) stimulated to think out their objectives and strategies, and (2) motivated to achieve their goals.

One major task for the planning director is to develop a calendar for the planning process. The normal calendar steps are:

1. Develop a set of relevant environmental facts and trends to distribute to everyone in preparation for their planning.
2. Work with top management to develop a set of overall firm objectives for the coming year to pass on to everyone in preparation for their planning.
3. Work with individuals to complete their marketing plans by a certain date.
4. Work with top management to review, approve, or modify the various plans.
5. Develop a consolidated official plan for the organization for the coming period.

This calendar sequence underscores the critical role of marketing planning in the overall management planning process. Individual account supervisors, client managers, and so on start the process by setting marketing goals for their areas for the coming period, along with proposed strategies and marketing budgets. Once top management approves these marketing goals and strategies, decisions can be made on how much personnel to hire, how much supplies to order, how much money to borrow, and so on. Thus, a commitment to a set of marketing goals precedes decisions on personnel, supplies, and financial requirements.

The Format of a Marketing Plan

Another major task of the planning director is to design the appropriate standard format that firm personnel should follow in preparing their marketing plans. The topics and their sequence can make a difference in the quality of planning results. We believe a marketing plan should contain the following major sections: (1) *executive summary*, (2) *situation analysis*, (3) *objectives and goals*, (4) *marketing strategy*, (5) *action program*, (6) *budgets*, and (7) *controls*. These sections will be discussed in the context of a situation where only a single marketing plan needs to be developed for a small organization. Here is the situation:

> Harris-Johnson Associates is a New York City architectural firm with two partners, four additional design professionals, and a secretary. The firm has been in existence for six years and has done a wide variety of design work on everything from shopping malls to libraries to prisons. A lack of focus in their previous business development efforts has left the firm in a somewhat precarious financial position, and Leslie Harris, the managing partner, has decided that it is time for him to develop a marketing plan.[4]

Executive summary. The planning document should open with a summary of the main goals and recommendations presented in the plan. Here is an abbreviated example:

> This year's marketing plan for Harris-Johnson Associates seeks income from fees for the year of $400,000. Bringing in this amount will require billing 10,000 hours at an average hourly rate of $40. The corporate and local government markets would be targeted, and the type of work sought would involve the design of retrofits and rehabilitations, solar energy projects, and correctional facilities. To accomplish this, the plan calls for a total marketing expenditure of $50,000. Of this, $5,000 will be spent on information sources and marketing research studies, $5,000 will be spent on producing and mailing a brochure, $4,000 will be spent on materials and design work for proposals and presentations, and $3,000 will be spent entertaining existing and prospective clients. The remaining $23,000 will be for time spent by Harris and others in marketing activities.

An executive summary can be particularly useful in those organizations that have several marketing plans developed each year. Higher management can preview the major thrust of each plan and read further in search of the information that is critical in evaluating the plan. Executive summaries are also helpful to outside consultants or newcomers to an organization's staff who may want to obtain a quick overview of past marketing efforts by examining the summaries of several years' plans.

Situation analysis. The first major in-depth section of the plan is the *situation analysis*, in which the major features of the situation facing the organization are described. The situation analysis consists of four subsections—background, normal forecast, opportunities and threats, and strengths and weaknesses.

BACKGROUND. This section starts with a summary of key performance indices for the last few years. For example, a plan for Harris-Johnson Associates would have a table (and accompanying explanation) showing the movement of the following indices over the last three years:

1. Income from fees
2. Net profit (loss)
3. Number of desirable leads identified
4. Number (and percent) of "short lists" made with desirable leads
5. Number (and percent) of commissions obtained once on the "short list"

The table would show that the firm's income from fees has declined from over $400,000 to only $231,000 in three years and that losses have mounted at the same time. A consistently low level of "leads identified" and "short lists made" would also be revealed. But the data would indicate a high percentage of commissions obtained once a short list had been made.

These data should be followed by a description of major developments occurring in the profession, such as changes in client preferences, technology, competition, and other factors that could influence the success of selected marketing strategies.

NORMAL FORECAST. The background information should be followed by a forecast of what the values of the key performance indices would become in the next year if no major changes were to occur in the *marketing environment* or *marketing strategies*. In other words, if the organization continued to pursue its old marketing strategies for another year, while competitors and other environmental forces did not change, what type of performance would occur? Such a forecast could be developed based on extrapolation from past data, the opinions of experts (from both inside and outside the organization), or more sophisticated forecasting tools.

Of course, if the figures in the normal forecast look disappointing or ominous—without even taking into account any competitive or environmental threats that could materialize—then the need for more dramatic shifts in marketing strategy will be clearly highlighted.

OPPORTUNITIES AND THREATS. The normal forecast should be followed by a section in which the main opportunities and threats facing the organization are stated. The "grand ideas" and "nightmares" that people think about but rarely articulate should be considered for inclusion at this point. Those that have the highest probability of occurring and/or the largest financial consequences (either positive or negative) should be explicitly discussed in the plan.

Table 14–1A shows the main opportunities and threats facing Harris-Johnson Associates. The opportunities and threats describe *outside* factors facing the organization. They are described to suggest some actions that might be warranted.

STRENGTHS AND WEAKNESSES.   The plan should next contain a list of the main internal strengths and weaknesses of the organization (see Table 14–1B). The list of strengths has implications for strategy formulation, while the list of weaknesses has implications for investments to correct weaknesses.

Objectives and goals.   The situation analysis describes where the organization stands and where it might go. Now a statement is required of where the organization should go. Specific objectives and goals have to be set. Desired levels for the performance indices covered in the background and normal forecast sections should be determined. These goals should be attainable and not a "wish list." Thus, Harris-Johnson would set a goal of $400,000 for income from fees, $40,000 for net profit, 50 for number of desirable leads identified, and so on.

Marketing strategy.   The marketing strategy describes the "game plan" by which the organization hopes to "win." It consists of decisions about target markets, positioning, the strategic marketing mix, the tactical marketing mix, and the marketing expenditure level. The strategy should capitalize on opportunities, thwart threats, build on strengths, and correct weaknesses. The strategy should be described with its supporting arguments.

Harris-Johnson's strategy would involve the *targeting* of corporate and local government prospects who require design work for retrofits and rehabilitations, solar energy projects, and correctional facilities. The firm would be *positioned* as highly experienced (and award-winning) in these areas and as providing very personalized service. The *strategic marketing mix* would have a basic emphasis on personal communications, with lesser but significant use being made of a brochure and well-done presentations. Another feature of this strategic marketing mix would be its emphasis on charging clients on an hourly-rate basis rather than on a fixed-fee basis or a percentage of construction cost basis. The *tactical marketing mix* would consist of the procedures to be used to identify leads, mail out the brochure, and perform other more mundane aspects of the marketing effort. Finally, the marketing expenditure level would be set at $50,000.

TABLE 14-1
AN EXAMPLE OF OPPORTUNITIES, THREATS, STRENGTHS,
AND WEAKNESSES

A. Opportunities and Threats Facing Harris-Johnson
Opportunities

1. The high cost of constructing new buildings in New York City has created great interest in retrofitting and rehabilitating old buildings.
2. The "Energy Crisis" has made managers in all types of organizations more conscious of the energy efficiency of buildings.
3. Tougher law enforcement and rising crime rates throughout the United States have swelled the size of prison populations, creating a need for more correctional facilities.

Threats

1. State and local governments in the Middle-Atlantic region are being pressured to cut spending drastically, particularly spending on construction.
2. Several large New York architectural firms have become extremely aggressive in terms of marketing and have been actively pursuing some of the same, smaller jobs Harris-Johnson is seeking.
3. Corporations are moving out of New York City toward the Sun Belt areas.

B. Strengths and Weaknesses of Harris-Johnson
Strengths

1. Harris and Johnson both have excellent reputations among their peers because of the prestigious design awards they have won and because of the teaching they have done at local architectural schools.
2. The rest of the staff are well trained, technically competent, and highly loyal to Harris and Johnson.
3. The firm does extremely well at getting jobs once they are on the "short list," as prospective clients seem to be impressed by Harris and Johnson's skills and the extent of personal involvement they plan to have with each project.

Weaknesses

1. Nobody in the firm has any background in marketing.
2. Telephone inquiries are not followed up in a systematic way with return calls, visits, or mailings.
3. Many of the firm's existing clients, including several real estate developers and local-government agencies, have been unreasonably slow in paying their bills.

Action program.   The overall action plan can take the form of a table, with the 12 months (or 52 weeks) of the year serving as columns and various marketing activities serving as rows. Dates can be entered when various activities or expenditures will be started, reviewed, and completed. The individuals responsible for performing various actions could also be listed. This action plan can be changed during the year as new problems and opportunities arise.

Budgets.   The goals, strategies, and planned actions allow the planner to build a budget, which is essentially a projected profit-and-loss statement. On the revenue side, it shows the forecasted number of hours or projects to be worked and the expected fees for that work. On the expense side, it shows the costs of marketing and all other activities. Once settled upon, the budget is the basis for marketing operations, financial planning, and personnel recruitment.

Controls.   The last section of the plan describes the controls that will be applied to monitor the plan's progress. This section might also include a short discussion of what actions will be taken if the controls reveal that the plan is not working as well as anticipated. We give further attention to the subject of marketing control in the remainder of this chapter.

MARKETING CONTROL

The purpose of marketing control is to maximize the probability that the professional service organization will achieve its short-run and long-run objectives. Many surprises are likely to occur during the plan's execution that will call for new responses or adjustments. Marketing control systems are an intrinsic part of the marketing planning process.

Marketing control is far from being a single process. Three types of marketing control can be distinguished. *Annual plan control* refers to the steps taken during the year to monitor and correct performance deviations from the plan. *Profitability control* consists of efforts to determine the actual profit or loss of different services, market segments, cases, or projects. *Strategic control* consists of a systematic evaluation of the organization's marketing performance in relation to its marketing opportunities. We describe each form of marketing control in the following sections.

Annual Plan Control

The purpose of annual plan control is to make sure during the course of the year that the organization is achieving the marketing objectives that it established in its annual plan. This calls for the four

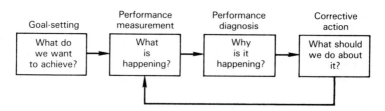

FIGURE 14–2.   The control process

steps shown in Figure 14–2. First, the various planners set well-defined goals for each time period during the plan year. Second, steps are taken to monitor the ongoing results and developments during the year. Third, the organization's managers seek to diagnose the causes of serious deviations in performance. Fourth, the managers choose *corrective actions* that will hopefully close the gap between goals and performance.

This system is called *management by objectives*. What control tools can be used to implement such a system? Four main ones are revenues analysis, marketing expenses-to-revenues analysis, "pipeline" analysis, and market attitude tracking.

Revenues analysis.   *Revenues analysis* is the effort to measure and evaluate the actual revenues being achieved in relation to the revenues goals set for different units of the organization. Thus, the managing partner of a CPA firm might examine quarterly revenues for auditing, tax, and management services—and perhaps also look at this broken down by certain industries or geographic territories. If revenues were lower than desired in any area, the reasons would be sought out. Blame would not be assigned too quickly, since research should be done to uncover the problems. It might be found that revenues are off because of (1) the fee-cutting tactics of certain competitors, (2) the failure to identify enough high-potential leads, (3) inadequate proposals, (4) poor word-of-mouth about the firm stimulated by the unfriendly behavior of certain staff members, and so on. The proper corrective actions would vary with each cause.

Marketing expenses-to-revenues analysis.   Annual plan control also requires checking on various marketing expenses as a ratio to revenues to make sure that the organization is not overspending to achieve its goals. The ratios to watch include total marketing expenses-to-revenues, personal contact expenses-to-revenues, advertising expenses-to-revenues, public relations expenses-to-revenues, and marketing research expenses-to-revenues. The organization should continuously check whether these ratios are appropriate compared to previous time periods or compared to the ratios other similar organizations are known to have. In addition, an eye should be kept on any other ratios that say something about the efficiency of the marketing effort. Well-managed professional service organizations will monitor the percentage of time staff members spend on marketing and on billable activities, the percentage of inquiries received per month that are converted into face-to-face meetings, the amount of revenues obtained per cold call made to a prospective client, and similar ratios.

"Pipeline" analysis.   A professional service firm, in addition to monitoring its revenues and costs, must also examine its "pipeline" statistics. Every firm hopes to have a healthy stream of leads, proposals, and closings in its pipeline. The key statistics to watch are shown in Figure 14–3 and described below.

NUMBER OF LEADS.   The professional service firm needs to continuously search for new leads which can hopefully be turned into future clients. The lead stream consists of suspects (people that might be called on) and prospects (people who look promising). The greater the lead stream, the greater the number of proposals that can be written, and the greater the number of closings that might occur. Many professional service firms actively decide what prospects to go after, and call this their "hit list."

NUMBER AND VALUE OF OUTSTANDING PROPOSALS.   The quality of a firm's leads will reflect itself in the number of proposals that the firm is able to submit. Firms need to track the number and dollar value of the total proposals outstanding. If these numbers slip overall, or fall for certain branch offices of the firm, the firm will have to take corrective actions.

PROPOSAL CYCLE.   The firm must also monitor the average proposal cycle, that is, the time elapsing between proposal invitation, submission, and decision. An East Coast management consulting firm normally spends three weeks preparing a proposal and waits four weeks to hear the prospect's decision, a total of seven weeks. In a recession period, the firm can prepare the proposal within two weeks because the staff has more time available, but they don't hear of the client's decision for about eight weeks. Clients are tougher to sell to, and they take more time to make a decision. Firms get concerned when the proposal cycle stretches out.

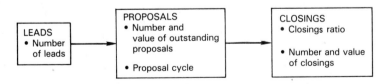

FIGURE 14–3. Key "pipeline" statistics

CLOSINGS RATIO.   The firm wants to maintain a high ratio of closings to proposals (sometimes called the "hit rate"). Each proposal costs money and time to prepare. Losing the account to a competitor is always disappointing. If the hit rate starts slipping overall, or for certain branch offices, the firm needs to find out why. Are the proposals prepared too hastily? Do the staff members lack skill in presenting proposals? Did the client really want a proposal in the first place? Every time a proposal is lost, the staff must ask the prospect why they lost so that they can do a better job in the future.

NUMBER AND VALUE OF CLOSINGS.   The firm needs to keep statistics on its new business backlog. If it has accepted too much new business, it will be slow in starting each assignment. Some clients will not want to wait several weeks for the staff to get started on the project. On the other hand, if the firm lacks enough new business backlog, then it will have excess staff capacity and unbillable hours on its hands. The staff will have to devote more time to new business marketing and less in "production" and "profit generation."

Market attitude tracking.   Organizations should periodically check on the attitudes of existing and prospective clients toward the organization. If market attitudes start eroding, they can lead to later declines in revenues. Knowing this early can lead to preventive actions. Market attitudes can be measured through regular surveys of clients and referral sources.

Profitability Control

Besides annual plan control, organizations need to carry on periodic research to determine the actual profit and loss attributable to various relationships, cases, projects, persons, or categories of services. Marketing profitability analysis requires a procedure for identifying all revenues generated by a particular set of activities and all costs associated with it. Sometimes this is fairly easy to do. It may only be necessary to take the fees earned on a set of activities, subtract the cost of the time people spent on the activities, and then subtract an allocated portion of the office overhead and marketing expenses.

But in other situations marketing profitability analysis is more troublesome. Take, for example, the problem of assessing the profitability of the management services activities of a CPA firm. How should marketing expenses be allocated to this work if most of it is obtained as a result of casual cross-selling done during audit engagements? Which persons, the auditors or the management consultants, should receive credit for bringing in management services work in this way? How profitable should this work be judged to be if it brings in little revenues by itself—because low fees are charged—but plays a major role in helping the firm keep some of its most profitable audit clients?

Marketing profitability analysis may raise many difficult questions about the contributions of various activities and persons. However, it is something that can help an organization reach important decisions about which services to drop, which marketing ventures to restructure, and which personnel to give bigger rewards.

Strategic Control

From time to time, professional service organizations need to take a critical look at their overall marketing performance. Marketing is one of the major areas where rapid obsolescence of objectives, policies, strategies, and programs is a constant possibility.

A major tool in this connection is the marketing audit. Organizations of all types are increasingly turning to marketing audits to assess their marketing opportunities and operations. A marketing audit is defined as follows:[5]

> A **marketing audit** is a *comprehensive, systematic, independent*, and *periodic* examination of an organization's marketing environment, objectives, strategies, and activities with a view to determining problem areas and opportunities and recommending a plan of action to improve the organization's marketing performance.

The four main characteristics of a marketing audit are expanded below:

1. *Comprehensive.* The marketing audit covers all of the major marketing issues facing an organization, and not only one or a few marketing troublespots. The latter would be called a functional audit if it covered only personal contact activities, fee setting, or some other marketing activities.

2. *Systematic.* The marketing audit involves an orderly sequence of diagnostic steps covering the organization's marketing environment, internal marketing system, and specific marketing activities. The diagnosis is followed by a corrective action plan involving both short-run and long-run proposals to improve the organization's overall marketing effectiveness.

3. *Independent.* The marketing audit is normally conducted by an inside or outside party who has sufficient independence from the marketing personnel to attain top management's confidence and the needed objectivity.

4. *Periodic.* The marketing audit should normally be carried out periodically instead of only when there is a crisis. It is a good thing to have done when an organization is just getting started with marketing, and it should be done periodically after that whether the organization is seemingly successful or in deep trouble.

TABLE 14–2
MARKETING AUDIT GUIDE

PART I. MARKETING ENVIRONMENT AUDIT

MACROENVIRONMENT

A. *Demographic*
1. What major demographic developments and trends pose opportunities or threats for this organization?
2. What actions has the organization taken in response to these developments?

B. *Economic*
1. What major developments and trends in income, prices, savings, and credit have an impact on the organization?
2. What actions has the organization taken in response to these developments and trends?

C. *Ecological*
1. What is the outlook for the cost and availability of natural resources and energy needed by this organization's clients?
2. What actions has the organization taken in response to these developments and trends?

D. *Technological*
1. What major changes are occurring in relevant product, service, and process technology?
2. What major generic substitutes might replace the products or services of the organization or its clients?

E. *Political*
1. What new legislation could affect this organization? What federal, state, and local agency actions should be watched?
2. What actions has the organization taken in response to these developments?

F. *Cultural*
1. What changes are occurring in consumer life styles and values that might affect this organization?
2. What actions has the organization taken in response to these developments?

TASK ENVIRONMENT

A. *Markets*
1. What is happening to market size, growth, and geographic distribution?
2. What are the major market segments? What are their expected rates of growth? Which are high-opportunity and low-opportunity segments?

B. *Clients*
1. How do current clients and prospects rate the organization and its competitors, particularly with respect to reputation, service quality, helpfulness, and fees?

TABLE 14–2 (cont.)

2. How do different classes of clients make their buying decisions?

3. What are the evolving needs and satisfactions being sought by clients in this market?

C. *Competitors*

1. Who are the major competitors? What are the objectives and strategy of each major competitor? What are their strengths and weaknesses? What are the sizes and trends in market shares?

2. What trends can be foreseen in future competition and substitutes for this service?

D. *Channels of Distribution*

1. What are the main distribution channels bringing services to clients?

2. What are the efficiency levels and growth potentials of the different distribution channels?

E. *Suppliers*

1. What is the outlook for the availability of different key resources used in providing services?

2. What trends are occurring among suppliers in their pattern of selling?

F. *Facilitators and Intermediaries*

1. Who are the main referral sources and suppliers of supplementary services?

2. What trends are occurring among facilitators and intermediaries?

G. *Publics*

1. What publics (financial, media, government, citizen, local, general, and internal) represent particular opportunities or problems for the organization?

2. What steps has the organization taken to deal effectively with its key publics?

Part II. Marketing Objectives and Strategy Audit

A. *Organization's Objectives*

1. Is the mission of the organization clearly stated in market-oriented terms? Is the mission feasible in terms of the organization's opportunities and resources?

2. Are the organization's various objectives clearly stated so that they lead logically to the marketing objectives?

3. Are the marketing objectives appropriate, given the organization's competitive position, resources, and opportunities?

B. *Marketing Strategy*

1. What is the core marketing strategy for achieving the objectives? Is it a sound marketing strategy?

2. Are enough resources (or too much resources) budgeted to accomplish the marketing objectives?

3. Are the marketing resources allocated optimally to prime market segments, territories, and services of the organization?

TABLE 14–2 (*cont.*)

---

4. Are the marketing resources allocated optimally to the major elements of the marketing mix, i.e., service quality, personal contact, public relations, and advertising?

Part III. Marketing Organization Audit

A. *Formal Structure*

1. Is there a high-level marketing officer with adequate authority and responsibility over those organizational activities that affect the client's satisfaction?

2. Are the marketing responsibilities optimally structured along functional, service, end-user, and territorial lines?

B. *Functional Efficiency*

1. Are there good communication and working relations between marketing personnel and professionals doing selling?

2. Are there any groups in marketing that need more training, motivation, supervision, or evaluation?

Part IV. Marketing Systems Audit

A. *Marketing Information System*

1. Is the marketing intelligence system producing accurate, sufficient, and timely information about developments in the marketplace?

2. Is marketing research being adequately used by managers?

B. *Marketing Planning System*

1. Is the marketing planning system well conceived and effective?

2. Is forecasting and market potential measurement soundly carried out?

C. *Marketing Control System*

1. Are the control procedures (monthly, quarterly, etc.) adequate to insure that the annual plan objectives are being achieved?

2. Is provision made to analyze periodically the profitability of different services, markets, territories, and channels of distribution?

3. Is provision made to examine and validate periodically various marketing costs?

Part V. Marketing Function Audits

A. *Services*

1. What are the service line objectives? Are these objectives sound? Is the current service line meeting these objectives?

2. Are there particular services that should be phased out?

3. Are there new services that are worth adding?

4. Are any services able to benefit from quality, feature, or style improvements?

TABLE 14–2 (*cont.*)

B. *Fees*

1. What are the fee objectives, policies, strategies, and procedures? To what extent are fees set on sound cost, demand, and competitive criteria?

2. Do the clients see the organization's fees as being in line or out of line with the perceived value of its offer?

C. *Distribution*

1. What are the distribution objectives and strategies?

2. Is there adequate market coverage and service?

D. *Personal Contact and Selling*

1. What are the organization's selling objectives?

2. Are professionals adequately trained, assigned, motivated, and supported in their selling efforts?

E. *Public Relations and Advertising*

1. Is there a well-conceived public relations program?

2. What are the organization's advertising objectives? Are they sound?

3. Is the right amount being spent on advertising? How is the budget determined?

4. Are the ad themes and copy effective? What do clients and the public think about the advertising?

5. Are the advertising media well chosen?

A marketing audit is carried out by an auditor who gathers information that is critical to evaluating the organization's marketing performance. The auditor collects secondary data and also interviews top managers, staff members, clients, referral sources, and others who might throw light on the organization's marketing performance. The auditor cannot rely only on internal management opinion, but must seek the opinions and evaluations of outsiders regarding the organization. Often the findings are a surprise, and sometimes a shock, to management.

Table 14–2 is a guide to the kinds of questions that the marketing auditor will raise. Not all of the questions are important in every situation. The instrument will be modified depending on whether the organization is a law firm, accounting firm, management consulting firm, architectural firm, and so on. However, the sequence of topics should be maintained.

The purpose of the audit is to judge whether the organization is performing optimally from a marketing point of view. The auditor will produce some short-run and long-run recommendations of actions that the organization could take to improve its performance. Management has to weigh carefully these recommendations and implement those which it feels would contribute to improved marketing performance.

The marketing audit is not a marketing plan, but an independent appraisal by a competent consultant of the main problems and opportunities facing the organization, and what it can do about them.

SUMMARY

The marketing planning and control system guides the professional service organization's operations. Organizations can be found operating planning systems of various degrees of sophistication, from simple budgeting systems to annual planning systems to long-range planning systems. The planning process starts with marketing forecasting and planning, followed by the development of a detailed organizational plan. The marketing plan contains the following sections: executive summary, situation analysis, objectives and goals, marketing strategy, action program, budgets, and controls. The marketing strategy section of the plan defines the target markets, positioning, marketing mix, and marketing expenditure level that will be used to achieve the marketing goals.

Marketing control is an intrinsic part of marketing planning. Organizations exercise at least three types of marketing control. Annual plan control consists of monitoring the current marketing performance to be sure that the annual goals are being achieved. The main tools are revenues analysis, marketing expenses-to-revenues analysis, "pipeline" analysis, and market attitude tracking. If underperformance is detected, the organization can implement a variety of corrective measures. Profitability control consists of determining the actual profitability of different marketing entities, such as different cases, projects, or categories of services. Strategic control consists of making sure that the organization's marketing objectives, strategies, and systems are optimally adapted to the current and forecasted marketing environment. It uses the tool known as the marketing audit, which is a comprehensive, systematic, independent, and periodic examination of the organization's marketing environment, objectives, strategies, and activities. The purpose of the marketing audit is to determine marketing problem areas and recommend corrective short-run and long-run actions to improve the organization's overall marketing effectiveness.

NOTES

1. Melville C. Branch, *The Corporate Planning Process* (New York: American Management Association, 1962), pp. 48–49.

2. See D.D. McConkey, *MBO for Nonprofit Organizations* (New York: AMACOM, 1975).

3. See Douglas McGregor, *The Human Side of Enterprise* (New York: McGraw-Hill, 1960).

4. The situation described here is adapted from Linda Carlson and Christopher M. Lovelock, "Harris-Johnson Associates," Case #9-580-158, HBS Case Services (Boston: Harvard Business School).

5. For details see Philip Kotler, William Gregor, and William Rodgers, "The Marketing Audit Comes of Age," *Sloan Management Review*, Winter 1977, pp. 25–43.

NAME INDEX

SUBJECT INDEX

Note: Entries set in boldface indicate classification of particular service groups.